K-DRAMA
SCHOOL

K-DRAMA SCHOOL

A Pop Culture Inquiry into
Why We Love Korean Television

GRACE JUNG

Running Press

PHILADELPHIA

Text copyright © 2024 by Grace Jung
Interior and cover illustrations copyright © 2024 by Sunny Wu
Cover copyright © 2024 by Hachette Book Group, Inc.

Running Press
Hachette Book Group
1290 Avenue of the Americas, New York, NY 10104
www.runningpress.com
@Running_Press

First Edition: April 2024

Published by Running Press, an imprint of Hachette Book Group, Inc.
The Running Press name and logo are trademarks of Hachette Book Group, Inc.

The Hachette Speakers Bureau provides a wide range of authors for speaking
events. To find out more, go to www.hachettespeakersbureau.com or email
HachetteSpeakers@hbgusa.com.

Running Press books may be purchased in bulk for business,
educational, or promotional use. For more information, please contact
your local bookseller or the Hachette Book Group Special Markets
Department at Special.Markets@hbgusa.com.

The publisher is not responsible for websites (or their content)
that are not owned by the publisher.

Print book cover and interior design by Justine Kelley

Library of Congress Control Number: 2023950603

ISBNs: 978-0-7624-8572-7 (hardcover); 978-0-7624-8574-1 (ebook);
978-0-7624-8816-2 (international trade paperback)

Printed in the United States of America

LSC-C

Printing 1, 2024

TABLE OF CONTENTS

WATCH TEN THOUSAND HOURS
OF KOREAN TV AND GET A PHD

PEOPLE SAY TV ROTS THE BRAIN. IF THAT'S TRUE, MY BRAIN OUGHT to be mush. Pour it into a bowl and call it oatmeal. Stir it around and give it to your kid. It's gooey! Sell it as a slime toy to ASMRtists! It's mushy! Call now! I'll give it to you for a good price.

Like many Americans, I am in debt because I went to college, but because I am addicted to self-inflicted cycles of abuse, I quit my New York office job in 2015 and went to graduate school in Los Angeles, deepening my debt. So please buy my goo-brain. It's stamped with "PhD" from a prestigious R-1 university. How much would you spend on a brain like mine?

Did you know that you can watch ten thousand hours of television and validate it as "research"? That's what I did. Hurray, America! I got a doctorate in film and television studies from the nation's top film school at the University of California, Los Angeles, and my research primarily involved watching ten thousand hours of Korean TV shows over five years. Afterward

I was awarded a PhD, and I am now officially a doctor. Can you believe that? It doesn't matter if you don't—it happened. My PhD award is sitting in my desk drawer underneath my golden weed grinder and rolling papers. So the next time some know-it-all lectures you on how bad TV is for your brain, tell them that you're conducting very important research on North and South Korea relations through the Bin-Jin couple's chemistry on *Crash Landing on You* (2019–2020). If anyone questions you, tell them that Dr. Grace said it's okay. *It's okay!* You're participating in the very important work of expanding your awareness.

◇◇◇◇◇◇◇◇◇◇◇◇◇◇

The word "television," broken down to its Latin and Greek roots, means "far sight." "Tele" means distant, far out (far out!), or operating across a distance. Vision, as we know, is sight. Television refers to the transmission of information entering your vision from a distance. This transmission also refers to *where* the information is getting blasted from, such as a station, satellite, cable, Wi-Fi, your dreams—basically any imagery that comes together in your view from somewhere afar. Even the distance from the front of an actual television screen is far. "Don't sit too close to the TV. You'll ruin your eyes!" my mom shouted at ten-year-old me. I was sitting close to our analog television because my eyes *were* ruined. It's genetic. My mother and I come from a long line of nearsighted relatives. Also, it's a myth that TV wrecks your eyes. Stare at the screen all you want. Oh wait. You already do, except now it's called a "phone."

As a culture and society, we're used to talking shit about television, just like how we talk shit about the rich. We like TV just as much as we like money, but for some reason, we're taught to disparage both. What's that about? So many film scholars and cinephiles haughtily pronounce, "I don't watch TV. I don't have the time. I don't even *own* a television set." This makes me eyeroll like crazy because the declaration is a self-righteous lie. Everyone watches TV, bro, even if it's just a little. News counts as TV. Videos on your phone count as TV. Episodic series on streaming services you watch on your laptop and tablet count as TV. Your Instagram stories, mukbang videos, ASMR, Yoga with Adriene, and Maangchi's bulgogi recipe on YouTube, as well as TikTok dance videos with Gen-Zers drinking dalgona coffee in comfortable pants—yes, all TV. These are another's vision crossing a great distance to enter yours. We exist in a culture inundated with an infinity of television.

I'm obsessed with Korean TV. I watch it all the time. Korean shows—whether they are K-dramas, reality, or variety—bring me a homey comfort. The combination of language, humor, crying, and music in a K-drama generates a warm familiarity. At the same time, Korean TV shows deeply disturb me. They trigger flashbacks and make my mind traverse back to some of the worst moments in my life that I endured as a child in South Korea and in the States. Watching Korean TV is a very private and personal ritual for me, but I know it is also a shared experience with people around the globe. K-dramas today offer a great deal of reprieve and healing while also addressing trauma. This is why I love Korean television: it offers a multiplicity of experience and reflection.

This book is a journey in analyzing K-dramas in the context of local and international politics, sociocultural issues, histories, and traumas as Hollywood's TV distribution systems acquire rights to more and more Korean shows due to high demand.

CINEMA AND MEDIA STUDIES, PHD X K-DRAMAS

In any form of Korean studies—whether it be from the department of anthropology, history, sociology, literature, or film and TV studies—there's always an encounter with national trauma. Korean trauma colors everything in Korean media, but academia cannot effectively nudge trauma toward a productive space for healing because academic language does not give space to feeling or subjectivity.

It is impossible to discuss Korean history without understanding trauma, just as it is impossible to give trauma full attention without inviting feeling. I know this because I'm a trauma survivor. I live with a developmental trauma disorder known as Complex Post-Traumatic Stress Disorder, or C-PTSD. It's a fairly new diagnosis, first named in 1988 by American psychiatrist Judith Herman.

PTSD, which is more commonly known, is often associated with war veterans and survivors of near-death experiences. PTSD gets diagnosed after someone experiences a big trauma ("big T") in their adulthood, and treatment focuses on helping them return to what their normal self was like before that trauma. But C-PTSD occurs during a child's formative years when they are still in development, so the person grows up normalized to trauma. There is no return to a self who existed before the trauma. The person's baseline is a traumatized state, and throughout the years they learn to manage and cope as best they can.

My own trauma disorder originates from my childhood, starting at age four due to prolonged parental abandonment and neglect, physical abuse, sexual assault, emotional abuse, mental abuse, and spiritual abuse in my home, schools, community, and church. One of my C-PTSD symptoms is daily emotional flashbacks. When I get triggered by something in my external environment or by my own thoughts and memories, my mind/body get thrown into an intense feeling of threat, danger, or dissociation as if I am right back in my past. My other symptoms include a constant feeling of worthlessness and defectiveness as well as psychosomatic migraines and insomnia that plague me regularly. With all that said, I've been exploring my disorder over the years with a psychologist whose treatment methods and tools have shown effective results. I see evidence of my healing daily, and I know I am making progress because I feel that change inside of me.

When I analyze K-dramas throughout this book, I do so by following my personal language of trauma as I observe characters make their way toward healing. I then reflect this onto my knowledge of modern Korean and Korean diaspora history, culture, politics, and society to offer a layered scope for the shows we watch and love. K-drama is not a single genre of television but rather an umbrella term used to describe a diversity of styles, tones, and stories across genres.

Korean television is here, and everyone—regardless of region, cultural background, gender, sexual orientation, race, or ethnic identity—is into it or, at the very least, has been exposed to it because of Hollywood's keen attention to Korean media. In 2022 Disney+ acquired exclusive rights to over twenty serialized K-dramas, twelve of which are their own original titles. Disney is harnessing the global fandom power of K-pop stars who spill over to K-dramas, drawing viewers into an expanding market. In 2021 Netflix invested half of a billion US dollars to acquire exclusive worldwide streaming rights for an undisclosed number of K-dramas and films.

Korean entertainment is a multibillion-dollar globalized media ecosystem that closely knits K-pop with K-dramas through their hallyu star system. The K-drama industry also capitalizes on its high production value and compelling storytelling. Netflix's *Squid Game* (2021) won six Emmy Awards. Apple TV optioned Min Jin Lee's bestselling novel *Pachinko* and turned it into a K-drama written by Korean producer and showrunner Soo Hugh. *Pachinko* (2022), which won an Emmy for Apple TV, stars top hallyu actors Lee Min-ho and Oscar winner Youn Yuh-jung. Hollywood stars like Steven Yeun and Ki Hong Lee balance jobs with both Korean and American productions. As K-dramas rack up more awards in Hollywood, they continue to gain far greater global attention than they've already received.

The old adage among Asian Americans is that we grew up without sufficient media representation. Although things are changing, ample media representation for Asian Americans and Pacific Islanders (AAPIs) is still an uphill battle with many complex issues to sort through. This is why Korean television was a comfort to me in my youth. I did not feel completely left out because I had access to all the K-dramas, sitcoms, and variety shows my mom rented from our local Korean video store. I saw faces like mine regularly on Korean TV. Growing up, fandom debriefing on seasonal K-dramas was an exclusive community ritual for me and other Korean American kids. Today, we witness a diversity of fan-generated discussions of K-dramas that resounds globally.

I write these pages as a cultural observer and participant in Korean television's ecosystem. Like all identities, mine is a complex medley. I am a Busan-born émigré, formerly undocumented citizen, cis-woman, neurodivergent, writer, stand-up comedian, Hollywood industry worker, and filmmaker with a PhD and publications in peer-reviewed journals who lives by her virtues as a professional creative and thinker. I wrote my doctoral dissertation on serialized Korean variety shows, but before all that, I am simply a lifelong fan of Korean television.

K-Drama School demonstrates the extent of my learnings through personal accounts melded with academic perspectives on family, gender, sexuality, disability, romance, economics, politics, and education. This book is meant for fans and audiences who want to know more about K-dramas through modern Korean history and the social ailments overcome or currently in battle that produced the shows we binge today. I encourage you to ask questions as an active participant when you watch K-dramas: Why does a particular character, scene, or plot point move you? What is it about this show that has you returning to it? What are you personally seeking when you watch a K-drama, and did you find it? What are the shows you love, and why?

Please don't think of me as a teacher who is here to "school" you. I'm not that professorial. Imagine me more as the hippie art teacher at an alternative school who doesn't give out grades, smokes weed, and goes by her first name. Imagine me in big flowy pants, platform shoes, and gigantic costume jewelry. I encourage you to "go deeper," "explore further," and "yes!" I don't walk around with a stick. Screw sticks. Screw grades. Also, I'm not just the teacher at this school; I am also the pupil, textbook, lunch lady, composition notebook, and custodian mopping up some kid's barf in the hallway.

I want this book to be a source of conversation for you and your friends, colleagues, family, community, and the chatty supermarket cashier to bond over K-dramas you love. *K-Drama School* is a resource for answering some of your questions and a launching pad for asking more. It is a guide for you to read when you're onto an interpretation of a show, and you can agree, disagree, subtract from, or add to my analysis however much you please because your analysis is valid! I want these pages to be part of a broader dialogue that I am already having with people through my podcast *K-Drama School*, which discusses comedy, mental health, culture, education, politics, relationships, society, psychedelics, spirituality, and how we consume and relate to our media as they reflect our subjective and collective experiences.

These pages are meant to be a fun and healing source for you to enjoy these shows just as much as I do. It's meant to be a deeper reflection on our social psyche and individual minds. Korean TV shows have been a steady companion throughout my life, offering me deep insights, comforts, revelations, agonies, and catharses. I am happy to offer you a friendly and personal reading to carry with you on your journey through today's maze of K-dramas while you unearth a bigger and deeper you.

Psychoanalyst Clarissa Pinkola Estés says, "Stories are medicine."[1] This point is essential to all my work. Human stories get recycled throughout lifetimes because they offer reprieve.

Although stories are by no means a replacement for therapy and treatment, I do know that engaging in stories is a timeless remedy that expands our understanding for greater compassion. That's why we read bedtime stories to children to lull them to sleep. That's why folk traditions from all cultures include stories at their heart. That's why we tell stories to friends, families, therapists, and ourselves. I apply the same concept when I analyze K-dramas. Stories on TV are stories no less significant than those in literature, cinema, and conversations with Halmŏni.[2] I mine K-dramas for medicine to help mend my wounds, face my fears, address what went ignored, speak to my subjective past and present, and inform me with valuable lessons to carry into my future with confidence and anticipation.

Anyway. Class is now in session.

---

1   Clarissa Pinkola Estés, *Women Who Run with the Wolves: The Myths and Stories of the Wild Woman Archetype* (New York: Ballantine Books, 1992), 504.

2   "Halmŏni" means "grandma" in Korean.

LESSON 1:
KOREAN OVERACHIEVEMENT AND *SKY CASTLE*

MY FAVORITE FILM IS THE COEN BROTHERS' *THE BIG LEBOWSKI* (1998), which balances brainy profundity and stupid humor in equal measure. What makes this film so lovable to me is Jeffrey Lebowski, aka The Dude, whose rug has been micturated upon in the fair city of Los Angeles. His outfit alone—that vintage knit sweater and jelly sandals from Jeff Bridges's own closet—should've garnered an Oscar nomination for Best Costume. The Dude is an unemployed middle-aged white man living in the Valley who enjoys the company of friends and White Russian cocktails. He represents the kind of lifestyle I strive for—one with simple pleasures like bowling, bubble baths, whale songs, Bob Dylan, a joint, and the occasional acid flashback. He is everything that an anxious overachieving Korean student is not: chill as fuck.

◇◇◇◇◇◇◇◇◇◇◇◇◇

SKY Castle is a good starting point for this book because the protagonists idolize education and schools in a pathological way, getting to the heart of the stereotype that plagues the Asian diaspora around the globe. Where does a Korean parent's die-hard obsession with their children's education come from? What does it allegorize in the larger schema of modern Korean history and its "tiger" economy? I don't know, man. Let's get there slowly and steadily, starting with the title.

SKY is an acronym for the three most coveted universities in Seoul—Seoul National University (SNU), Korea University, and Yonsei University. Sky Castle is the name of the residence for the show's characters, although I do wonder why they call their townhouses a "castle." These houses are swanky but do not aesthetically resemble a castle. Like, where's the moat? Sky Castle is a gated community of residents obsessed with hierarchy and power. They buy into the fantastical dream that education promises a royal lifestyle, fully lapping up the fruit punch.

EMOTIONAL FLASHBACKS AND POVERTY TRAUMA

The romantic Korean melodramas I grew up watching in the 1990s and early 2000s recycled the same dichotomy repeatedly. There's the morally upright working-class girl who the rich boy falls in love with, and there's the bitchy saboteur who spitefully tries to steal the man for herself. Of course, the morally upright one always wins the man, but SKY Castle flips the known premise: What if the bitchy saboteur did win the rich boy and the morally upright girl was abandoned? What if the bitchy saboteur and the rich boy got married and had children? What if the morally upright girl died and the bitchy saboteur is now the show's protagonist? Oh, ho ho.

The anti-heroine we follow in SKY Castle is Han Seo-jin, and she's a real piece of work. Seo-jin is the reimagined nineties K-drama mean girl who bagged the rich man by successfully kicking the poor, morally upright girl to the curb. Seo-jin's whole identity, however, is a complete and utter fabrication. While Seo-jin's neighbors think that her mother travels to Germany to buy her daughter expensive chinaware and that her father is the former president of Sydney Bank, her childhood friend Soo-im knows the truth: Seo-jin's original name is Mi-hyang, and she is a working-class daughter of an alcoholic butcher who vends at an outdoor market.

Seo-jin hides her poverty out of shame. In a flashback to her high school days, she runs away from her drunken dad after he berates her in public and throws her a bag of clotted blood to take home to her "bitch" of a mother. Blood leaks from the bag and covers Seo-jin's clothes and shoes. Then she hears other high school girls badmouthing her.

Poverty is imbued with shame because of class systems that human civilizations built over the eons. Ancestral struggles over limited resources reside in our survival brain. In premodern Korea, prior to the Gabo Reform of 1894, the nation functioned under a rigid caste system. The 백정/*paekchŏng* (aka the butcher) was regarded as an untouchable—just a notch above slaves. Those in the paekchŏng class not only handled animal carcasses but also worked as executioners. In the present day, paekchŏng is used euphemistically as "butcher" to describe the executioner in organized crime circles like in the show *Bloodhounds* (2023). In the 1920s members of the paekchŏng community organized to oppose social discrimination, poor working conditions, and low wages, but they were met by opposition from the rest of the country and the Japanese colonial government.[3] Socioculturally, the paekchŏng were openly mistreated and looked down upon for generations. Seo-jin's trauma lies in the shame of identifying with this lower-class rank, which remains stigmatized even after the reform. Seo-jin does everything she can to control her external image through the elaborate lies she constructs out of fear.

In 1992 my parents and I left Busan for New York, where our poverty and ethnic difference cast a shadow over me. Since kindergarten I always felt the need to hide my heritage in this country. It was not welcome. Bringing kimbap to school was unacceptable. Not knowing English was a defect. Not having a pair of formal shoes except for beat-up sneakers to wear on picture day was an outrage. I understand Seo-jin's pain. Being poor and different creates turmoil and a warped self-perception in a young person's life. Poverty is a trauma.

3   Ian Neary, "The Paekjong and the Hyongpyongsa: The Untouchables of Korea and Their Struggle for Liberation," *Immigrants & Minorities* 6, no. 2 (1987): 117–150, DOI: 10.1080/02619288.1987.9974654.

When I was four I was sent to nursery school in my neighborhood of Dong-nae, Busan—yes, the city where the train full of zombies with Gong Yoo went to. My school was perched on the second floor of an old building that was a Protestant church on Sundays and a nursery school from Monday through Saturday. My teacher was a tall and lanky woman named Miss So, and she was violent. Corporal punishment was exercised freely at this school. During art class, all the kids used the same spiral-bound sketchbook and cray-pas. We sat in long rows, shoulder to shoulder, and were told to draw our family. I drew my parents and me on a sketchpad and colored in my family's hair with black craypa. "Make sure you save the color black for last. If you use black before you color in the background, it will smudge," Miss So announced. I immediately felt fear-induced adrenaline shoot down my legs and arms. In a panic, I grabbed a brown craypa and frantically colored in the background because I knew I was going to get hit. I initially wanted to color the background sky blue, but I figured brown would hide the smudges. Miss So caught me before I could finish. The boy sitting to my left had made the same grave mistake. In fact, most of the kids in class had done this because everyone's hair color was black. Our teacher ruthlessly grabbed my head and smashed it against the boy's skull next to me. She went around the whole class of four- to six-year-old kids and did this to every child who made the same error, chastising us all the while.

This was fucking *art* class, bro.

Arithmetic was hell. I did not understand math. Why would a four-year-old be good at math, anyway? Doesn't make sense. But there were pop quizzes every single day, and I got numerous problems wrong. Instead of teaching math, the teacher would have us stand and wait in a line while she marked the quizzes and ripped through the pages with red ink. She'd raise her switch, a short wooden stick about a foot long and wrapped in black electrical tape to prevent splinters (how considerate!), and make us raise our palms faceup so she could whack the switch over our little hands. If I got four out of ten problems wrong, that would be four whacks. If I got ten wrong, that would be ten whacks. I usually got all ten wrong. I never got better at math. My GRE score in math was in the fortieth percentile even though I studied my ass off every single day for three months, and these were the same few math questions I had studied my ass off every single day since middle school through high school in prep for the SATs. Yup! Beating a kid into learning anything does not work. Even if it does, that kid is now broken elsewhere.

I get triggered multiple times daily. My flashbacks cause obsessive negative thinking and engage imaginary fights with my abusers, but this engagement only causes physical agony and emotional drainage. The only way for me to return to myself is by acknowledging my vulnerabilities and tending to my pain with loving care. I do this by asking questions or mentioning words that land with me until my upset transmutes into an emotional breakthrough. This is a tool I learned in therapy, which serves me well today.

Our anti-hero, Seo-jin, doesn't have this tool yet. The description I gave you about her is only from the first two episodes of *SKY Castle*. If Seo-jin went on a healing retreat to Mount Shasta and acquired this tool, there would be no show because screenwriting rule 101 is *have conflict*. Instead of tending to her triggers, Seo-jin avoids them and does everything to make up for her shortcomings by putting her pride and hopes all into one basket—her eldest daughter, Ye-seo.

OVERACHIEVING TO BE LOVED AND TO LIVE

Ye-seo is a terror. She's smart as a whip and fiercely ambitious. Her goals as a high school senior are to be the top of her class, get accepted to SNU's premed program, and become a third-generation doctor for the Kang household to please her paternal grandmother. Ye-seo harbors a protective love for her mother, who is repeatedly disrespected by her paternal grandmother. Ye-seo's determination is frightening. She throws tantrums when she doesn't get her way and fawns over authority figures who wield power. She is demanding, narcissistic, and sociopathic in how condescending she is toward her peers. And she's loud as hell. Ye-seo's obsession to win and be the best at all costs is driven by spite, and she could not be a more perfect delight in Seo-jin's eyes.

I invited Dr. Jacob Ham to speak on my podcast about overachieving and trauma. Dr. Ham is a Korean American clinical psychologist serving as the director of Center for Child Trauma and Resilience at Mount Sinai in New York. I asked him why traumatized Koreans have a need to overachieve. He said, "Well, there's the cultural motivator, which is that the only way you're going to have food, the only way you're going to have any status or be able to survive at all is accomplishment. . . . So there's this life-or-death urgency to succeed."[4] Dr. Ham followed this with:

> On a deeply interpersonal psychological level, I find that over-achievement is actually a proxy for seeking love. My thesis is that when our parents are so focused on surviving physically, then our emotional health is put aside. And it's the next generation's job to deal with the emotional health once the financial and physical health are secured. And so I think that people just don't feel loved or valued as individuals. It's only through what you can produce. And so accomplishment is the only way to garner attention, garner praise. All of those feel good. They feel like love.[5]

Striving hard feels like a productive means toward staying alive—hence the intensity in characters like Ye-seo. This survival mechanism is tied to the struggle for love. Psychiatrist and trauma specialist Bessel van der Kolk has a similar view in his book *The Body Keeps the Score*: "Children and adults will do anything for people they trust and whose opinion they value."[6]

Educational success for Ye-seo contains an urgent tremor for survival that has been transmitted down from her mother's life-or-death anxiety around achievement. This life-or-death mentality behind educational success driven by fear dates to the 1970s in South Korea. Only the privileged elite attended universities back then, as South Korea's middle class was still coming into existence. Historian Nam Hee Lee writes, "Anyone with

---

4   Grace Jung and Jacob Ham, "Ep 112: Save Me and When Two Pisces Dream of Yin Yang Cheese with Dr. Jacob Ham," *K-Drama School*, February 20, 2023.

5   Ibid.

6   Bessel van der Kolk, *The Body Keeps the Score* (New York: Penguin Books, 2014), 350.

a university diploma was on the road to becoming bourgeois regardless of his or her current socioeconomic background."[7] South Korean men were more likely to attend schools and enter universities than women; parental sacrifice as well as labor sacrifice by a family's daughters and sisters were a given in order to send sons to college who were then expected to raise their families out of poverty. My mother and her older sister are examples of this sacrifice. My mother, who desperately wanted to go to school in the 1970s, was not permitted by her farmer father, who considered school a waste of money, especially on a girl. After years of laboring on the farm, my fourteen-year-old mother was sent over sixty miles outside of her village to work at a factory in Ulsan.

Historian Bruce Cumings states, "South Koreans experience a knot of terrible loss, tragedy, bitterness, fate, invisible burdens, an inner negation pushing them down and bending them inward, which they call *han*."[8] The money my mother sent home while laboring alone as a teenager was put toward educating all five of her younger siblings. The fact that my mom could not attend college is her *han*—a deeply painful resentment. Her trauma. She still does not stop harping on the injustice she feels for her lost opportunity and the sacrifice she made for her siblings' upward mobility. My master's and doctoral degrees don't mean a whole lot to me right now, as I do not work in academia. They were not even particularly difficult for me to get because reading, developing an argument, writing, and keeping deadlines come easily to me. I wonder if I chased higher ed to its tippy tops in an effort to detangle this han for my mom the way Ye-seo tries for Seo-jin.

This familial sacrifice speaks to the life-or-death urgency behind South Korea's education fervor. It's not just one person's future on the line but rather an entire family's economic stability. This is why I've seen so many Korean families get drunk and fight at reunions. Everyone feels like a victim, and they all point fingers in a drunken rage over what they personally sacrificed for the greater whole. They do this because the roles they each took on

---

7   Nam Hee Lee, *The Making of Minjung: Democracy and the Politics of Representation in South Korea* (Ithaca, NY: Cornell University Press, 2007), 19.

8   Bruce Cumings, *The Korean War: A History* (New York: Modern Library, 2010), 63.

did not feel like a choice. They felt like they were pressured into these decisions rather than allowed to make them with clarity, autonomy, and intention. Lee writes that "students agonized deeply over balancing their desire to fulfill their parents' and their own wishes for success and their sense of responsibility to society."[9]

It is no accident that *SKY Castle* repeatedly mentions the need to create a third-generation doctor within each household. The history of South Korea's intellectual class as well as the nation's fledgling middle class that developed in the 1970s was built out of familial pressures, which were rooted in a larger political-economic mobilization by a military dictatorship that envisioned a South Korea with healthy middle and upper-middle classes in its economy. This ambition was driven by the pain of national poverty. This pastime continues into the present day through intense pressure on and high expectations of schoolkids living in the twenty-first century.

My grades throughout elementary, middle, and high school were not great, but they were not shit, either. I was a firm B-average student. When I got to college, however, my grades were stellar. I was also an alcoholic who drank every single night and went to my restaurant jobs and classes hungover in a sleep-deprived foggy haze, but I majored in English, read all the books, wrote excellent papers, and won awards in writing contests for poetry and fiction. A college friend casually observed that I seemed to overcompensate by excelling in school while my personal life was in the shits, and I thought this was an apt assessment. I overcompensated for my self-loathing by overachieving academically. I did not realize I had an addiction to overachievement and overworking until I read Stephanie Foo's *What My Bones Know*, in which she mentions workaholism as a C-PTSD symptom—one that causes "moments of intense joy through achievement followed by anxiety over finding my next success."[10] I felt like I needed high achievements because underneath I felt that without such bells and whistles, I am not worthy of anything good. On my podcast Dr. Ham mentioned that praise and recognition for

---

9 Nam Hee Lee, *The Making of Minjung*, 19.

10 Stephanie Foo, *What My Bones Know: A Memoir of Healing from Complex Trauma* (New York: Random House, 2022), 132.

accomplishment *feel* like love: "It's the closest thing we know to love, so we chase it with a life-or-death energy that a baby chases being close to their parent 'cause they would die without being close to their parent."

I added, "Or die without love."

He replied, "Exactly."

In a 2019 study by Chae Woon Kwak and Jeannette R. Ickovics published in the *Asian Journal of Psychiatry*, the authors note that, among the thirty-eight Organization for Economic Co-operation and Development (OECD) nations, South Korea is ranked first when it comes to suicide. Suicide is the leading cause of death among Korean adolescents. In the journal of *Child and Adolescent Psychiatry and Mental Health*, research documents suicides among Korean children in elementary school as young as the third grade, and many children end their lives by jumping off of high buildings.[11] South Korea, according to Kwak and Ickovics's research, currently lacks "an organization dedicated to mental health research and development," thus limiting resources and prevention strategies.[12] The pressure to achieve academic success and the stress of that pursuit, which determines Koreans' college entry and job security, are marked as the "major driver" of suicide among South Korean children: "Academic stress accounts for 46% of depression among high school students in Seoul."[13] What drives a student to overachieve to the point of death? They are chasing their parents' love, because without it, they will die.

REBELS AND THE EDUCATIONAL BATTLEFIELD

My favorite character on *SKY Castle* is Seo-jin's younger daughter, Ye-bin, played by the tremendous actress Lee Ji-won. She is in middle school and doesn't care about grades. She is a rebel cut from a different cloth who doesn't understand her mother's and sister's drive. Ye-bin is an example of a child who remains impervious to the Establishment and the Man. She has no

11   Minha Hong, Han Nah Cho, Ah Reum Kim, Hyun Ju Hong, and Yong-Sil Kweon, "Suicidal Deaths in Elementary School Students in Korea," *Child and Adolescent Psychiatry and Mental Health* 11 (2017): 1–5.

12   Chae Woon Kwak and Jeannette R. Ickovics, "Adolescent Suicide in South Korea: Risk Factors and Proposed Multi-dimensional Solution," *Asian Journal of Psychiatry* 43 (2019): 150–153, 151.

13   Ibid., 150.

deference to a tyrannical superego like the rest of her family. Ye-bin walks to the beat of her own drum (good for her!), but she does act out by shoplifting at a convenience store.

When Seo-jin finds out about her daughter's kleptomania, she doesn't say a word. This breaks Ye-bin's heart because she was shoplifting to get her mother's attention. Because Seo-jin is so focused on Ye-seo's schooling, she neglects her younger daughter's emotional needs. Ye-bin is highly adept at hiding this need. Most tough girls are needy and hypersensitive empaths skilled at masking their vulnerability with a thick, scaly skin like unfeeling reptiles. Perhaps this explains the punk aesthetic full of leather, chains, metal bolts, and sometimes snakes for pets. Ye-bin has a rough-around-the-edges, Riot grrrl exterior that seems impenetrable, but she is, in fact, merely a child seeking her mother's love.

Growing up in New York, I used to listen to an East Coast FM morning radio show called *Elvis Duran and the Morning Zoo* on Z-100. One morning I heard one of the deejays deliver a news story about abused dogs, and she immediately commented that people should be good to dogs because they only want to be loved. I remember wondering, *How are people any different? And why is it so hard to admit that?*

A Sky Castle resident named Young-jae gets accepted to SNU, and his parents and neighbors praise him, but a dark resentment festers beneath his veneer of smiles and good graces. Young-jae's mother, Myung-joo, gifts all the mothers at Sky Castle a ceramic Madonna holding a child. The figurine symbolizes a mother's unconditional love for her baby, but in the parenting styles among Sky Castle parents, the actual holding and bonding are largely absent, especially between Myung-joo and Young-jae.

Young-jae seeks solace in other women due to the lack of warm maternal bonding. One of these is the housekeeper, Ga-eul, who he develops a romantic relationship with. The other is his tutor, Kim Joo-young, a private instructor whose supplementary education guarantees the students' acceptance into their parents' dream institution. Her fee costs up to millions. Parents seeking Joo-young's aid can only access her through invitation as a VIP member at a bank. Her services are reserved for the one percent; she is the Bentley of tutors. Her demeanor is cool, calm, and distant. Her hair is slicked back, and her gaze smolders like hot coal. Her intentions are difficult to read. When Joo-young works with her students, she tends to their emotional needs, knowing full well that their parents are starving them of such. Joo-young harbors a sinister ulterior motive to destroy families by encouraging her students to disappoint their parents.

Myung-joo's greatest pride as a mother at Sky Castle is successfully getting Young-jae enrolled at SNU's premed program, which puts Young-jae on track to becoming a third-generation doctor in his family. But as soon as he fulfills his parents' wish, Young-jae runs away to live with his former housekeeper, Ga-eul. When Myung-joo tracks him down, Young-jae unleashes his pent-up wrath for all the abuse he put up with since he was seven: "You said I didn't deserve to eat if I wasn't the top of my class. Didn't you tell me to go out and die if my grades dropped? I was living in hell. I wouldn't have survived if it weren't for Ga-eul."

Young-jae finds liberation by disappearing as soon as he satisfies his mother's wishes. Once Myung-joo loses Young-jae, her identity shatters. Myung-joo's ego had become glued to her son's achievements. Once this is gone, she loses herself and ends her own life by blowing her head off with her husband's hunting rifle.

Now, in my talk with Dr. Ham, he noted my way of othering Myung-joo in my analysis. Dr. Ham turned my gaze inward toward my own heart center and got me to see behind Myung-joo's urgent drive by wondering why she felt the need to go to such lengths. He said,

> Somehow this was instilled in her. That if you're not number one, you will die and you will not eat. She was living that viscerally in her parenting. It was all misattuned to him 'cause he was not hungry or going to get shot if he wasn't number one. But her survival instincts hardwired into her from the histories of trauma that are hardwired into us intergenerationally— that's what was ruling her. So, it's not about ego. It's just about survival.[14]

---

14   Grace Jung and Jacob Ham, "Ep 112: Save Me and When Two Pisces Dream of Yin Yang Cheese with Dr. Jacob Ham," *K-Drama School*, February 20, 2023, https://youtu.be/GYkzYIlJgGk.

Modern Korean history offers context for such urgent survival methods and where they stem from. It's more than apparent in the show's mise-en-scène that Young-jae's family luxuriates in a lavish lifestyle without any immediate threat of death by starvation and houselessness like Korean civilians constantly felt during the war years. Research investigations conducted by South Korea's Truth and Reconciliation Commission in the early 2000s found nearly ten thousand cases of wrongful deaths and civilian massacres during the Korean War. These are the number of *incidents*—not the complete death toll.

One incident documented by Cumings mentions a massacre from July 1950 in Daejeon, where anywhere between four thousand and seven thousand men, women, and children were killed and thrown into a pit. He writes, "American officers stood idly by while this slaughter went on, photographing it for their records but doing nothing to stop it."[15] The photos were classified and only released in 1999. Even prior to the official declaration of the Korean War in 1950, there were numerous peasant uprisings and guerrilla rebellions that led to countless civil conflicts throughout the divided peninsula, which was occupied by the US and USSR. The country was pulled apart over ideological differences that most locals didn't understand.

An estimated one hundred thousand bodies—although the exact figure is eternally unknowable—were buried in mass graves or thrown into the sea.[16] The names, faces, and stories of these individuals are lost. For this reason, shamanic rituals in South Korea continue the heavy work of appeasing the misery of countless souls. Korean War casualties range between an estimated three to five million. The Korean War's heated battle where people clashed and killed one another ruthlessly or were mangled, tortured, bombed, and shot by American, Soviet, Chinese, North Korean, and South Korean troops may be a distant memory, but the war rages on in other ways in South Korea's hypercompetitive society; parents, teachers, and students treat the education system as a war to be won.

---

15 Cumings, *The Korean War*, 173.
16 Ibid., 202.

In episode nine of *Extraordinary Attorney Woo* (2022), which is entitled "The Pied Piper," there's a character who legally changed his name to Bang Gu-ppong—essentially naming himself "Fart." Gu-ppong is a self-ordained Commander-in-Chief of the Children's Liberation Army and wears an army-green jacket as he mobilizes a group of elementary students into excitement before hijacking the school bus and taking the kids to a park to play. Gu-ppong treats his mission to break children out of classrooms like he would a war mission. This is evident in his military rhetoric and outfit. Gu-ppong's earnestness in his belief that children must play and not be trapped in a classroom lands him in prison for illegally kidnapping grade schoolers. It reveals Gu-ppong's high-stakes and warlike mentality against adult-induced pressures placed onto children.

Similarly, in episode six of *Juvenile Justice* (2022), protagonist Shim Eun-seok is a judge overseeing a school case in which over twenty high school students are tried for looking at leaked answers of an exam prior to the test date. One of the defendants is Seok-hyun, whose mother stands on trial and lists what her son's daily curriculum consists of: private coaching with a required list of books he must read, volunteer job options he should start, clubs he should join to boost his extracurricular activities, 학원/*hakwon* (aka cram school) for multiple subjects, private lessons to keep up with hakwon, grad students who offload the student's assignment load, tutors, school reports, contests, admission interviews, and résumé preparation. Seok-hyun's mom flatly tells Judge Shim that all of this requires money, and therefore the wealthiest students are the ones who get accepted to SNU. She says, "We're in the middle of a bloody war here." Seok-hyun's mom brazenly admits that while her son breached ethics, she does not see how this necessitates legal intervention when the entire educational system is rigged by money for ready-made elite students who come from wealth. War unearths madness. Morality and ethics must go out the window for there to be no regard for human life. The parents of Sky Castle are participants of the same bloody war locked in a vicious cycle of blind ambition for success.

South Korea in the 1960s all the way through the late 1980s was in a constant state of violent political instability. The presidents who came into power in South Korea were not known for being poets, artists, philosophers, or lawyers. They were known for their military service to the Japanese imperial government during World War II and the Korean War. During the military dictatorships of Park Chung-hee and Chun Doo-hwan, many student protestors were arrested and tortured to death. Their bodies were discarded and eternally lost from their family's reach, just like the civilians who were massacred and then thrown into mass graves during the war.

South Korea witnessed people disappear constantly. Given these historical occurrences, I hear the fear of death in Myung-joo's extreme parenting methods. It's possible that Myung-joo's memory contains headlines of politicians and students getting shot, sights of endless violence on television, and news of losses within her local community and family, not to mention the deeper traumatic well of the Korean War and its devastation that reside within her. South Korea did not develop a stable middle class until the late 1980s, and that class formation was possible through education. Most of the nation was living in poverty after the cease-fire was declared in 1953. Houselessness, illness, and starvation were realities for most Koreans during and immediately after the war. Abject poverty and hunger are part of my own parents' and grandparents' memories. Hunger and health neglect due to poverty are part of my own immigrant millennial history in Korea and America. The Korean War never ended. It lives on within me.

◇◇◇◇◇◇◇◇◇◇◇◇◇◇

My favorite Korean comedian is Yoo Jae-suk. One of the many shows he hosts is *You Quiz*, where he invites model, comedian, and kimchi-business entrepreneur Hong Jin-kyung and her daughter Rael to the show. Hong comments that as an uneducated mother, she finds herself needing schooling to support her daughter, who is in middle school. Jin-kyung visits the SNU campus to interview students for advice and quickly learns that not a single student had a parent who helicoptered over them and forced them to study. The students say that they forged their own interest in education out of their love for learning.[17]

---

17 Entretenimiento Koreano, "[#YouQuizontheBlock] Hong Jinkyung X Kim Rael | #EntretenimientoKoreano," November 1, 2021, www.youtube.com/watch?v=1_IfNq3yuDw.

So for those of you wondering whether South Korean students and parents really are like the ones you see in K-dramas, there's your answer. Also, don't believe everything you see on TV, man. C'mon.

COMBATTING OVERACHIEVEMENT WITH PLAY

We love K-dramas because they use extreme forms of storytelling to moralize the importance of self-care. I see so many ailments among overachieving characters. In *Crash Course in Romance* (2023) Choi Chi-yeol suffers from an eating disorder, insomnia, headaches, and panic attacks due to gross physical self-neglect caused by overwork. In *Reply 1988* (2015) Choi Taek suffers from insomnia, migraines, and an eating disorder due to overwork. In *It's Okay, That's Love* (2014) Jang Jae-yeol suffers from a sleep disorder, tics, and schizophrenia that get triggered by his overwork. In *Extraordinary Attorney Woo*, attorney Jung Myung-seok develops cancer from overwork and rebukes himself for chasing upward mobility while neglecting his health and partner. All these characters prioritize achievement over self-care, and their overexertion is framed in a pitiful light via the show's mise-en-scène through sentimental music and sympathetic responses from their loved ones, who rescue them from their dogged routines and habits. Overachievement is self-destruction.

In the portrait documentary *Matter of Heart* (1986), which is about psychiatrist Carl G. Jung, one of his students recollects how Jung used to take a shovel down to the lake outside his home office and play there for a couple of hours every day before going inside to sit at his desk and work. I came to learn in recent years that I produce my best work when I am in good condition. Balancing work with rest and play are essential to maintain this.

How does one play? Just follow your own joy and curiosity. For more techniques, consult any dog or child. Go on and goof off.

We love *SKY Castle* because it confronts us with a universally applicable question: Are we motivated each day by fear of our inner critic—the amalgamation of every judgment, criticism, and harsh word we ever heard from authority figures we were so eager to please but were impossible to satisfy—or are we driven by love for ourselves and this life, which is our own and not anyone else's?

UNSCHOOL YOUR SCHOOLING ASS

I often hear bitter declarations that school is irrelevant. With the massive debt that young adults dig themselves into for higher education, which offers no guarantee of a livable wage in the future, this declaration is understandable. After I graduated with a doctorate degree in 2021 to a desert of an academic job market, recession, and inflation, I sat down and asked myself: Why did I get higher degrees that incurred more debt and didn't help my relevancy in the job market? A very honest answer came to me: *Because I felt stupid.* I wanted to prove that I was not a fungible idiot. The abuse and discrimination that I grew up with made me feel like my whole existence was wrong, and my feelings of inadequacy made me chase after higher degrees to compensate for this lack.

Culturally, we go around using the colloquial expression "schooling" like it's a diss—a way to shut someone down with our intellect, leaving them speechless and floored. Why does knowledge need to be wielded so violently? Also, why do people receive it so violently? When people learn that I have a doctorate, some react with defensiveness and hostility. It's jarring when it happens, and although I do not to take it personally, I also do not feel the need to dumb myself down or apologize for what I am.

Learning is not a competition, just as not knowing something yet is not a weakness. Furthermore, information and knowledge aren't necessarily power. That's an illusion. Our culture has a sick way of making us feel inadequate, then sells us the idea that we need to pay an unreasonable amount of money to go to an institution that teaches us how to arm ourselves with knowledge, like picking up guns as if we're about to head into battle. All of this estranges us further from ourselves and others.

This false logic makes intellectuals seem threatening. Intellectuals can also remind us of a teacher who made us feel stupid, small, and powerless in the past. Everyone can recall at least one prick of a teacher. Grading one's intellectual aptitude feels personal, especially to a vulnerable child, and yet we send kids to school when they are just toddlers and use an arbitrary barometer like grades to decide who is better or worse than others, assuming that intellect is singular and measurable: "Get used to it, kids! You'll never be good enough. Good luck!"

Some schools, like my Busan nursery school, used to beat me on top of making me feel stupid, conditioning me to believe that I deserve to be abused for making errors in class. I only recently learned in therapy that I never deserve to be abused, no matter what. This was radically eye-opening. I didn't realize how much abuse I tolerated regularly for over thirty years because I believed I deserved it.

Grading never stops. Every job interview triggers the same feelings of panic, worry, and lack, along with the anxiety that some giant stick will come crashing down onto my body. Every Yelp review and every judgmental comment on social media are grades. Grades are judgments. High grades bring on a temporary high by inflating the ego. Low grades trigger shame. But grades are just an illusion. They do not define you or me. Acquisition of knowledge doesn't make a person any greater or lesser than another. I pursue knowledge the same way I pursue anything else—it expands my conscious awareness by nursing an interest and creating my own meaning to enrich life. It is a very personal experience that matters solely to me.

Knowledge and information are not weapons to use against human vulnerabilities. They are not for "schooling" people to make them feel inferior, even if someone *is* being ignorant and perhaps hurtful based on their ignorance. Knowledge and information are for sharing and offering people freedom from their miseries by enhancing their consciousness, helping them solve problems, and giving their hearts reprieve through understanding. Grades aren't real, man. Criticism and judgment from others don't matter because, as The Dude says, "That's just, like, your opinion, man." Opinions are not facts, no matter *who* tells them.

The great irony to being a scholar is that the more knowledge I acquire, the more the pool of potential knowledge expands. Every subject or idea has a whole field of study behind it with communities, literatures, methodologies, theories, discourses, debates, and histories that I couldn't possibly master in a single lifetime. The scholar, however, does not give up on her quest for knowledge. That is why PhD is "doctor of philosophy," as philosophy is a love for knowledge. My degrees are only that—pieces of papers that remind me of what I love. What I'm saying is that it's okay to not know, even though many of us pretend to know. News flash: scholars are mad insecure. One can argue that I do not know *most things*, but no one is going to hit me for not knowing something. At least not anymore. And if they do, well, I know how to clap back. 👏! 👏!

Did you know that you have nothing to prove? Did you know that you're not an idiot? Did you know that the only thing that matters is whatever you decide for yourself to matter—whatever lights up your eyes and gets your blood moving? Did you know that it is possible to study whatever you want, and find others who share your interest, and have a community that supports and leads you closer to what makes you feel good? Did you know that you never need to waste your precious time or energy on anything that bores you or makes you miserable? Did you know that it's okay not to be perfect and excel at everything? Did you know that other people's opinions about you have nothing to do with you and everything to do with themselves? Did you know that it's okay to live a life that pleases you? I sure as hell didn't. I only came to these realizations in recent years, and not from school, either. Korean TV played a part in some of these revelations. The rest came from trusty doctors, books, friends, meditation, and acid trips.

I used to wonder what drew me to *The Big Lebowski* so much when I was a nineteen-year-old college student. I just love The Dude because he wears loose pants, grows out his hair and belly, and lives by his own virtues to stay chill and enjoy life for what it is while doing a J, and I abide. 🙏

LESSON 2:
A BRIEF HISTORY OF K-TRAUMAS AND EARLY KOREAN TELEVISION

THE NEXT FEW PAGES ARE A CRASH COURSE ON K-DRAMA HISTORY. Seriously, you won't get this quality of knowledge anywhere else. This is top-shelf stuff, baby. Not even $100,000 a year at some private institution is going to bring you the kind of gems I'm about to drop right here and now. Lucky you, man! Oh, my stars! You're so lucky! I'm excited for you! Grab a highlighter! If any of this stuff bores you, just skip it! All you need to do is read the parts that speak to you and serve you. The rest are just words, man. There are no rules!

COLONIZATION, WAR, AND TV

My first memory of watching and retaining the contents of a K-drama was from an MBC series called *Eyes of Dawn* (여명의 눈동자), which aired between 1991 and 1992. It's a historical period drama set during pre-war Korea under Japanese colonization and through the Korean War. It stars Park Sang-won, Choi Jae-sung, and Chae Shi-ra. I was at my maternal grandparents' farmhouse in Hapcheon, sitting in the living room, watching TV with my youngest aunt and grandparents. It was winter, so the floor was warm from the 온돌/*ondol*—a rock bed beneath the yellow vinyl that was heated by a fire pit that my grandmother stoked from outside with wood that my grandfather brought from the mountains. I sat beneath the blankets and watched a man on TV scream in agony from an injury as another soldier tied a tourniquet around his wound. Melodramatic music accompanied this noble act. I recall this because it was viscerally intense and I was probably too young to be watching, but I also remember because I heard my aunt utter sympathetically, "Imagine how painful that must be." This is the power of melodrama. It evokes an emotional response in the viewer through an excessive emotional reaction on the screen, and the image accompanied by that feeling burns into the memory of the viewer.

Eyes of Dawn is a war epic that ran for thirty-seven episodes, and it documents some of the most tumultuous times in modern Korean history, starting at the turn of the twentieth century and continuing through mid-century. The show is based on a ten-volume novel written by Kim Seong-jong, adapted for the screen by screenwriter Song Ji-na.

Song Ji-na is a legendary TV screenwriter who not only wrote *Eyes of Dawn* but also followed it up with *Sandglass* on SBS, which changed Korean TV history in 1995 by breaking ratings records. (Fun fact: Song's son Jin Han-sae is the writer of *Extracurricular* [2020].) *Sandglass* features some sexy actors of that era like Go Hyun-jung, Choi Min-soo, and Lee Jung-jae. You all know who Lee Jung-jae is. He's the lead actor in another historic series: *Squid Game* (2021). A lot of non-Koreans mistake Lee Jung-jae for some dopey-looking dude, but back in the 1990s he was a model and a stud. Everyone wanted a piece of him. *Sandglass* made Lee a star, and he led a prolific film career ever since. *Sandglass* was well received by audiences and critics because it depicted the post–Korean War years, primarily the 1970s and 1980s. South Koreans were mourning and processing their country's century-long oppression through television. K-dramas are dramatic because Koreans understand the theater and grief of war. The drama is always roiling inside Koreans from intergenerational trauma dating back to colonization, national division, the Korean War, and military dictatorships.

If you've seen K-dramas, there's always a nationalistic bias when handling Japan and Japanese characters. It's because Japan colonized the Korean peninsula in 1910. Technically, Japan already had control over Korea in 1905, when they barged into the Korean monarch and told King Gojong that they were now policing Chosŏn with Japanese officers. The Japan-Korea Treaty of 1905 wasn't an agreement between the two nations but rather an annexation as Japan took away Chosŏn's sovereignty by force. I personally am not a fan of the show *The King: Eternal Monarch* (2020). I think it's a shit show, but I do love its what-if fantasy of what an undivided Korea might look like today if the nation retained its monarch and was never divided. In 1910 Japan officially annexed Korea, and the nation lived under Japanese colonial rule until 1945—the same year World War II ended.

During World War I and World War II, Japan put many Koreans in the frontlines to fight for Japan's imperial war cause. Korean men, women, and children were kidnapped from their homes and forced into slave labor on Hashima Island to mine for coal. Korean girls and women were forced into sex slavery for Japanese soldiers during World War II. This exploitation continued among Korean and American soldiers during the Korean War. Exploitation of vulnerable Korean bodies continued through its own government systems even after the cease-fire in 1953, when the Republic of Korea (ROK) began its reconstruction. Children, women, the disabled, and the economically disadvantaged built South Korea into what it is today. That exploitation persists now through othered bodies from Asian, African, Latin American, and Eastern European countries that migrate to South Korea for economic mobility.

During Korea's colonial occupation from 1910 to 1945, Western technology was introduced to Korea via Japan, which was already modernizing from British influence during the Meiji period (1868–1912). There was a great deal of political suppression in Korea by Japanese imperialists during this time. The Korean monarch of the Chosŏn Dynasty disintegrated. The Korean language was made illegal. Koreans were required to use Japanese and to adopt Japanese names. In fact, this is the reason why Fred Armisen, formerly of

Saturday Night Live (1975–present) and *Portlandia* (2011–2018), thought he had Japanese family lineage for so long until he found out that his great-grandfather was actually Korean but had adopted a Japanese name in the colonial era. Many Korean identities were erased due to colonization. For instance, in 1936 Korean athlete Sohn Kee-chung competed in the Berlin Olympic Games representing Imperial Japan and won gold. The Japanese army recruited Koreans as Japanese soldiers to fight the Americans, the British, and Soviets. In the midst of this political oppression, however, Korea also gained access to Western technologies like the gramophone and record players, as well as new styles of music, film, and literature via Japan.

On August 6, 1945, the US dropped a nuclear bomb on Hiroshima. Three days later the US dropped a second nuclear bomb on Nagasaki. Hundreds of thousands of Japanese civilians were killed. Tens of thousands of Koreans living in Japan were also killed. Five days after the second bombing, Japan surrendered, and Korea declared August 15, 1945, as its national Independence Day. But the US and USSR split Korea into two countries immediately after its independence from Japan and reoccupied many of its existing colonial systems. Due to "cold war" tensions over the two powers' ideological differences, the Soviet Union occupied North Korea and America occupied South Korea. In 1950 North Korea invaded South Korea, effectively triggering Soviet and US forces into the heat of battle during this so-called cold war.

Korea got embroiled in a civil war now known as the Korean War (1950–1953). Tens of thousands of American soldiers served in the Korean War, and millions of Koreans died. The Korean War came to a standstill on July 27, 1953, and a cease-fire was declared. However, no peace treaty was ever signed between North and South Korea. The two countries are, to this day, technically still in a state of war. Shortly after the Korean War, American television and its production crews made their way into South Korea in the form of military technology for American troops on Korean soil.

KOREA'S INTRODUCTION TO TELEVISION

South Korea's first television sets were placed in public squares in Seoul in May 1956 and aired programs that blended theatrical entertainment such as dance and drama. The first-ever K-drama produced and broadcast for viewers was called *Heaven's Gate* (1956) and the second was *Death Row* (1956). Both shows were one-off theater pieces that were shot and broadcast live, so it was like watching live theater but through a small screen. South Koreans' introduction to TV was a public event.

That same year, South Korea established its first television station, called HLKZ-TV, with the aid of Radio Corporation of America (RCA), which at the time had a Korean division in Seoul, called KORCAD. This station shut down in 1959 due to an electrical fire. The American Forces Korea Network (AFKN) was established in South Korea so American troops could watch live television like *The Tonight Show*. AFKN was the sole TV broadcaster in South Korea in 1959.

By 1960 more Korean households owned televisions. The Korean military dictator Park Chung-hee encouraged Koreans to own television sets. As a staunch military man, Park understood the power of visual media, and he used TV to control the population with propaganda and to suppress any media insurgence against him. On December 31, 1961, South Korea's very own broadcasting station HLKA-TV was established for the nation's first public broadcaster, Korea Broadcasting Station (KBS), and Park's office offered it to the people as his "Christmas present." Park believed in the influence television had over the masses because he spent a great deal of time studying and working in Japan, which was a war ally to Germany.

Germany and the Third Reich saw the power of visual media to transform civilians into Hitler supporters and anti-Semites who would turn a blind eye to the murder of millions of Jews during the Holocaust. One example of such visual propaganda is *Triumph of the Will* (1935) by Leni Riefenstahl. Because of the history of Nazism in Germany, the Frankfurt School was highly leery of television, so they wrote essays questioning the scary potential of television as a mind-control medium that might destroy humanity again. This is expressly shown in Theodor Adorno and Max Horkheimer's essay "The Culture Industry: Enlightenment as Mass Deception."

Park Chung-hee, inspired by the Nazis, exploited television's potential to maintain authoritarian power. Little did Park realize that all reception is subjective, and no matter how many guns he pointed at people in broadcasting stations, newspaper headquarters, and college campuses, there would always be dissent. Although the media's influence on the masses is real, subjectivity is also real. That's why some of you love *Squid Game* while others had nightmares after the first episode and stopped watching. Television viewers are not a singular unthinking body. Viewers are made of individuals, each with their own tastes and opinions. While all this political drama was happening in the backdrop of South Korean society, KBS began live broadcasting K-dramas in January 1962.

By 1964 the electronics company Samsung established its own broadcasting network called Tongyang Broadcasting Company (TBC). It makes fiscal sense as to why Samsung would do this; they sold television sets, and they wanted to sell more sets to entice viewers with popular content. Fun fact: the first Korean-made TV set in 1966 is not from Samsung but rather its competitor LG, although back then the company was called GoldStar. If you've seen *Reply 1988*, you'll recall seeing "GoldStar" on Jung-hwan's dad's jacket. TBC became the nation's first-ever commercial broadcaster, and upon their establishment, the network took some sleazy measures to talent scout at their competitor KBS to poach their producers, better known as PDs in Korea. Unlike KBS, TBC developed and produced prerecorded serialized dramas from 1964 onward, starting with the show *First Snow* (초설). TBC was also the first network to air a daily serialized drama that ran from Monday through Friday called *Where It Snows* (눈이 내리는데). These serialized dramas are called 연속극/*yŏn-sok gŭk*, which my mother's generation grew up watching. The most popular TV drama in the 1960s was *Mr. Gu at Sajik Village* (사직골 구서방), which first aired in 1967. The attraction was its comedic genre. People wanted to laugh. Who can blame them? The country was in political and economic turmoil, and television was an excellent way to escape.

Munhwa Broadcasting Corporation (MBC) is a commercial broadcaster established in 1969. By this point, around two hundred thousand television sets had entered South Korean homes. But MBC came into formation during Park Chung-hee's military reign, and to remain in operation, the network was forced to align its interests with the authoritarian ruler by submitting monthly activity reports. The Korean government dictated what kind of content and subject matter could air. MBC, similarly to TBC, broke away from live broadcasting and made itself stand out from KBS by adopting new strategies. MBC took a lot of influence from Japanese broadcasting programs and techniques. MBC producers were encouraged to watch Japanese shows from the Japanese Broadcasting Corporation (NHK), and they took notes to copy them. KBS did the same. I interviewed a former PD at KBS who told me that, in the 1990s, he and other PDs would fly to Japan for a weekend, sit in a hotel, and just watch TV for hours at a time, and then fly back to Seoul to hold a meeting on Monday with notes on what they saw. Koreans had to do this because of geoblocking, which banned Japanese content from airing in Korea due to its contentious international politics. Japanese influence on early Korean television is as significant as American militarism and domestic military dictatorships in the ROK that shaped the nation's media history.

In the 1960s censorship and family-friendly television became issues in the press. In 1968 an anxious professor named Kim In-ja told journalists that if television broadcasting is crude and lowbrow, it could lead to crude and lowbrow civilians. Newton Minow, the former chair of the US Federal Communications Commission (FCC), also propagated this paranoid idea in the States—that television's baseness will debase society—referring to American television as a "vast wasteland" in 1961 and giving rise to concepts like television being trash that rots the brain. Television programs that were deemed unhelpful to the growth and development of minors were relegated to broadcasting slots after 10:00 p.m. Korea's paranoia about television, however, is tied to real fears associated with fascism, which Korean society had already fallen victim to at the hands of colonizers prior to the Korean War and their own government after the war.

Present-day suspicions around television still abound. It's fascinating just how disruptive television is as a cultural concept and artifact. TV in our culture today is associated with sin. Anything pleasurable—like lust, gluttony, and excessive indulgence—is considered sinful. The film *Chocolat* (2000) is a decent examination of institutional skepticism of pleasure. Television has been and is still viewed as a threat to our culture's superego—the one constructed out of authority figures like parents, politicians, religious figures, and intellectual experts—all concerned with control.

There were moments throughout television history when people tried to rationalize away the guilt they felt while indulging in the pleasure of television. To do away with this guilt, America developed educational networks and programs. That's why you have PBS in the US and EBS in South Korea. Government spending on something as entertaining as television required a heavy-handed rationale. Make TV a little *boring*, I guess. Turn television viewing into *homework*, and you will have a justifiable TV-viewing experience according to these weird, old, and repressed men who remain eternally suspicious of pleasure.

I attended an academic conference centered on Korean screen studies a few years ago, where the majority of scholars presented on Korean films. Park Chan-wook's *The Handmaiden* (2016) had just come out, and scholars could not stop gushing about it. I couldn't understand why. It's a pervy film, and while I think Park is accomplished in his filmic stylization, he's also a pervy director who overemploys the male gaze in his work to fetishize women's bodies as objects of lust or victimization to sadistic male violence. When scholars talk about cinema, they don't smile or laugh. Everything's serious, urgent, and lofty. But when I and a couple of other scholars presented on TV shows, the room could not help but grow softer, as people began smiling and chuckling. It's impossible to discuss K-dramas without *feeling*. We all know what it is. There are shows we *love*. There are shows we grew up watching next to our mothers, friends, and siblings. There are shows we turned to on a weekly basis as a pleasure ritual and went to school the next day to chat about with friends. Discussions of K-dramas break open fissures in the cold, dry concrete block of high theory in a room full of people wearing stuffy, unfeeling, intellectually driven, left-brain façades of "serious" scholarship. Out through these cracks oozes a pink light of tender feelings attached to sweet and sour childhood memories, nostalgic longing, and an affection for our younger selves who loved TV so much that we glued ourselves to the screen.

EARLY K-DRAMAS

I asked my mom who her favorite actress was when she was a teen. She said, "Jang Mi-hee." You've seen Jang Mi-hee in *The Black Knight: The Man Who Guards Me* (2017), where she plays a witch who bends actress Seo Ji-hye over her knee and spanks her ass for misbehaving. Even though *The Black Knight* is a lousy show, this one scene made the whole experience for me. I screamed and threw crumpled dollar bills at my iPad. It felt like church, and by "church" I mean a drag show on a Monday night at a gay bar in West Hollywood.

Actors like Jang Mi-hee were hired through an open-call recruitment organized by TV networks. The first of these was at KBS in 1961, and 2,600 actors showed up to audition, but only 26 were selected. Among these was Kim Hye-ja, who you've seen in *Princess Hours* (2006), *Unkind Women* (2015), *Dear My Friends* (2016), *The Light in Your Eyes* (2019), and *Our Blues* (2022), as well as in films like *Mother* (2009) by Oscar-winner Bong Joon-ho. Kim Hye-ja was also in the 1969 show *Frog Husband* on MBC.

Frog Husband was extremely controversial because the storyline included adultery. It follows a white-collar working man who is having an affair with his secretary at his office. The show was highly entertaining for viewers who had never seen such a conflict displayed so publicly on TV. Although criticized for being scandalous, *Frog Husband* also made MBC famous. The reason why sex sells is precisely because so many people make a big stink about squashing it, which garners even more curious attention. The producers at MBC who made *Frog Husband* were fully prepared to deal with any penalties or wrist-slaps they would receive from the higher-ups. The show caused upset in the reviews, but it also shattered the sociocultural illusion of a happy and monogamous marriage. Korea's early TV writers and producers learned through *Frog Husband* that scandal, sensation, and shock draw viewers' attention.

In 1970 *I Love You* (너를 사랑해) aired on MBC and was the first to include a ten-second sex scene on television. It was a major hit in ratings despite receiving a warning from the censorship board. That same year MBC aired *Let's Live by the Riverside* (강변살자), which features a relationship between an older woman and a younger man, and censors at the time deemed it socially inappropriate. There's a start to everything. This, of course, is in great contrast to how regularly contemporary K-dramas feature relationships between older women and younger men. Although MBC received flak from the Korea Communications Commission (KCC) for *Let's Live by the Riverside*, they also gained high ratings from curious viewers at home who craved content that pushed conservative boundaries and explored scandal.

To compete with MBC's high ratings, TBC aired the show *Assi* (1970), a historical drama spanning the 1930s through the 1950s. The show focuses on a young woman who marries a cold-mannered man and faces obstacles from him and his family. The show was a major undertaking that featured over twelve hundred actors and aired a total of 253 episodes over the course of a year.

In 1972 Park Chung-hee declared martial law and passed the Yushin Constitution, causing greater injury to South Korea's democracy. Under this constitution Park was able to centralize all authoritarian power to himself, giving him permanent presidency. Any criticism of Park's government was outlawed. KBS became a public service broadcaster and a state resource for Park to disseminate his propaganda. Communism was a perfectly convenient scapegoat. Anything that appeared to be dissent against the government was potentially a communist crime, including hairstyles, music, fashion, and television programs. As censorship laws tightened, television sets were more sought after than ever before. Serialized dramas were hot because they featured the nation's favorite stars, who represented fantastical aspirations, desire, love, and beauty.

Park was assassinated in 1979. Choi Gyu-ha was briefly Park's successor, but Major General Chun Doo-hwan staged a coup d'état to take office in 1980. Chun's military authority rule over South Korea included the Basic Press Law, which made any media criticism against the government illegal. The government-controlled broadcaster KBS absorbed both TBC and MBC by force. PDs voiced their concerns over the integrity of public programming, but Chun put his closest people in the presidents' seats at both stations, and all insurgence was squashed within the network. 1980 is also when color television sets began to proliferate throughout South Korea.

Part of Chun's mass control through media was the "3S" policy, refer-ring to sex, sports, and screen. Chun's logic was that as long as the masses were watching the latest game, sex in movies, and entertainment on tele-vision, the people would be too dull and complacent to participate in any political protest against his military dictatorship. Chun used the paranoid logic that screens rot the brain as a political tactic to distract civilians from generating insurgence against him, echoing Park's practices.

Yeah. That didn't work. The 1980s was a heated time in South Korea on both the silver screen and in the streets. Wherever there is oppres-sion, there is also an equal amount of rebellion. That's why in *Reply 1988*, while Deok-seon sits at home glued to the TV without a care in the world, her older sister Bo-ra marches in the streets through tear gas and police brutality to fight for her country's liberty. But Park's suppressive meth-ods of controlling people through media have lasting consequences to this day.

KBS and MBC today completely avoid political discussions on televi-sion, and PDs take active measures to self-censor political topics. As the original public broadcaster, KBS shows tend to be more family oriented and didactic, particularly around issues such as divorce. SBS is a commercial broadcaster that is somewhat more lenient with socioculturally dicey top-ics, but it generally strays from any political discussions. South Korea today has numerous cable-outlet alternatives to these three channels, and they also stray from political discussions. Reasons for this vary, but one big influ-ence is who owns these networks. A great number of them are tied to major corporate conglomerates, and these conglomerates have historically been bedfellows with the Korean government.

It's no wonder that conglomerates and patriarchal figures appear so frequently in K-dramas as ruthless. They played a major role in Korea's television history alongside militaristic governing tactics. Pay careful attention to how chaebols and political leaders get portrayed in K-dramas. Taking these sociopolitical, cultural, and historical contexts into consid-eration the next time you watch a show might add a deeper flavor to your viewing experience.

A BRIEF KOREAN AMERICAN HISTORY OF K-DRAMA RECEPTION

Nineteenth-century French gastronomist Jean Anthelme Brillat-Savarin said that if we tell him what we eat, he'll tell us what we are. Korean immigrants like myself will tell him to ask our moms because I don't exactly know what I just ate. I ate whatever she gave me without questioning what was on the table because if I did, she'd smack me across my backside and say, "Shut up and eat."

On an episode of *Conan*, Conan O'Brien goes to South Korea and asks Korean American actor Steven Yeun what every side dish on the table of a "traditional" Korean restaurant contains. Yeun replies, "It has whatever my mom puts in it. I don't know."[18] For those of us in America raised by a Korean mother, 엄마/*Umma* was our first tastemaker, not just in the form of food but also the shows we watched. She was the ruler of the remote control and the VHS machine. Television was not only our hearth of culture, entertainment, and pleasure but also a means to access the motherland from a distance. It warmed and nourished our dual identities as Koreans living as Americans and vice versa.

A disconnect formed as we grew into Korean American adults in this country with the language we acquired as first-generation children of immigrants in an English-speaking society. When we went to Korean restaurants, non-Korean friends often turned to us for answers about the food they were about to partake: What is this? How is it prepared? What goes into it? Is it gluten-free? Does it have soy? Does it have meat? Does it have fish sauce? Does it have shellfish? How annoying. By virtue of being Korean, we were automatically expected to be chefs and nutritionists too. If only we could get away with just slapping their backsides while barking, "Shut up and eat."

When I was a child, whatever banchan my mother put out became the thing that wound up in my mouth without question, becoming a part of me and turning me into the *what* to Brillat-Savarin's observations—the being I am in the world.[19] As an adult, however, I continuously encounter questions I never bothered asking my own mother. I don't know how to reply to

---

18 Team Coco, "Conan & Steven Yeun Enjoy a Traditional Korean Meal," *Conan*, YouTube, April 12, 2016, www.youtube.com/watch?v=tsTZ2iFRSmw&list=LLGNGXH1XI5STOJYDsHVK_qQ&index=2063, accessed November 25, 2020.

19 반찬/*Banchan* refers to small Korean side dishes.

questions about Korean food other than how Yeun replies to O'Brien: "It has whatever my mom puts in it. I don't know." Yeun's declaration is a light brush-off of O'Brien's white American interrogation and ignorant expectation that Yeun *must* know what all these food items and ingredients are simply because he is Korean. This ignores the fact that Yeun is an American-born actor. Yeun's brush-off, however, contains an unspoken explanation: we, as Korean Americans, don't have all the answers to questions about Korea because we are also American—culturally disjointed because we have mastered neither country's cultures and live with enormous gaps of cultural knowledge due to our upbringing.

We, the Korean diaspora, are just as lost as O'Brien is at the "traditional" Korean dinner table. While the chef, maître d', and servers might have an explanation for the things we point to on the table and ask about, we as consumers have no way of discerning what it is we are mindlessly consuming today in the state of global hype around Korean culture. With all that said, questioning does open our eyes to wondering what the specificities of these cultural objects are and how they came to be a part of who and what we are. If I am what I consume, there are whole parts of me made of serialized Korean TV shows—or what we call in our current zeitgeist "K-dramas."

Let me expand Brillat-Savarin's declaration. If you tell me what you watch, I'll tell you what you are. If you watched K-dramas all your life since you were a child with those VHS tapes that your mother picked up at the Korean supermarket when she went food shopping, I know you. I see you. We grew up with Korean immigrant mothers who shaped our habitus, and there is a continuation of that influence as well as a discontinuation as we've become vocal about our own preferences and envision off-menu items that differ from what our mothers raised us on. K-dramas have evolved significantly alongside social progression, globalization, and an expanded sociocultural awareness.

It is natural to associate food with internationally available K-dramas. In the 1990s video stores in New York were always next to or a part of the Korean supermarket where my mom did her shopping and picked up VHS tapes of Korean TV. The shopkeepers of the VHS mom-and-pop businesses would record and copy numerous tapes of different shows simultaneously in their cubby that was filled with dozens of VHS machines and television sets stacked on top of one another. There wasn't quite the deluge of K-dramas that we find online today back then. It's akin to K-pop groups in that contemporary K-dramas are hard to keep up with because there are just so many. When I was a kid, my mom would simply ask the shopkeeper, "What's a good drama these days?" The shopkeeper would grab a tape from behind her and say, "This is pretty popular." Or I'd ask my Korean American friends what they were watching lately, and there would be a loud consensus over what show grabbed their attention as of late. It's how I came to see shows like *Asphalt Man* (1995), *Star in My Heart* (1997), *Into the Sunlight* (1999), *First Love* (1997), *LA Arirang* (1995), *Three Guys and Three Girls* (1996–1999), *All About Eve* (2000), *Hur Jun* (1999–2000), *Autumn in My Heart* (2000), *Successful Story of a Bright Girl* (2002)—man, I could go on. But if you recognize any of the above, you have K-drama OG status in my heart, along with the kids who grew up calling it "HanAhReum" and not "H-Mart."

The shows on VHS tapes that our mothers brought home back then have become a part of our collective memory and shaped who we are today as Korean Americans. Some left a greater impression on us than others, but we're collectively united by a few titles that link us generationally (I'm a millennial 😊). These shows connect us to our ethnic culture and social networks. That connection has now broadened and become transnational through the internet, making niche content globally accessible with fan-translated subtitles. Rakuten's Viki harnessed this multilingual fandom love into economical labor for their shows and movies.

The Korean supermarket and video store were part of Korean immigrant mothers' domestic management since the 1980s into the early 2000s. Historically, the first generation of working-class Korean immigrants who came to the US worked mostly as greengrocers. In the 1980s, as competition began to increase, mom-and-pop shops started to distinguish themselves with add-on services such as flowers, salad bars, and Korean videos. The VHS tapes came from distributors with ties to Korean broadcasters like MBC, KBS, and, later, SBS. Video store shopkeepers were given a single copy of the master tape from distributors two weeks after the program aired in Korea and then were required by contract to hold back releasing the tapes for another four weeks, which forced diaspora Koreans to wait a total of six weeks before they could see the shows that their family and friends back in the motherland were already chatting about. Some of my Korean friends were recent emigres who had earlier access to K-dramas as they aired in Korea in real time through online access. These kids were generous enough to share their passwords with the rest of us, and we'd binge whole shows before the other suckers could see them and give away major spoilers just to see them cry about it.

This enhanced anticipation of shows in America through holdbacks led to greater demand and resulted in about $7 million a year in profit for KBS in US video rights sales in the 1980s and 1990s. By the late nineties, however, this mom-and-pop distribution system rapidly disintegrated as digitization, video uploads, and pirating on the internet made K-dramas more accessible.

In some ways, this was a relief because there were plenty of days when I grabbed the videotape of my latest show, ran to the VCR with excited anticipation, popped it in, and saw nothing but a black screen because the ajumma's recording system went awry that day.[20] What a mood killer. There were also times when I would re-rent video tapes of shows I'd already seen because I wanted to rewatch them. I rewatch a lot of films and shows regularly. Whenever I would grab a tape from a series that was already over, the owner would eye me weirdly, saying, "You already saw this." Sometimes the shows I wanted to revisit would no longer be available because the owner taped over that show with the latest series, and I could see the remnants of my beloved show through the white sticker with a new title. With streaming, I can revisit all the shows I want as many times as I want whenever I want. But I do mourn the death of these video stores in the early 2000s as YouTube and streaming companies shifted our entire culture of viewing to monetized online content, which outdid the mom-and-pop VHS system. Although the actual stores are empty, I still see worn-down Korean "Video Store" signs in Los Angeles's Koreatown, and they are beautiful relics to my eyes.

---

20 아줌마/*Ajumma* is "auntie" to informally address a middle-aged woman in Korean.

LESSON 3:
REALISM AND TRAUMA RECOVERY IN *MY MISTER*

I'M A NINETIES-TO-EARLY-MILLENNIA K-POP FAN THAT FOLLOWED groups like S.E.S., H.O.T., T.T.Ma, and 1TYM. I also loved Yoon Mi-rae. I still do, and she's recorded a lot of K-drama original soundtracks for shows like *Master's Sun* (2013), *It's Okay, That's Love* (2014), and *Descendants of the Sun* (2016). K-pop and K-dramas have always had a symbiotic relationship through K-pop stars' musical talents and acting abilities.

My favorite K-pop soloist is IU (née Lee Ji-eun). She is not only an immensely talented singer but also a force to be reckoned with as an actress. I first saw her in the 2013 K-drama *You're the Best, Lee Soon-shin*, where she played opposite Jo Jung-suk (another phenomenal actor I admire) and supported by fan-favorite Yoo In-na and veteran actresses Go Doo-shim and Lee Mi-sook. The show's reception was okay. The ratings weren't stellar, but IU won the Best New Actress award at KBS that year—and for good reason. She's quite talented. Then I saw IU again in a devastating and tacky show called *Moon Lovers: Scarlet Heart Ryeo* (2016), which is based on a Chinese novel entitled *Bu Bu Jing Xin* by Tong Hua. I thought that show did IU's character Hae Soo real dirty, but IU still delivered a very controlled performance. Then, in 2018 IU appears in *My Mister* and shakes my world.

C-PTSD AND ASSESSING A THREAT

My Mister is an excellent case study for analyzing a person afflicted with developmental trauma and how she copes as an adult. The protagonist appears hopeless but eventually finds healing, thanks to a sturdy mentor who does not give up on her. It is one of the most radical examples of love I've witnessed on television between two characters who are not romantic partners or family. They are colleagues at an office and fellow neighbors. *My Mister* is a slice-of-life realist text about how a person reconnects to their inner humanity after experiencing a disconnection due to trauma.

My Mister's protagonist, Ji-an, suffers from Complex Post-Traumatic Stress Disorder (C-PTSD). I first heard of PTSD in grade school when I learned about war veterans who returned home "shell-shocked." PTSD is common among veterans who experienced battle where their lives were threatened or witnessed atrocities—getting caught in crossfires, killing, raping, bombing, surviving torture when taken prisoner, and witnessing the deaths of their comrades. But trauma does not just erupt from war and accidents.

With PTSD, there is a clear picture of a person before and after the trauma. For example, before going to war, my friend J was a humorous and outgoing guy. After high school, he joined the US Army. When he returned from his tour in Afghanistan, he was withdrawn, silent, and depressed. Our mutual friends told me, "He's not the same." With C-PTSD, however, there is no identifiable self before the trauma because survivors of this disorder were children when they were traumatized. Trauma gets coded into a child's brain when they experience prolonged neglect from their caretakers or suffer long-term physical, emotional, mental, spiritual, and/or sexual abuse as a child. In my case, I am a survivor of all of the above, and the abuse I suffered began at age four and persisted throughout my teens and twenties.

C-PTSD victims like me live life in a state of trauma as the norm because that is all we've known since the development of our consciousness. There is no before-the-trauma state of being that I can return to or recall. My perception of life has always been a default state of fear, defense, and alarm. Many people afflicted with C-PTSD grow up with other ailments. In my case, I suffer from anxiety, depression, ADHD, insomnia, migraines, numbness, dissociation, addictions, eating disorders, physical pains, and recurring emotional flashbacks that turn into obsessive negative thoughts. Love and intimacy feel like threats. Depending on the day, these symptoms are either better or worse.

When I began watching *My Mister*, I immediately recognized my younger self in Ji-an. She is closed-mouthed, shuts out the world with her earphones, and overexerts her body with infernal physical labor while disregarding her health. She is reticent and not personable. Ji-an is in a perpetual state of either dissociative numbness or anger, and the only person she reserves any affection for is her disabled elderly grandmother, who is deaf and mute. Watching Ji-an is like watching me in my late teens and twenties. Ji-an is not living. She is only surviving, and her existence passes through the atmosphere of life without indulging in its substance mindfully. Under the cloud of C-PTSD, life does not appear to be one full of options and choices. Life seems like a matter of getting through each day. While some people make future plans for fun activities, joyful encounters, or hopeful events, I would be knotted up with anxiety, anticipating the worst possible outcome in everything, putting on armor to protect myself from others, and preparing for battle with trembling fingers. To cope with feelings of inner chaos, numbness, or agony, I frequently turned to alcohol. In my default mode, I am enshrouded in a dark cloud of depression, with zero appetite for anything.

At the time I did not know why I felt this way. I thought that being tense, insecure, and afraid was the norm. I came to understand through treatment that the basis of my C-PTSD stems from abandonment as well as physical and emotional abuse I had been subject to since nursery school, which carried into my formative years at home in the US after my immigration in 1992. Besides the trauma of poverty, I grew up with microaggressions and racism that I dealt on my own and witnessed my parents be subject to. Between ages five and eighteen, I experienced sexual assault multiple times by male predators in my community. Throughout my twenties and early thirties I continued to experience sexual assault from male partners and strangers. I struggled with shame, depression, anxiety, and rage for years.

Ji-an is not a pleasant person to watch. She's not the IU we know and love in bright and bubbly music videos with her whispery high soprano. Ji-an is a quiet and sullen twenty-one-year-old woman who works as a temp at a large engineering company in Seoul. Her parents died when she was very young, leaving behind a massive debt to loan sharks. Ji-an is not only required to pay back this debt but is also continuously intruded upon and harassed by a thug named Gwang-il. He assaults Ji-an and her immobile grandmother. There's a permanent shadow cast over Ji-an's face. Her lips are always chapped from malnourishment. She wears dark clothes and a knock-off pair of black Converse sneakers with low socks, even in the dead cold winter. She is brusque in her mannerisms, sullen and silent. Just about everyone at the office where she temps abhors her. Watching her is like watching me at her age.

The male protagonist is Dong-hoon, a structural engineer and general manager of the safety inspection team at the same office. Despite Ji-an's rough and insolent demeanor, once Dong-hoon learns of Ji-an's hardship, he shows her compassion. This puts Ji-an at odds with herself, as she spies on Dong-hoon by tapping his phone and recording his conversations in an attempt to blackmail him and profit. Complicated feelings of attraction arise within Ji-an as she stalks Dong-hoon through his phone, spying on his life as a father, husband, brother, and son. After witnessing his humanity, it becomes impossible for Ji-an to go through with her plans to exploit him.

Ji-an's sonic voyeurism of Dong-hoon through phone tapping points to a larger social malaise plaguing contemporary South Korea in the form of spy cameras—aka spycams—that infest hotels, motels, pools, guest houses, and restrooms to peep on female victims who are unaware of being photographed. There are thousands of spycams installed in public places by perpetrators who target women. Some predators who are close to their female victims film the women they have sex with and keep the footage to use as collateral against them. Victims, however, often avoid seeking justice because they are conscious of gender-discriminatory police bias but also afflicted by self-directed shame.[21] *My Mister* reimagines surveillance objects that violate women's privacy into one that can exploit men for monetary gain.

Tapping phones to determine which men are safe or not becomes a means for Ji-an to play god. It gives her the power of choice as to who she will open up to and who she will protect herself from. Judith Herman observes that hyper-vigilance, along with anxiety and agitation, are constant for the chronically traumatized.[22] Hypervigilance is a symptom of C-PTSD that helps survivors assess any threats or threatening persons quickly. This paranoid social outlook, however, leads to intimacy and interrelationship problems due to trust issues. To keep things simple, Ji-an generally deems everybody around her as "unsafe" and keeps them at a distance with her unfriendly demeanor because any close relationship feels like a threat of potential abandonment or injury.

In a restaurant scene with Ji-an and Dong-hoon, she bitterly reflects on the people who had initially been kind to her when they found out that she was an orphan single-handedly caring for her disabled grandmother. People brought food and showed kindness up to about four times, but they eventually stopped. As Ji-an comments on how this limited altruistic act must've made them feel righteous, Dong-hoon softly chides in reply that four times is a lot considering there are numerous others who haven't done a single act of good.

In my own trauma therapy I am consistently encouraged to work through my triggered state until my energy transmutes, enabling me to see the good in humanity again. When I am triggered, my worldview turns red or black. Everything gets labeled with an anxious permanence: *It's never going to work* or *It's hopeless* or *It's* always *like this for me.* This is a defense mechanism I developed to preserve myself from further damage. It feels safer to predetermine everything as shit rather than wait out uncertainty because I was assaulted as a child. In Ji-an's case, it is easier for her to see these do-gooders as self-righteous jerks who did not commit to their charitable acts, because the pain of being abandoned again is too much. Rather than let Ji-an linger on this

---

21 Birru Dereje Teshome, "Spy Camera Epidemic in Korea: A Situational Analysis," *Asian Journal of Sociological Research* 2, no. 1 (2019): 1–13, 7.

22 Judith Lewis-Herman, *Trauma and Recovery: The Aftermath of Violence—From Domestic Abuse to Political Terror* (New York: Basic Books, 1992), 86.

painful mindset, Dong-hoon gently turns her attention toward the fact that there *were* charitable people in her life and that their contributions matter just as much as she does.

A MENTOR WHO RECOGNIZES THE GOOD

Ji-an has a dark past. She killed a violent loan shark who incessantly beat Ji-an and her disabled grandmother while demanding money that her dead mother owed. Ji-an was in middle school at the time, and the law found her not guilty because she was a minor acting out of self-defense. The violent man's son Gwang-il, however, continues to hound Ji-an for money and takes out his vindictive rage through physical and verbal abuse. When Ji-an takes another beating from Gwang-il and goes to work battered while running a fever, she collapses in the office. Her coworkers then mutter judgmentally that she must've slept at her desk. Dong-hoon later sees Ji-an drinking beer at a convenience store to soothe her pain and notices bruises on her hand. He tells her, "Take medicine if you're sick." Dong-hoon alerts Ji-an to her own lack of self-care by offering sensible advice.

When I was in college, I stopped eating. I used to pass out constantly from low blood pressure and malnutrition. I stopped eating because I wanted to disappear. I was in endless pain and a state of self-loathing, but I didn't know what to do. I just lived life in a dense fog of depression, wondering when it will finally end and give me peace. I genuinely felt as if I did not deserve anything good because I saw myself as only bad.

When Dong-hoon sees Ji-an steal a shopping cart to push her immobile grandmother outside to see the full moon in the sky, he takes a moment to recognize the good in Ji-an and tells her, "You are good." The translation that appears in the Netflix subtitles says, "You are nice," but the phrase "착하다" is more heartfelt and profound. It is a declaration of one person's acknowledgment of another person's inner good. It's a recognition of one's radiating inner spirit. Ji-an repeatedly listens to this utterance recorded on her phone to absorb its warmth. The image of her playing this phrase over and over reveals how starved Ji-an was of such humane acknowledgment. It shows a tiny spark of tender vulnerability left in her.

After this exchange, Dong-hoon shows Ji-an more attention as a mentor and boss at work. When Ji-an overhears one of Dong-hoon's subordinates drunkenly complain about Dong-hoon's passivity at a work dinner, Ji-an slaps him in the face. Upon hearing this, Dong-hoon firmly instructs Ji-an on proper decorum in a calm tone without judgment while also showing his appreciation for her support. *My Mister* brims with such complex and nuanced exchanges that strive to address the wholeness of human interrelationships and feeling and not just a stark contrast of extremes. Dong-hoon's instruction of Ji-an is an amalgam of disappointment, frustration, tenderness, and gratitude packed into one solid teaching moment on how to trust human relationships again. These experiences whittle away at Ji-an's emotional guardedness.

Dong-hoon understands that, given her orphaned status, Ji-an grew up with no proper parenting and can't help but be how she is, even though it disagrees with the people in her social environment. Rather than take their side, Dong-hoon risks his own reputation by guiding and directing Ji-an toward the embrace of a community. When Ji-an starts to express her attraction to Dong-hoon, he remains firm on his boundaries while also being mindful of her emotional and mental vulnerability. He does not prey upon her naiveté. He views her as a child and mentors her in not just work but also life.

At one point Ji-an asks Dong-hoon if he really doesn't hate her. To this he responds, "Once you know someone—once you really get to know someone—there comes a point where you don't care what they do. And I know you."

Dong-hoon's nonjudgment contributes to Ji-an's healing and step-by-step unlearning of words and actions that cause her further alienation. Dong-hoon invites Ji-an to socialize with his close network of neighborhood friends. He offers her more than just compassion; he gives her instruction, community, and love. When Ji-an's past for killing a man out of self-defense gets exposed company-wide, Dong-hoon remains firm in his position as her ally. When his colleagues say that his defense of Ji-an raises eyebrows, he says that he would do the same for any one of them.

Dong-hoon encourages Ji-an to work on her social life, telling her that there's nothing wrong with growing close to people. Ji-an remains suspect: "Will anyone be close to me after they find out that I'm a killer? Even those closest to me hesitated once they found out what kind of person I am." To this Dong-hoon casually responds, "As long as it means nothing to you, so it will be to others." Dong-hoon helps Ji-an restore her self-esteem and self-worth. Ji-an believes she is unworthy of being close to anyone. Parental abandonment and abuse have made love and intimacy feel unsafe to her. Trauma literature shows that when a child experiences abandonment from their caretakers, they start to think they were abandoned because there's something wrong with them. But Dong-hoon tells Ji-an that it is up to her to decide who and what she is to the world, not the other way around. This helps clear the cobwebs that had been obstructing the path to her inner locus. As Van der Kolk writes, "Change begins when we learn to own our 'emotional' brains."[23]

When I was in college, school began to feel friendly to me because I had a choice in where I wanted to put my attention and energy. I took a creative writing course in poetry led by the poet-in-residence Charles North. Charles always took the time to compliment my work. He later asked if I would be interested in taking an independent study with him for one-on-one mentoring in creative writing. To everyone's shock, I said no. Charles smiled graciously and said okay. When I later mentioned this exchange casually to another professor, he told me, "Grace, Charles does not offer an opportunity like that to just anyone. It's incredibly rare. You have to take that independent study. Email him immediately and tell him that you changed your mind."

Charles's kind attention was so alien to me. I did not believe I was talented. I was running from my own imposter syndrome, which, while common, was inevitable in my case, as everything was completely new to me and my parents. Because my parents did not have a grasp of the English language, I was their translator and interpreter since age six. I became the family's navigational guide and voice, but it was not my decision. It was just decided for me. My family and I were undocumented immigrants residing in the US "illegally" for over a decade until we finally got our green cards and eventually became naturalized US citizens. I questioned my belongingness to this country and my rights as a citizen. My parents were always eager to take advice

---

23 Van der Kolk, *The Body Keeps the Score*, 129.

from other people they deemed more qualified, even if such advice was irrelevant or harmful in raising me. I am the first in my family to go to college. This turned the entire college experience into a giant question mark. It took me many years to feel like I was back in the driver's seat of my life again.

I spent a very creatively productive semester under Charles's tutelage, writing new poems, essays, and fiction that sharpened my voice. I also received the Academy of American Poets Prize through my university, which had been established by John Ashbery—a poet I greatly admire. Charles encouraged me to get to know my roots by reading and translating Korean literature. These explorations led to my Fulbright research stint in Seoul in 2009, and I eventually translated two books of Korean fiction.

But my skewed self-perception and distrust of people continued to alienate me from myself and others, and I was severely depressed throughout college. During one of our office meetings, I told Charles that I am a misanthropist. He balked and said, "I do not believe that. Not in the least." Charles was doing for me what Dong-hoon was doing for Ji-an: releasing me from my own skewed self-perception and limiting belief that stemmed from fear. The physical assault and ridicule I experienced as a child made me feel constantly embarrassed, stupid, unsure, and not good enough. I thought I was a piece of shit who deserved to neither give nor receive love. Trustworthy mentors and teachers like Charles and Dong-hoon are lifesavers to C-PTSD survivors like me and Ji-an.

During Ji-an and Dong-hoon's commute home from work, they run into Dong-hoon's friends in front of their neighborhood bar. Everyone walks Ji-an home together while chatting. Ji-an chimes in and says she wishes to grow older soon because life will be easier than it is now. This stops everyone in their tracks. The group of adults twice her age encircle Ji-an, looking at her silently with warm compassion because they know the truth: it doesn't get any easier with age, but they adore Ji-an for naively believing this. Her comment reflects the light of her youthful hope.

Ji-an often gets locked into a myopic view of her own life filled with self-pity and agony. But this small moment offers her healing, as she finally looks up to notice the bigger circle of community surrounding her and that the world is more than just her own pain. Dong-hoon tells Ji-an to reach out to him anytime Gwang-il shows up and that the whole neighborhood has generations of family and friends who will run to her aid at the drop of a hat. In these moments of humanity, Ji-an's defensive shell cracks.

Toward the end of the show, at a politically tense company hearing that deliberates on Park Dong-hoon's promotion, Ji-an is invited to speak openly about her relationship with him, given the suspicious rumors in the office. Ji-an says, "Even if I am fired today, I'm grateful to the company and Mr. Park for treating me like a human being for the first time in my life and for making me believe that perhaps I am a good person."

THE REAL ME

Discussions of realism in media are typically imbued with cynicism. In the post–World War II atmosphere, Italian neorealists used working-class conditions as inspiration for their movies, exhibiting their desperate straits in poverty, as well as state and patriarchal oppression, through gritty aesthetics and long takes that illustrate a detached perspective, employing an apathetic lens to the injustice their characters suffer. Realism in cinema is defined by telling the observer to accept life's cruelty as is, with no hope for improvement or change. In these so-called realist films, however, while the bulk of the plotline may be filled with despair, tension, and injustice, there are also moments of magic that transcend the brutality of the characters' circumstances, offering momentary reprieve. Aren't these moments just as *real*?

Think of the way we use the word "real" in our everyday rhetoric. When something serious, shocking, or overwhelming takes place, people say, "Shit got real." When people want to rain on someone's parade, they start by saying, "Let's be real," then nitpick over the alleged impracticalities of a given idea. When relationships end, one party usually mentions how they finally saw the other party's "real" side—meaning their absolute worst—which then led to the demise of that connection.

My question is, when we are at our absolute worst, are we in fact being our *real* selves? When shit hits the fan, is that really the life's *real*? Why is that the general outlook? The realism in *My Mister* relies on the surreal—a very delicate divine moment that hangs on sheer chance and luck. When Ji-an's abuser Gwang-il overhears her telling Dong-hoon that she knows Gwang-il is inherently good despite his appearance now, Gwang-il returns the evidence he stole from Ji-an, which helps get Dong-hoon's enemy indicted. Justice is served and order is restored. Just as Dong-hoon's recognition of Ji-an's inner good ignited a turning point in her to change for the better, Ji-an chooses to remember Gwang-il for the good person that he had been as a boy rather than the violent man he grew up to be. This acknowledgment moves Gwang-il to override his malice.

My Mister redefines realism as a display of human redemption in the face of life's absurd cruelty and injustice. The show places its bet on hope for humanity with the promise for change and healing even among the most egregious characters. The "real" in a person is not their worst qualities but rather their inherent good. Realism doesn't have to be limited to moments of life at their worst. Realism can be defined by an unexpected opening that streams with light.

Maybe that's why I watch so many K-dramas. I'm seeking answers to my own anguish through these protagonists' journey toward healing from past wounds.

We love a show like *My Mister* because we witness a traumatized woman find healing and inner peace. The show provokes a cultural nerve by holding a mirror up to its social malaises—namely toxic masculinity, social inequity, and capitalist inhumanity—while also exhibiting compassion, resilience, and respect. We love *My Mister* because it shows a traumatized woman learning how to trust people again through the support of a sturdy mentor and community that embrace her with no questions asked. We love *My Mister* because the members of that community choose to see Ji-an as their own, nurturing her back to a healthy, bright, and joyful person who shines light onto the world—her real self.

LESSON 4:

PENTHOUSE AND FOOD-SLAPPING MAKJANG DRAMAS FOR THE EGO'S SOUL

ACTRESS KIM SEO-HYUNG, WHO PLAYS COACH KIM JOO-YOUNG IN *SKY Castle*, is an icon in the *makjang* world. In 2008 she appeared on an SBS show, *Temptation of Wife*, as a jealous saboteur and homewrecker. Watching an ego-driven theater of chaos is great fun when it is safely contained within a screen. Well, pretty much all TV is this—a safe means to voyeuristically experience.

Shows like *SKY Castle*, *World of the Married* (2020), and *Penthouse* (2020) are spectacles of infernal ego-driven conflicts. Characters claw for more money and power as a way to hide and run from their deepest insecurities while envying one another's rank and material wealth. Juicy shit. Pour me another white wine spritzer. Let's get into it.

SOAP OPERA FOUNDATIONS OF MAKJANG

I once taught an undergraduate seminar entitled "K-Dramas on Netflix." I asked my students whether they'd ever heard of the word "makjang" before, and quite a few nodded. When asked to describe it, they used the following excellent descriptors: attention-grabbing, wild turns, unexpected, outrageous circumstances, suspension of belief, and traditionalist/conservative ideals clashing with modern takes. Makjang describes the absolute end—the pit of despair and point of no return. Makjang references the train wreck you can't avert your eyes from. It's the same feeling you get when you watch antics on American reality television or ridiculous plotlines in soap operas, such as twins conceived by one mother but each fathered by a different man (hi-oh!). Makjang dramas suspend your belief to hallucinogenic levels of camp.

A makjang drama always includes a twisted villain. Viewers tune in to enjoy despising the villain's treacherous ways while the protagonist remains frustratingly naïve. Many makjang scenes are hyperbolic to the point of making us question how on earth anyone could return to normalcy after such a cataclysmic event. Makjang was never intended as a genre, but it slowly became one via social media discourse, fandom responses, and the cheap, fast-paced production of shooting serialized dramas with scripts written overnight. Makjang dramas raise the emotional stakes by following the characters' ego-driven motives like jealousy, vindictiveness, and greed, which lead to long-term revenge plotting.

Makjang K-dramas, aka "weekday dramas" (연속극 드라마), air every weekday, typically in the late morning hours just before lunch. The industry calls these daily serialized soaps "partial script dramas" (쪽대본 드라마) because a new script gets written each day. A good crash-course on makjang drama's fast-paced production process and outrageous storylines based on hackneyed tropes is available on *Infinite Challenge* (2005–2018) in the "Part Script" series.[24]

Media scholar Youjeong Oh writes,

> *Broadcasting firms and drama producers share the interests in viewer ratings; higher ratings not only generate more sales of*

---

24 MBCentertainment, *Infinite Challenge*, March 10, 2012, "Infinite Challenge, Part Script #이, 쪽대본 드라마 20090214," www.youtube.com/watch?v=0YWDmaRIrVI.

commercials, but also raise the unit price of commercials. . . . This critical commercial logic has created a system of what is called jjok-daebon (a slice of script) or "hasty script" in the Korean drama indus-try. Under this system, extremely short sections of scripts arrive on set, barely meeting the live-shoot schedule.[25]

This time compression contributes to the nonsensical aesthetic of mak-jang shows. *Goblin: The Lonely and Great God* (2016) satirizes these weekday dramas when the grim reaper Kim Woo-bin is at a restaurant gasping while watching morning TV. These shows are also called "morning dramas" or "mom shows" because stay-at-home mothers tend to watch them after sending their kids off to school. This is also how soap operas got their name in the US.

Radio shows in the 1930s were sponsored by soap companies and tar-geted the domestic manager—women listeners at home. These women did laundry and dishes while listening to radio shows that advertised soap prod-ucts. This trend carried into television. The daily serialization of these shows is meant to match the daily work ritual and rhythm of homemakers, but the shows also include crazy unexpected narrative turns with outrageous sce-narios and extreme plot twists for shock entertainment. Over-the-top narra-tive choices keep viewers glued to TV in wonderment: *How are they gonna get out of this pickle?* Makjang dramas typically have a secret surrounding some-one's birth, scandals, affairs, deception, murder, and debt. Consider the show *Penthouse.* Even before the show aired, it was anticipated as a makjang due to the reputation of the show's creator, Kim Soon-ok, whose writing is expected to be ridiculous, camp, and outrageous, requiring the viewer to truly suspend their belief.

THE IMF CRISIS AND MATERIAL EXCESS ON TV

Media studies scholar and journalist Choi Ji-hee claims that the phrase "makjang drama" appeared in the press when shows like *First Wives' Club*

---

25 Youjeong Oh, "The Interactive Nature of Korean TV Dramas," in *Hallyu 2.0: The Korea Wave in the Age of Social Media,* ed. Sangjoon Lee and Abé Mark Nornes (University of Michigan Press: Ann Arbor, 2015), 135.

(2007–2008), *You Are My Destiny* (2008), and *Temptation of Wife* were on the air. Choi calls 2009 the "heyday" of makjang dramas when Kim Soon-ok's *Temptation of Wife*, Moon Young-nam's *Three Brothers* (2009–2010), and Im Sung-han's *Assorted Gems* (2009–2010) were all on the air at once. Choi argues that the aesthetic of makjang is a result of low-cost production while trying to reel in high viewer ratings.[26]

Makjang, therefore, serves a strategic purpose. It's to keep people cemented to the screen. Television and production labor studies scholar John Caldwell calls this strategy of emphasizing the aesthetic of excess and style "televisuality."[27] Caldwell discusses this term in the context of 1980s television, with its rise of cable in America and the hypercompetition that broadcasters faced with their own decline in ratings and profits. Out of this crisis, serialized shows, reality TV, and the news got all wacky, excessive, sensational, and gaudy. Quite on-brand for the 1980s, I'd say, considering its hairstyles, fashion, and accessories were so over the top. Makjang mirrors the same paranoid and hypercompetitive attitude that defines all sensational television.

Makjang is an extension of televisuality, with television's hellbent intention to keep people focused on their channel. One way of keeping viewers invested is through serialization's addictive regularity, fueling the daily rhythm and comfort that satisfies the ego's immediate craving. K-dramas are great at episode cliffhangers, such as a birth reveal, a smooch, a car screeching toward headlights, and so on. If cliffhangers are designed to make the ego crave more and quickly, then K-drama cliffhangers are designed to give you televisual blue balls. Makjang dramas have ridiculous narratives because they are produced under the guise of stress aesthetics—the visual result of a high-stress creative environment.[28]

---

26 Choi Ji-hee, "Makchangdŭramaran muŏshin'ga," in *Tŭramaŭi modŭn kŏt*, ed. Hong Sŏk-kyŏng (Seoul: Culture Book, 2016), 229–249.

27 John Thornton Caldwell, *Televisuality: Style, Crisis, and Authority in American Television* (New Brunswick, NJ: Rutgers University Press, 1995).

28 John T. Caldwell, "Stress Aesthetics and Deprivation Payroll Systems," in *Behind the Screen* (New York: Palgrave Macmillan, 2013), 91–111.

Makjang shows are written and produced with time and budget constraints. The cast and crew work long nights, so the final cut of each episode emerges like a hysterical sleep-deprived delirium. New scripts are written, memorized, shot, and aired daily. South Korea's makjang drama phenomenon is similar to the rise of New Wave B-films in 1960s Japan; Japanese filmmakers produced hundreds of movies in a single year under a tight budget with high sensationalist elements to compete against Hollywood films playing in domestic theaters and the television sets at home. These Japanese films were also meant to incite and provoke with taboo topics like sex, queerness, violence, and discrimination against Zainichi Koreans.[29]

A standard K-drama typically spends approximately one to two hundred million won per episode; the bulk of this budget goes to the star cast, and the production must make the most out of what's left over. Ratings competition for K-dramas was fierce among KBS, SBS, and MBC. By 2009 Korean cable channels like tvN and JTBC also gained popularity with original programs. Choi states that the shortening of episodes also contributes to the makjang quality of shows. While a show traditionally had sixty episodes for characters to develop an arc, many are now only thirty episodes and move at a much faster rate, proving difficult for viewers to keep up with its logics.[30]

Makjang televisuality is also a response to the IMF crisis (Asian Financial Crisis). It was a way to get people to tune in, watch, and buy during a time when folks were not opening their wallets. Viewers would see accessories exchanged on TV and go buy them. The star-shaped necklace of Polaris worn by Yoo-jin in *Winter Sonata* (2002) became a bestseller thanks to the show. The hats and scarves on *Stairway to Heaven* (2003) also became part of the fad. This embedded marketing for accessories was quite common in the early 2000s. Makjang is a visual display of excessive *affect*. There's always too much emotional display in makjang K-dramas, and that's part of the fun. How could there not be?

---

29 Dan Geary, "Butts, Blood, and Bombs: The American Occupation's Effect on Japanese Cinema," *Cinesthesia* 10, issue 2, article 3 (2020): 1–13.

30 Choi, "Makchangdŭramaran muŏshin'ga," 233.

The IMF crisis was scarring for Koreans. Check out *Twenty-Five Twenty-One* (2022) for a glimpse on this. *Reborn Rich* (2022) and *Reply 1994* (2013) also cover this history. *Miss Korea* (2013) is an excellent show that illustrates how the IMF crisis forced all hands on deck, including a young uneducated woman who had nothing else to turn to except her looks and figure as a Miss Korea pageant contestant for the sake of her family's survival. I love this show! So much heart!

The IMF crisis was a shameful period for the whole country, as it required international funds to bail South Korea out economically, triggering memories of the same financial dependency South Korea had on the US. This economic crisis in South Korea upturned people's lives completely. Upper-middle-class and middle-class households that took decades to develop went broke overnight. It set back decades of social progress, as women in white-collar jobs were the first to be fired, forcing them to take pink-collar jobs to support their families. It was also greatly emasculating for unemployed fathers who became filled with dread and shame. My paternal aunt's husband never recovered after he lost his office job in the late nineties. As a result, my aunt started selling makeup and umbrellas to get by, and my cousin immediately went to work to carry the financial burden for his family. Not too long thereafter, he died very suddenly at the age of twenty-seven due to a brain aneurysm.

One way that humans respond to shock is excessive consumption, including food, alcohol, and shopping. The visual excess in K-dramas in the late 1990s and early 2000s is a response to the barrenness people felt due to their bankruptcy or job loss. Korean fashion was excessive. So many accessories and clothes were designed with rhinestones and layered fabric. There were pins shaped like flora and fauna. Cell phones had chains that dangled with accessories or whole entire stuffed animals. Bell-bottom jeans were acid washed, torn up, and printed with cat whiskers. On top of that, Korean fashion was full of hats with furs and brooches. Some of that over-the-top flexing through consumer goods is meant to say, "I'm hiding my poverty. Forget being poor. I got money to spend." Middle-class consumers expressed similar decadence but through fast fashion and cheap spending, emphasizing exterior excess to hide or combat fiscal woes. The excess in makjang is also evident in the episode quantity. Kim Soon-ok's *Temptation of Wife* had 129 episodes that ran every weekday. Prior to that was *Hearts of Destiny*, which had 138 episodes.

Some of the greatest makjang moments in history have taken place on daytime TV. In *Everybody Say Kimchi* (2014) a former mother-in-law takes a handful of kimchi and smacks her former son-in-law across the face with it. The scene went viral online and the food slap has been recycled numerous times in other shows. This includes spaghetti in *Eve Love* (2015), pasta in *The Lady in Dignity* (2017), pork ribs in *Welcome to Waikiki* (2018), toenjang and kimbap in *Happy Sisters* (2017), and maple syrup in *SKY Castle*. *Search WWW* (2019) parodies food-related slaps in a meta K-drama within the show with wet seaweed thrown across a male character's head. K-dramas have distinguished themselves from American soaps by using food to make a point rather than a classic splash of plain old water to the face. K-dramas love food so much that they'll have food fights with it too. When I was growing up, wasting food was sacrilegious because starvation was a real calamity that my parents' generation lived with, but on television, food is so abundant that it's weaponized to deliver a point.

MAKJANG'S BOUNDARY EXPANSION AND CENSORSHIP

K-dramas were produced under the influence of military dictatorships since the advent of television broadcasting in South Korea. Park Chung-hee initially encouraged TV shows to cultivate national consciousness with wholesome entertainment. Shows like *Annyŏng* (1975) on MBC and *Dad* (1975) on TBC included extramarital affairs. This subject matter on television was so unconventional and shocking to critics and the board that the shows were prematurely taken off the air. As a result, the government regarded K-dramas as more than just entertainment and reconceptualized TV programs as educational tools. This brought on stricter standards from the KCC as concepts like public broadcasting started to take shape.[31] The KCC is like the Federal Communications Commission (FCC) in the US in that they primarily handle censorship and viewer grievances. Choi argues that part of the reason why K-dramas today cannot help but be over the top is because they are reacting against severe political oppressions.[32]

Hollywood cinema from 1933 through 1968 was similarly oppressed through the Hays Code, named after Republican politician Will H. Hays, who presided over the Motion Picture Producers and Distributors of America (MPPDA). His main administrator, Joseph Breen, was a censor on the MPPDA and strictly enforced the Hays Code within Hollywood films to set guidelines on what should and should not be shown. When I wrote my master's thesis, I spent many hours at the Margaret Herrick Library flipping through correspondences and microfiche of notes that Breen had given after watching films or reading scripts, negotiating what films would or would not receive the MPPDA's stamp of approval. These discussions always stemmed from a hetero, cis-male, WASP perspective that cringed at implied miscegenation between white and nonwhite characters, sex or the implication of sex, queerness, profanity, and violence. In 1968, after decades of rebellion against the code that tread on screenwriters' and filmmakers' constitutional right to freedom of speech, the Hays Code was replaced by the Motion Picture Association of America's ratings system—that big green or red card during trailers at the movies that states whether a film is rated G, PG, PG-13, or R. Even while the Hays Code was in place, however, Hollywood always figured out creative ways to get past censors and sub-vert. Japanese new-wave filmmakers did the same, and K-drama writers, producers, directors, and actors are no different, because wherever there is oppression, rebellion coexists.

We love makjang K-dramas because even though Korean television that is broadcast through airwaves has restrictions that censor profanity,

---

31   Ibid., 247–248. For more on Korean television's history and public broadcasting, check out Ki-Sung Kwak's *Media and Democratic Transition in South Korea* (New York: Routledge, 2012) as well as my article, "Aspirational Paternity and the Female Gaze on Korean Reality-Variety TV," in *Media, Culture & Society* 42, no. 2 (2020): 191–206, https://doi.org/10.1177/0163443719853506.

32   Ibid.

nudity, sex, and queer love, the creators always figure out a way to get their point across by employing all kinds of out-of-the-box methods that lead to wacky results. Makjang dramas entertain through rebellion. They punch a big hole through our chest when we feel suffocated by the heavy lead of oppression, and they incite laughter, tears, outrage, and awe. That's why we love them.

Who among us can't relate to ego-driven feelings such as jealousy, lust, and greed? We've all felt the desire to rebel, stir the pot, and go bonkers. Part of what drove me to write my dissertation on Korean variety shows filled with absurdity and ridicule was to rub it in stuck-up scholars' faces and encourage them to pull the sticks out of their asses. Baby, I'm a clown. Thoughts and feelings that stem from the ego are relatable shadows that people live with on a deeply human level daily. Television is a safe screen space for viewers to watch characters follow through on these no-no thoughts and feelings while they make life-altering decisions that make us gasp, laugh, or scream.

Choi states that a makjang's "provocative" storyline is a reaction against social or familial conservatism.[33] Makjang dramas often vilify the family; while some of these shows air during "family hour" at 8:00 p.m. and their metadata promote the shows as family-friendly programs, the enemy in these narratives is usually the family unit.[34] There's something about a makjang show and the way it pushes boundaries of what's acceptable that I find therapeutic and cathartic. It activates change socially and culturally through television in subversive ways.

In *Penthouse*, Oh Yoon-hee is a single mother who once dreamt of becoming an opera singer when she trained at Cheong-ah Arts School. Now her daughter Rona also dreams of becoming an opera singer and wishes to train at Cheong-ah Arts School. This forces Yoon-hee to confront her past nemesis, Cheon Seo-jin, who sabotaged Yoon-hee's career out of jealousy when they were both students. Yoon-hee goes above and beyond to get Rona admitted by running down a long table at a parent-teacher school meeting to kick a

---

33 Ibid., 230.
34 Ibid., 234.

teacher in the face. Yoon-hee also flirts with her enemy's husband, throws a teenaged girl down a tall building to her death, and betrays her best friend who turns out to be the biological mother of the girl she just killed. Jesus Christ. *Penthouse* is exhausting.

Makjang elements abound on *Penthouse* not because Kim Soon-ok's shows have a limited budget. Nope. She's a big-time showrunner who is worth her salt, and *Penthouse* had a substantial budget to produce twenty-one episodes. The makjang quality of *Penthouse* at this point is an aesthetic that captures the showrunner's touch. Auteurs in cinema are often equated with highbrow arthouse filmmakers like Wes Anderson and Wong Kar Wai, but I place K-drama showrunners like Kim Soon-ok up there alongside such figures in recognition of their auteurship in creating entertaining TV writing.

Part of my own trauma therapy involves taking risks to develop a healthy ego. I regularly put my ego on the line whenever I perform stand-up. Going onstage to crack up a room full of strangers is high risk. If a joke does not land, the pain and suffering from that humiliation make me feel like an absolute bottom. Makjang. The lesson there is that even though I've hit absolute bottom, I'm still alive. My organs are still functioning. My life continues. It teaches me resilience. When a joke works, especially in a big room where the laughs are loud, there's no greater high in the world. Every comedian understands this feeling and what this sound does for our soul. That's why we do it.

I take creative risks to show myself what I'm capable of against the torrent of self-criticism that I hear regularly in my head and to combat low self-esteem. When I'm onstage, I talk about sex, shit, weight, trauma, family discord, and failed relationships. I've even shown my bare ass. None of this embarrasses me when it's done to get people laughing. My performance offers my soul release. I stop taking myself so goddamned seriously, and I just entertain by turning my worst fears into jokes with a clear intention solely to delight.

Makjang dramas are too stressful for me to watch these days. There's too much yelling and plot twists to keep track of. But that doesn't mean I see them as trashy entertainment. I find makjang TV comparable to 1920s German expressionist cinema like *Nosferatu*, *The Cabinet of Dr. Caligari*, *Faust*, and *Metropolis*. Expressionist films generate drama through the use of long shadow effects, highly artificial set designs, surprising camera effects, gothic distress, and nightmare aesthetics. The set design on *Penthouse* is also gaudy. The dramatic shadow effect is visible in the Korean actors' faces through extreme expressions to deliver an emotion or evoke mood, such as widening their eyes, facial twitches, and evil grinning. *Penthouse* also includes a lot of screaming, hyperventilating, maniacal laughing, and hysterical crying. Excess is the name of the game in makjang!

Penthouse's characters live in a ridiculously tall building where only the wealthiest people can afford to live, winking at *SKY Castle*'s residential premise. In this way, makjang also reacts to shows that broke ratings records to the point of becoming a cultural phenomenon. *Penthouse* characters are all in strained relationships. There's a persistent low-level frequency that hums beneath the shiny surface of everyone's tense façade of kempt appearances that drip in expensive clothes, jewelry, accessories, hair, and makeup. The mothers are obsessed with their high school children's education, career, and well-being. They are willing to do anything for them, including murder and infidelity. Makjang dramas showcase the impossibly high standards and pressures women function under by making them look ridiculous, gaudy, and laughable on the small screen, and then shatter those expectations by taking characters to the point of no return through makjang's twists and turns. *Penthouse* satirizes the ridiculously lofty capitalist expectations in a hyper-competitive high society. Makjang, therefore, is not just aesthetic and style; it is also a visual trauma-processing through camp art that mocks sociocultural trends that turn humans into cretins.

I once heard a K-drama actress speak on a variety talk show called *Happy Together* (2001–2020), telling the audience that although television scenes like throwing water in someone's face, slapping them, and grabbing people by the hair are not actions that we normally perform. These shows' bizarre performances serve a cathartic purpose for emotionally repressed viewers at home, especially mothers. Makjang dramas are oxygen for those living in a stuffy society. Makjang also serves a critical function. It points a finger at you to ask yourself what back-breaking and soul-crushing decisions you live with daily just to survive and whether it is worth it as you smash avocado toast in your nemesis's face.

I see queer makjang queens in K-dramas constantly. These relentless female characters have been wronged and their feelings are valid! These celebrated antiheroines in K-dramas exhibit vindictive rage to create the makjang spectacle we can't avert our eyes from. The moral boundary between what is right and wrong in a makjang gets blurred constantly, and the meaning behind this is actually quite profound: everything is in forward motion and everything changes. Everything comes in waves of up and down, light to dark and back again, repeatedly ad infinitum. The heroines' flaws are just as great as their strengths, and all heroines are potentially villains too. In fact, their flaws and strengths are hard to tell apart because I'm laughing at all their extreme choices on television as I whisper, "Yes, queen." This ambiguity that emerges from these awe-inspiring flaws in K-drama characters queers our righteous questions around morality. In a way, it's humbling, and it forces us to think outside the conventions we find in customs, social order, and mainstream culture. These makjang tantrums are a reaction to impossible patriarchal demands of a woman. We can cry about it while watching a weepy melodrama, but it's a lot more fun to laugh and scream at it when these queer makjang queens grab one another by the hair and slap faces, fighting for their dignity.

LESSON 5:
ORPHANS WITH LEUKEMIA IN K-DRAMAS

K-DRAMAS ARE TEEMING WITH PROTAGONIST ORPHANS, BUT I THINK
the most tragic orphan is Soo-jung in *What Happened in Bali* (2004). She
has no parents and didn't go to college. She has no extended family who supports her. She has an older brother with a gambling addiction. This show is very
unkind toward Soo-jung. She gets into a toxic relationship with an abusive guy
named Jae-min but also falls for her neighbor In-wook. But Jae-min is forced
to marry a wealthy girl who also happens to be In-wook's ex-girlfriend (uh-oh),
so Soo-jung decides to run away with In-wook (goodness gracious). Jae-min
tracks them down and, spoiler alert, shoots the couple dead with a gun. And
that's the end of the show. 😵

It makes sense to start a story with an orphan. There's nothing more tragic
than a child with dead parents. Focusing the narrative on a helpless orphan is
an easy way to anticipate melodrama and conflict right off the bat. A child with
no protective caretakers getting bullied by the world reels in audience sympathy. We are on her side: *Poor orphan child! You deserve to have whatever you wish!*

That's why orphans are common in literature like Oedipus, Harry Potter, Pip, Anne, and Annie.

Caroline Myss writes that the orphan trope is metaphoric of individuals who do not feel like they are part of their tribe or family from birth, forcing them to develop independence early on: "The absence of family influences, attitudes, and traditions inspires or compels the Orphan Child to construct an inner reality based on personal judgment and experience."[35] The orphan trope in K-dramas, however, has a deeper significance tied to colonization, war history, and adoption.

QUESTIONABLE BLOOD AND LEUKEMIA

Koreans are obsessed with blood. While I was growing up, Korean adults told me that we have a fiery blood built for tenacity. This mentality is constructed from Korea's nationalism, which was generated in reaction to colonization. Concepts like "purity" in blood and a preoccupation with national origin have histories linked to white supremacy and Nazism in Western countries, but they can also be traced worldwide. Every country has nationalism. In a global society dictated by capitalism, patriarchy, wars, inequity, and colonization, it's inevitable. In South Korea, nationalism was used to mobilize people out of economic and political rubble in the post–World War II years. It was used to motivate Koreans with anger, vengeance, and fury against their memory of foreign invasions. Anticolonial sentiment ran Koreans' blood hot and drove them to work like hell to establish Korea's national economic footing in just a few decades. Of course, this drive cost many lives, and economic stability doesn't mean the nation's traumas have been addressed, processed, and healed.[36]

Repressed pain and anger lead to cancer. Louise Hay's metaphysical interpretation of cancer is: "Deep hurt. Longstanding resentment. Deep secret or grief eating away at the self."[37] The prevalent trope of leukemia in

---

35 Caroline Myss, *Sacred Contracts: Awakening Your Divine Potential* (New York: Three Rivers Press, 2001), 373.

36 For more on this, see Chang Kyung-sup's *South Korea Under Compressed Modernity Familial Political Economy in Transition* (New York: Routledge, 2010).

37 Louise Hay, *You Can Heal Your Life* (Carlsbad, CA: Hay House, 1984), 158.

K-dramas at the turn of the twenty-first century was processing the nation's repressed traumas.

Autumn in My Heart is the most memorable show among millennial K-drama fans, featuring hallyu megastars Song Hye-kyo, Song Seung-hun, and Won Bin. These actors became so successful that Won Bin doesn't even work anymore. He's happily tucked away somewhere living life as a husband to actress Lee Na-young. The show was written by Oh Soo-yeon, who also wrote *Winter Sonata*. *Winter Sonata* is often referred to as *the* hallyu TV show in Korean studies literature that catapulted Choi Ji-woo into international fame and made Bae Yong-joon so rich that he too retired from being a working actor.

Autumn in My Heart was shocking because it (spoiler alert) killed off the female protagonist with leukemia. I was thirteen years old when this show aired, and it took me a year and a half to get over Jung-suh's death. In fact, the show was doubly shocking because it (spoiler alert) killed the male protagonist Joon-suh too. What kind of sadistic writer would do this to the people who've been loyally watching her show? With Oh's next big hit, *Winter Sonata*, there were rumors circulating in the Korean blogosphere that the writer was going to kill the male protagonist, but after many fans begged the writer and director not to hurl them into another depression, the writer-director duo compromised by just (spoiler alert) turning Min-hyung blind. What's with killing and blinding characters? What did they do to deserve such a punishment?

In the case of Jung-suh and Min-hyung, they share similarities related to questions of familial belonging. In *Autumn in My Heart*, Jung-suh was swapped with another infant girl at birth. Jung-suh's father is an eternal question mark because he died of leukemia as soon as she was born. The only thing Jung-suh knows about her father is that he was a drunk and a wife beater who died of a disease that she later inherits. In *Winter Sonata*, Joon-sang is raised by a single mother who does not explain who his father is. The mystery enshrouding the true identity of Joon-sang's father is similar to Jung-suh's: Jung-suh's blood-related father was a violent man who passed down his leukemia to a daughter he never met, and Joon-sang's father was an adulterer who already had a wife and child of his own at the time of his birth. These fathers' short-comings disrupt the harmony of heteronormative order. In the story world, the sins of these fathers require a punishment, and that punishment falls on their innocent children—the living proof of their immorality.

Leukemia returns time and time again in K-dramas. It is a trope just like the orphan trope. But I wondered why *leukemia*—a cancer related to blood? Leukemia is a cancer that causes white blood cells to multiply abnormally quickly through the bone marrow's excessive production. Many leukemia patients are on a list seeking a bone marrow donor whose stem cells can be transplanted, but the odds of finding the right match is a challenge. The ethnicity of the recipient and donor also matter because the human leukocyte antigen markers are passed down genetically.

Leukemia is common among K-drama protagonists who have a mysterious family tree surrounded by secrets or just a big question mark on their identity because they are orphans or raised by a single parent. With Jung-suh in *Autumn in My Heart*, her father is faceless and nameless. The family she thought was hers turns out to be strangers; no one is a bone marrow match, and Jung-suh dies. Two years prior to that, MBC aired an intense love triangle called *Forever Yours* (1998). An abusive man rapes and impregnates the orphan female lead, and she is later diagnosed with leukemia. Her violent abuser blinds her boyfriend, so when she dies, she donates her eyes to him and leaves behind her baby for him to raise. In 2001 there was another show with a similar ending called *Legend* (2001). The orphan female lead develops leukemia, gives birth to her ex-boyfriend's child, and donates her eyes to her male companion, who had been blinded during an attack while trying to protect her.

These female protagonists not only die from a fatal blood-related disease with no family to help them, but they also leave behind a family member (a child) and give away their body parts to the men who loved them. These characters physically become a blended family without sharing blood-ties, but there are literally parts of the female protagonist that hold them all together, albeit through her life's sacrifice. These blood-themed stories question Korea's patriarchy and patrilineal system, which emphasize birth right, national origin, and heteronormativity. K-dramas exhibit queerness by illustrating chosen families who find one another and blend onscreen to display a family unit and love that queers the status quo's definition of "family."

Leukemia also has a disruptive function in K-dramas. In *Beautiful Days* (2001) Yeon-soo and Sena are found-family sisters at an orphanage who make a promise to always be together. As adults their relationship strains when Sena runs away from the orphanage to be with Yeon-soo in Seoul. On the night of their meeting, Yeon-soo gets into a car accident and never shows up. Sena misinterprets Yeon-soo's absence as abandonment and harbors resentment. To make things worse, the two male characters fall in love with Yeon-soo and fight over her, while Sena crushes on one of them. To turn the sadness into makjang, Yeon-soo is diagnosed with leukemia. Jesus Christ.

Yeon-soo's leukemia illustrates the tragedy of this disease for an orphan who has no family to test for bone marrow transplant. The search is as impossible as the pursuit of her own parents, lost in a maze of erased histories. The melodrama is as painful as watching Yeon-soo fight for love and happiness despite everyone's family baggage stemming from childhood trauma and unforgivable parental sins. But when Yeon-soo is diagnosed with cancer, relationships that seemed impossible to reconcile are resolved, as everyone puts aside their beef to focus on her recovery. As such, leukemia can also work as a saving grace in the torrent of TV drama.

KOREAN WAR ORPHANS AND KOREAN ADOPTEES

During and shortly after the Korean War, Americans associated Koreans mostly with refugees, prostitutes, and orphans. The prostitute association is why "Asian" is an entire genre of porn. When I was a middle schooler in a WASPy suburban town, a couple of white boys asked me "what" I was, demanding an explanation of my ethnicity. I defiantly responded vaguely and said, "Asian." This got them excited, and they cracked up hysterically while repeating "Asian" over and over again as my humiliation deepened.

The plight of Korean orphans is linked to American neocolonialism, Civil Rights Movement, and "cold" war history. After the Korean War's cease-fire in 1953, television sets rapidly entered American homes, bringing the counterculture movement, the Civil Rights Movement, anticommunism, and the Vietnam War into people's living rooms.[38] The Montgomery bus boycott, Martin Luther King Jr., Malcolm X, the National Association for the Advancement of Colored People (NAACP), and the Urban League began to awaken Americans and people around the world to white supremacy and the country's deep denial of slavery, murder, and oppression of Black bodies. Television was visually exposing America's hypocrisy in its claim of being a democratic nation, highlighting its segregation laws, Jim Crow, and the beating and murdering of Black citizens. The USSR criticized America for its national hypocrisy.

The US also demonstrated its hypocrisy by rounding up and imprisoning Japanese Americans after the Pearl Harbor attack on December 7, 1941. Between 1942 and 1945 approximately 120,000 Japanese American civilians were forcibly removed from their homes and incarcerated in camps with poor living conditions. This was in direct violation of the US Constitution, but Franklin D. Roosevelt nonetheless issued the order after Japan's attack on Pearl Harbor in Oahu, Hawaii. Of course, many people forget to explain how a Hawaiian lagoon such as Pearl Harbor even became an issue for Americans. US forces annexed the Hawaiian Islands in the late 1800s after Hawaii's living monarch Queen Lili'uokalani was forcibly overthrown so that American businesses could access sugar plantations and cheap labor while avoiding high taxes on sugar.

The USSR called the US out: How could Americans call themselves democratic when they are racially divided, killing Black Americans at home and Asians abroad? As America's public image tarnished around the globe due to its anti-Black laws and anti-Asian wars, the government needed a facelift to improve its image and boost morale. This took place by combining US militarism and Korean babies with Christian and capitalist values. The American government had an opportunity to rebrand its national image by utilizing the faces of Korean refugees as literal poster-children for America's nationalist campaign. This nationalist propaganda touted Ameri-Christian values of charity, humanitarianism, and white salvation, despite

---

38   I highly recommend Lynn Spiegl's *Make Room for TV: Television and the Family Ideal in Postwar America* (Chicago: University of Chicago, 1992).

Americans having bombed, raped, brutalized, dislocated, and killed the same Koreans that caused orphans to be conceived and abandoned in the first place. Americans turned a blind eye to the devastation they left behind in Korea and haven't looked back until Koreans started making content that topped Billboard charts and won awards at Cannes, the Oscars, the Emmys, and the Golden Globes.

A K-drama's female orphan protagonist faces numerous social injustices given her waif status and economic poverty. The upper class has nothing but disdain for her. In pretty much all K-dramas, whenever a rich man brings home a poor orphan woman to his house and introduces her to his parents, his parents respond by saying she is unacceptable due to her low pedigree and questionable roots. Although unwelcome and impolite, questions about what one's father does for a living are commonly asked in South Korean social settings when people want to gauge one's social status, which is directly correlated to that circle's prioritization of patriarchal hierarchy. This is also a residue from premodern Korea's feudal caste society as discussed in chapter 1. Questioning one's unknown background, roots, and blood is embedded with classism, xenophobia, and a preoccupation with the heteronormative status quo.

There are many Korean adoptees around the world today living as artists, scholars, and activists who call for the end of adoption. Meanwhile, South Korean adoption agencies continue to persist. Despite South Korea's now-stable economy, its adoption agencies remain highly profitable in the face of white salvationists' desire for "cute Asian babies." American poet, activist, and Korean adoptee Julayne Lee, who was raised by a white Christian family in Minnesota, writes in her poem "For My Mother":

I've been told I need to be thankful to you

for giving me a better life

rescuing me from the war-ravaged country of Korea

here is what I have to be thankful for

when you told me

you paid a lot of money for me

when you told me

if you hadn't adopted me

I'd be living a life of prostitution

on the streets of Korea

I'd be homeless or dead.

Did it ever occur to you

I can do all of those things in America?[39]

There are many cases of adoptees hearing such insensitive and dehumanizing comments from their adoptive parents. In more extreme circumstances, I've heard of cases in which adoptees were sexually abused by their family members as children, but when they told their adoptive parents, they were not believed, and the assault continued until they could escape. Problems related to adoption corruption—such as deportation of Korean adoptees due to incomplete naturalization papers by adoptive guardians, the abuse of adoptees by adoptive families, and the high suicide rate of said adoptees who get deported—are critical human rights issues.

Meanwhile, the South Korean government and society are slow to offer support to single parents so they can stay together with their children. Single

---

39 Julayne Lee, "For My Mother," in *Not My White Savior: A Memoir in Poems* (Los Angeles: A Vireo Books, 2018), 42.

mothers are ostracized and shamed in Korea. *When the Camellia Blooms* (2019) is a decent exploration of this problem. South Korea's adoption rights activists see an urgent need to give single parents—especially girls and women—the support they deserve to have their babies and choose to raise them rather than give them up for adoption due to force of circumstances.[40] There have also been documented instances of newborns being swindled out of hospitals and sent into adoption black markets without their mothers' knowledge solely to fulfill a quota for agencies. American adoption agencies like Holt are historically linked to corrupt tactics like fabricating documents or identities that make reconciliation between original family members impossible.[41]

American studies scholar Susie Woo mentions in *Framed by War* that America's involvement in the Korean War was like creating a disaster, then coming to the nation's aid just after being the cause of that disaster: "Visualizing Korea's children was a necessary component of rescue, for it was through seeing the child in pain that viewers could envision themselves as rescuers."[42] This was an attempt by Americans to rationalize the military firepower they used against the Korean peninsula that caused so much ruin and death among civilians. There's a sarcastic Korean proverb used in situations like this: "Give disease then offer medicine."[43] Korean war orphans were used as political props for Americans to appease their guilt around their country's racist and imperialist war efforts as well as anti-Black violence. Organizations like the Christian Children's Fund used photographs of Korean orphans for American fundraising campaigns.

Korean women were also used as props in America's democracy campaign to maintain its hegemonic status. The US government supported American GI efforts to bring home Korean "war brides" to combat its negative global image. Woo writes, "In the context of the Cold War, Korean adoptees and brides became commodities in service to the post–World War II construction

---

40 I recommend the films *Broker* (2022) by Hirokazu Kore-eda and *Return to Seoul* (2022) by Davy Chou.

41 AP, "More South Korean Adoptees Who Were Sent Overseas Demand Probes into Their Cases," *NPR*, December 9, 2022, www.npr.org/2022/12/09/1141912093/south-korea-adoptees-fraud-investigation-western-families.

42 Susie Woo, *Framed by War: Korean Children and Women at the Crossroads of US Empire* (New York: New York University Press, 2019), 60.

43 병주고 약주고.

of benevolent US power."[44] Considering these histories, the political significance of the young orphan in K-dramas is even greater when she grows into a strong woman with her own voice and self-determination.

THE ADOPTEE'S VOICE IN K-DRAMAS

The orphan protagonist in K-dramas faces class issues, but she speaks up whenever she is insulted for her poverty and background. On the one hand, American newspapers, magazines, movies, talk radio, and television shows that framed South Korea as an impoverished nation of orphaned refugees in need of American charity completely excised the actual subjectivity of these children. On the other hand, orphans in K-dramas repeatedly show that while the cards are stacked against them, they persevere and win despite the odds. K-dramas allow the Korean orphan to reclaim her subjectivity and reimagine a new life for herself by pursuing her passions in both love and career.

In *Thirty-Nine* (2022) Cha Mi-jo is an adoptee who grew up in a well-off and loving family and now runs her own dermatology clinic. She has good friends and a loving boyfriend, but when she meets her original mother, she is stunned by how immoral she is. Mi-jo is ashamed of being related to a woman who blackmailed her wealthy adoptive parents for money over the years. But she later overcomes this and has a healing moment with her boyfriend's adoptive younger sister, So-won. So-won initially quits piano after her adoptive father disowns her, saying the only reason why So-won is good at the piano is because he spent too much money on her education. Mi-jo tells So-won that her talent in piano is actually a precious gift she inherited from her original parents. While I found *Thirty-Nine*'s storytelling weak, I genuinely appreciated this compelling address.

Another example of a multifaceted adoptee K-drama character is Morgan in *Search WWW*. There's a scene in which Morgan is on a video call with his white adoptive father in Australia, who instructs his Korean son on how to make toenjang jjigae using rinsed-rice water. Later, when his girlfriend, Tami, shows up, she asks him why he stopped cooking midway. Morgan replies, "I

---

44 Woo, *Framed by War*, 18.

needed it for a brief performance." Morgan's simple explanation indicates that cooking Korean food on his birthday is solely to satisfy his adoptive father's wishes rather than his own, illustrating a Korean child's need to fulfill a white parent's expectations of what he should be.

The short exchange between Morgan and Tami points to an array of repressed and unspoken thoughts and feelings that Morgan harbors as an adoptee with white parents. Although both parties are well meaning and have love for each other, there are complications stemming from Morgan's adoptive status and heritage that clash with his white parents' expectations of him as a Korean. Morgan also struggles with a physical ailment that strikes him every year on his adoptive birthday because it reminds him of the pain of being abandoned as a child by his original mother, indicating that this trauma lives in the body. Morgan is another example of contemporary K-dramas creating narrative space for adoptee issues, albeit played by a South Korean actor.

FROM WAR ORPHAN TO WORLD LEADER

Since the early 2010s there has been a gradual evolution in K-drama tropes. Killing off orphan characters began decreasing as South Korea emerged from the IMF crisis. Popular K-drama tropes from the mid-1990s and early 2000s contain national qualms stemming from postwar symptoms through tropes of impossible romance (unification) due to incest resulting from secret affairs or fatality through an incurable disease genetically inherited from faceless parents. These tropes in K-dramas have been left behind for first-world concerns such as office politics in *Incomplete Life* (2014), female insecurity around weight in *Oh! My Venus* (2016), female anxiety over looks in *She Was Pretty* (2015), and hypercompetition among wealthy helicopter parents in *SKY Castle*.

In recent years, Korean movie scripts written by male filmmakers are being adapted into Netflix TV series like *The Silent Sea* (2021) and *Black Knight* (2023), which center on environmental crises like water shortages and air pollution. Korean characters are at the forefront of technological and military advancements that rescue the world from such plights. These shows imagine

South Korea as a world leader competent enough to handle such rescue missions, positioning it as an elite nation. It is no accident that both *The Silent Sea* and *Black Knight* are globally accessible via Netflix.[45] These shows signal to the world that South Korea has graduated from impoverished war-related issues to those that are more relevant to first-world concerns. If we learned anything from how America used Korean war orphans for its nation's self-image, it's easy to see how K-dramas like these are being used for a politicized agenda today.

---

45 I discuss how South Korea utilizes television for international politics and projection of its global self-image in this study: Jung, "Aspirational Paternity and the Female Gaze on Korean Reality-Variety TV."

LESSON 6:
SUBWAY SANDWICHES, SOJU, AND COFFEE IN K-DRAMAS

I LIVED THROUGH EIGHT ANXIETY-RIDDEN YEARS OF THE GEORGE W. Bush administration throughout high school and college. Adults around me constantly said, "You're gonna have a very hard time in the job market," which never helped my anxiety.

After Lehman Brothers collapsed in 2008 and the recession comfortably settled into America's economy, nobody needed paintings. Nobody needed frames. These items became excesses—surplus purchases. Why? Because they are inedible. My parents' small business in art, frame, and antique furniture came to a full stop. Whenever any disaster strikes, the first questions people ask are: *What will I eat? How will I feed my family?*

We work to eat. We eat to live. Food is our sustenance, but in K-dramas, it is accessorized.

PPL

The Korean film and television industries are built on the backs of food conglomerates like CJ and Lotte. That's why you see the CJ Entertainment logo pop up during the opening of your Korean movie. "CJ" stands for Cheil Jedang—a conglomerate dealing in food manufacturing and distribution. CJ is an arm of Samsung. Lotte Entertainment is associated with Nongshim, which is also a food distributor and the maker of your favorite ramyun, such as Chapaghetti, Neoguri, and Shin. The Chapaguri that you see in *Parasite* (2019) is a combination of two ramyuns from Lotte—Chapaghetti with Neoguri. These food conglomerates are why you see so much eating in Korean movies and television. Corporate sponsorships fund K-dramas, and most of those sponsors are food and drink companies. Every single K-drama you watch— even fictionalized historical dramas like *Mr. Sunshine*—have cafés, bakeries, and restaurants where characters rendezvous.

This is because K-dramas rely on product placement. The concept of product placement—or "PPL" as the Korean TV industry abbreviates—isn't new and, of course, is not restricted to South Korea. Embedded marketing in media can be traced back to nineteenth-century American novels. Hollywood included cars like Ford, Plymouth, Chevy, and Packard, as well as beverages like Coca-Cola and cigarettes like Marlboro in early studio films from as early as the 1910s. The tradition of conspicuous brand placement continued into the age of television. One or two brands sponsored entire shows. *I Love Lucy* (1951–1957) has numerous cigarette breaks because Philip Morris was a sponsor. Some parts of *I Love Lucy* include whole segments that last several minutes dedicated to Lucy praising Carnation's condensed milk as she pours it into teacups because Nestlé was another corporate sponsor.

All this changed with Sylvester (Pat) Weaver at NBC in 1949 (fun fact: Pat Weaver is Sigourney Weaver's dad). Weaver shifted the operation by ensuring that the network controlled the programs, and companies purchased ad time through commercial breaks. This turned the table completely. Companies were now at the mercy of networks and popular programs, and this relationship continues to this day. That's why corporate sponsors clamor for ad space during the Super Bowl and spend millions of US dollars for small breaks in between the most watched sporting event annually.

In 1963, under the Park Chung-hee administration, KBS opened itself up to corporate sponsorship. PDs and screenwriters brown-nosed corporate sponsors to fund their shows, reflecting the pre-1949 model that American networks followed. Sponsors had a lot of power over these creatives and would dictate casting decisions for talent they preferred to see. The 1960s K-drama actors would take a shot of soju and then make comments in their lines on how excellent it is.[46] This flagrant embedded marketing hasn't changed very much to this day.

Commercial interruptions do not pervade South Korean shows as frequently as they do in American broadcasting. An entire Korean program can run without a single ad break. The downside is a prolonged series of ads in between separate programs, but this is also changing with the growth of cable and streaming in Korea. Thus, product placement still plays a major role in Korean series production. And it's not just one brand that owns the entire show; multiple brands sponsor each show. Percentages of how much screen time each product gets and the frequency of the product's appearance varies depending on the deal.

Writer Kim Eun-sook's earliest major hit is *Lovers in Paris* (2004). I still remember the characters going to Baskin Robbins to eat ice cream and how Soo-hyuk tells Tae-young the number of songs he has on his MP3 player. In *Descendants of the Sun* the characters eat tons of Subway sandwiches and ginseng squeeze packs. Song Hye-kyo's character applies Laneige lipstick and lights a 2S candle—products that get as many close-up glamour shots as her face. We see the same level of conspicuous PPL in *Goblin*. I watched that show multiple times because the fashion, jewelry, and makeup are such wonderful eye candy. Of course, *Goblin* had a *lot* of PPL, everything from perfume, handbags, lipstick, ice cream, fried chicken, furniture, watches, car, mobile phone, and beverages. Characters on *Descendants of the Sun*, *Goblin*, and *Mr. Sunshine* all went to Dal.komm Coffee to work out misunderstandings ("오해야!"). Cafés become a natural PPL strategy because so many K-drama storylines include one-on-one meetings over coffee. It only

---

46 Kim Hwan-pyo, 드라마, 한국을 말하다/*Tŭrama, Han'gukŭl Marhada* (Inmul: Seoul, 2012), 42.

makes sense that a café be included as part of the production, so why not make it a sponsor? It's an astute business strategy, except seeing Dal.komm Coffee in *Mr. Sunshine*, which is set in the same year as the Gabo Reform, is utterly unconvincing.

Product placement is never *not* noticeable. In fact, the beat that actors take when they are about to mention sponsors is very noticeable. In *Mr. Sunshine* Eugene Choi raises his Odense teacup in the middle of his quiet meditation, looks out his window, and makes an out-of-character observation: "Is this style of teacup in fashion now?" Like, dude, you're a former Korean slave whose parents were killed in front of you and you were adopted by a white man then raised to become a military officer in America. Why would a teacup's mode be on your radar?

Paris Baguette is very obviously a sponsor on *Mr. Sunshine*. We know this not only because it is one of the first banner bumpers to appear when the end credits roll but also because in episode two the brand's characteristic blue and white label appears where Lady Ae-shin makes a stop to enjoy some sweets. The signposts and lamps all read "French Bakery." During the show's airing, Paris Baguette sold *Mr. Sunshine*–inspired specialty pastries.

What would a K-drama be without a coffee sponsor? Dal.komm makes, perhaps, the most obtrusive display in *Mr. Sunshine*. Not only do the characters really push this 가배/*gabae* (Chosŏn lingo for "coffee") stuff, but the napkins and even background sign straight up read "Dal.komm Coffee" in English—something that would *not* have been common in that era. It's about as ridiculous as when Ji-an in *My Mister* holds her serious meetings at Quiznos to discuss how she's going to blackmail her male superiors at work, as if Quiznos is the most secure environment to do this.

Whatever. No need to get all worked up over how a show takes us "out of the moment." A complaint like that is nonsense. The nature of TV is self-reflexive, so eye-roll all you want. PPL in K-dramas isn't going anywhere. Not even in a period piece. In fact, given how subscription streaming doesn't have ads, product placement is now becoming a part of Hollywood's original shows as well. In this way, Hollywood streamers are now reappropriating their own business strategy by taking influence from K-drama productions like they do in *Stranger Things* with 7-Eleven, Sharp, Coca-Cola, and Cadillac.[47] In the Netflix original K-drama series *DP*, there are scenes where characters eat McDonald's fast food. While the press and social media went bananas over Netflix's subscriber loss in 2022, Netflix went on quietly accruing ad revenue from product placement.

Seeing as we TV lovers don't simply rely on broadcast and cable television to receive our shows but also subscribe to digital streaming, our lives are now dictated by both commercial interruptions *and* embedded marketing. The absurdity of synergistic ecosystems and our addiction to TV have turned us all into food- and screen-addicted consumers locked in a cycle of binge watching, binge eating, and impulse buying.

Are product placements effective? Hell, yes. Subway sandwiches saw a rise in their sales across Asia thanks to Song Hye-kyo ordering them so much in *Descendants of the Sun*.[48] I'm not even looking at numbers here. I don't need to. The shows speak for themselves as the same few products appear for years at a time because the marketing works. If it didn't, American fast-food corporations like Subway would not keep partnering with Korean production companies.

AMERICAN LUNCHEON MEAT AS KOREAN FOOD

South Korea's consumption of American luncheon meat dates back to the Korean War. SPAM is canned meat that was made for soldiers, but it entered the South Korean black market via the US military and became hybridized into Korean stews like *budaejjigae*, which literally means "military base soup." Is SPAM good? It's hardly meat. Koreans love meat, and their beef, hanwoo, is famous for taste and quality. Hapcheon, where my maternal family is from, is famous for their hanwoo. When I went to a restaurant with my family, I saw a huge glass encasement with different cuts of hanwoo to choose from. An aunty brought the selection to our table and grilled them

---

47   Katie Powers, "Product Visibility in 'Stranger Things 3' Valued at $15 Million," *American Marketing Association*, July 11, 2019, www.ama.org/marketing-news/product-placement-in-stranger-things-3-valued-at-15-million/.

48   Seth Berkman, "Korean TV's Unlikely Star: Subway Sandwiches," *New York Times*, March 14, 2021, www.nytimes.com/2021/03/14/business/media/subway-product-placement-korea.html, accessed February 21, 2022.

on a giant cast-iron skillet. After we finished eating the meat, she returned with rice and kimchi, and fried that baby over the beef fat and served it to us with a side of toenjang jjigae. Trust me: South Koreans know quality meat. SPAM is not up there in terms of quality, but Koreans are creative and resourceful in how to put canned pork to good use and bring SPAM giftsets to one another on holidays.

In budaejjigae, the gelatinous fat from SPAM melts nicely into a thick broth melding with kimchi, vegetables, and hot dogs that bring out a richness. Add ramyun noodles and cheese to that bad boy, then wash it down with soju. 크~. Forget about it.

Korean moms know how to dice up SPAM into tiny little cubes when making kimchi fried rice before placing a pretty sunny-side-up egg over it, topped with sesame seeds. Hell, yeah. Koreans know exactly what to do with nasty-ass overprocessed American luncheon meat: turn it into a yummy experience. They know how to turn a horrible situation like a foreign military occupation in their country into a creative meal opportunity. Koreans everywhere are preoccupied with food. That's why we greet one another by asking, "Have you eaten?"

CHICKEN AND BOOZE

Whenever K-drama characters are stressed, they order fried chicken from BBQ Chicken to pair with beer and soju. Chun Song-yi's go-to stress reducer in *My Love from the Star* (2013) is fried chicken and beer or chi-maek—a portmanteau of chicken and maekju.[49] Yoon Se-ri in *Crash Landing on You* shares this vice, and her eating habit is an homage to Chun Song-yi, as both beloved characters were created by the same screenwriter, Park Ji-eun.

Booze makes a regular appearance in K-dramas. TV characters also have sports drinks and hangover elixirs to appease their upset stomachs from the booze they drank the night before. Sometimes characters chat over ramyun or coffee, but they commune over beer and soju way more often.

Soju brands like Chamisul, owned by Jinro, regularly hire stars as brand ambassadors like IU and Park Seo-joon—the one with that haircut in *Itaewon*

---

49 멕주/*maekju* is "beer" in Korean.

Class. Itaewon Class was produced by Showbox—an arm of Korea's confectionary conglomerate Orion, which makes Choco Pie. Chamisul's rival soju brand, Chum-churum, is owned by Lotte, which owns entertainment businesses that produce TV shows and movies. Booze flows constantly in K-dramas because they are corporate sponsored. This is why there's a high tendency for K-dramas to glorify alcohol. For the most gratuitous form of K-drama binge drinking, see *Bloodhounds* (2023). Does booze sponsorship work? Absolutely. I've spent countless nights with ramyun and soju until my face and body bloated just because a K-drama drinking scene inspired me to action.

Meanwhile, South Koreans suffer from high rates of alcoholism in a very enabling society. Despite this, research on alcoholism in South Korea is limited. Treatment for the disease, let alone a broader recognition of alcoholism *as* a disease, is also limited. Research dating back to 2013 mentions that alcoholism treatment in South Korea struggles with social integration.[50] The nation's drinking culture, which includes after-work dinner functions, enables extreme forms of alcohol consumption. Work-related cases of sexual assault are frequently found in such spaces. There's a 2022 academic article that discusses how South Korea struggles with the highest rate of suicides in the world due to a number of social malaises, but it discounts high-risk alcohol consumption as a factor, stating that alcohol consumption in social gatherings prevents isolation and therefore encourages a willingness to live.[51] To that, I call bullshit, as anyone in Alcoholics Anonymous would. High-risk alcohol consumption is a form of long-term suicide, and plenty of studies have shown a link between suicide and extreme alcohol abuse.[52]

Despite such evidence, whenever a K-drama character goes through a breakup or a bad day at work, feels sad, feels angry, wants to celebrate, feels

---

50 Jee Wook Kim, Boung Chul Lee, Tae-Cheon Kang, and Ihn-Geun Choi, "The Current Situation of Treatment Systems for Alcoholism in Korea," *Journal of Korean Medical Science* 28, no. 2 (2013): 181–189, https://synapse.koreamed.org/articles/1022158.

51 Hyemin Jang, Whanhee Lee, Yong-ook Kim, and Ho Kim, "Suicide Rate and Social Environment Characteristics in South Korea: The Roles of Socioeconomic, Demographic, Urbanicity, General Health Behaviors, and Other Environmental Factors on Suicide Rate," *BMC Public Health* 22, (2022): 410, https://bmcpublichealth.biomedcentral.com/articles/10.1186/s12889-022-12843-4.

52 Maurizio Pompili, Gianluca Serafini, Marco Innamorati, Giovanni Dominici, Stefano Ferracuti, Giorgio D. Kotzalidis, et al., "Suicidal Behavior and Alcohol Abuse," *International Journal of Environmental Research and Public Health* 7, no. 4. (2010): 1392–1431, https://doi.org/10.3390/ijerph7041392.

bored, or wants to connect with someone, they *always* crack open a beer or twist a soju cap. South Korean law, which has a very low tolerance for any illicit drug use, including cannabis, is extremely deregulated when it comes to alcohol. My friends and I used to go to parks in Seoul with bottles of soju, and no one said anything because container laws do not apply. Corporate backing of the Korean alcohol industry is powerful within the nation's economy and has deep ties to its media ecosystem. It's about as strong as Korea's obsession with food and its deep corporate entanglement with sponsors like Lotte, CJ, and Orion.

WHAT'S KOREAN ABOUT KOREAN FOOD?

When my parents' small art business went kaput in 2008, my mother wanted to work. My mother did not go to college. She was born on a farm and worked as a laborer all her life before getting married at twenty-three and immediately having me at twenty-four. When I was a toddler, she briefly ran a small business making custom quilts and blankets in Busan. Upon immigrating to New York, she only ever worked with my father in his small business, but that work had dried up due to the 2008 recession. She'd never worked anywhere else in the States. As a mother and a homemaker, she had only one transferrable skill: cooking. My mother felt that her cooking skills could easily translate into any other kitchen. She naively believed she could work in a hotel kitchen as a line cook because she had fed a family for over twenty years. Although she probably could have, I know how competitive line cook positions at high-end hotel restaurants can be given my years of service-industry work at bougie restaurants in New York since age eighteen. My mother tried her hand at her own banchan business at local farmer's markets in New York—a lofty idea that did not take into consideration the language barrier, permits, and paperwork to meet FDA standards. It was a business that did not flourish.

My point is that *food* became my mom's fallback. It became the thing she felt she could profit from, just as South Korea rebuilt its economy and expanded its global outreach with exports like kimchi, bibimbap, bulgogi, galbi, and soju. We can now add dalgona to that list, and Trader Joe's sells ttŏkpokki (yikes). We'll be adding an endless array of new food inventions branded by South Korea to that list, which will become more trends for kids to share on social media while dancing. In *Run On* (2020–2021) I saw a character pouring honey from his parents' farm into his beer, calling it 꿀맥주/ honey beer and declaring it "a thing," as if it's a thing that everyone knows. This is just another way to sell Korean beer and honey through television. It's a means of selling a "Korean style" of drinking beer, much like dalgona coffee is a "Korean style" of drinking instant coffee and so-maek is a "Korean style" of drinking soju and beer together . . . you get the picture. "Korea" is now a marketed fad, aesthetic, brand, and lifestyle.

Korea is an agrarian land. It makes sense why food distributors became corporatized and branched out into entertainment—an easy transition because they understand the concept of distribution and consumer demands thoroughly. After its independence from colonization and rehabilitation after the Korean War, the memory of starvation was embedded in South Korea's not-too-distant memory.

As the land reconstructed from war rubble and agricultural systems were rebuilt, Korean women fed countless family members on their own to survive. Koreans knew what they had to offer: food and their cooking skills. When resources were lacking, it forced creative solutions, like turning a can of SPAM into a flavorful protein-packed soup. Food is an easy way to deliver branded constructs like cultural authenticity and traditional indigeneity to white nations that fetishize nonwhite nations with awe-inspired othering. This worked. It still works. Tradition is a vague cultural cloth.

Just because Maangchi has her way of making kimchi, it doesn't mean that's how my mom makes it. It doesn't mean that's how *I* make it. Every single household has their own way of making kimchi, fried rice, stews, soups, pancakes, dumplings, and so on. These are passed down generationally from the matriarch. For instance, people who know and love Korean food really dig yookgaejang (if you know, you know!), which is made from beef brisket. When I was a kid, however, my grandmother would kill a chicken in her yard and make a spicy chicken soup called dakgaejang in the winter months for me. The memory of that soup still warms my bones, and it doesn't exist anywhere else on earth because that was her thing, and she made it her own way.

Korea's obsession with excessive eating is an indication of the nation's trauma of starvation. Many Koreans still live with the memory of hunger and dying of starvation during and after the Korean War. We must also be mindful that North Koreans still struggle with hunger, as do people in many other countries.

The excessive and gluttonous eating on South Korean screens today projects, the nation's new-money status while revealing the country's pre-occupation with food and its potential lack—the anxiety that food might be taken away suddenly with no warning, so they must eat as much as they can right now and quickly. Excessive eating via mukbang videos reveals the pathological and unhealthy consumption habit South Korean influenc-ers have developed, reminding me of American hot-dog eating contests at county fairs. The instant foods that mukbang producers choose to eat—like fried chicken, cheese, ttŏkpokki, and ramyun—are overprocessed and high in starch, fat, sodium, preservatives, and sugar. Mukbang videos with exces-sive eating aspire to first-world diseases like high cholesterol, diabetes, heart disease, and high blood pressure. Beneath what these videos flash as new-money status is a self-destructiveness while trying to prove something that does not need proving. This tendency coincides with the overachievement preoccupation I point to in chapter 1. Trauma causes a person to relive some-thing over and over again in different ways until they come apart because they don't want to be here. Being here with the memory of these traumas is unbearable. The memory of hunger and deprivation is still prominent in the nation's subconscious, sloshing about beneath the shiny, sparkly, eye-popping, and mouthwatering veneer. Drill down just a tiny bit, and you'll strike a tarry thickness full of fear, suffering, and agony linked to poverty, hunger, and desperation from the brutality of war that still needs processing.

BINGE CULTURE AND MUKBANG

There is a fine line between satisfactory pleasure and overindulgence. When I was in college, Netflix introduced the "Play Now" option on their website—one of the early ideations of streaming. Binge watching started to proliferate around 2006 and 2007. I was still ordering DVDs through Netflix's snail-mail service and renting DVDs at my local Blockbuster in El Barrio, Manhattan, but the convenience of the "Play Now" button felt miraculous to me. I also watched a lot of pirated K-dramas uploaded onto YouTube with Vietnamese subtitles.

My television bingeing worsened when I worked an office job in New York. I was very unhappy. Offices make a lot of false promises and eat away at your humanity. When I got home from work, I would feel so drained and empty that all I could manage was to fix myself a big starchy dinner and a stiff drink before watching television for hours until I passed out, only to relive the same nightmare again the next day.

It wasn't until my thirties when I realized what I was doing. Binge watching television was a means of numbing myself out. What was I avoiding? What was I distracting myself from? What kind of unhappiness or disturbance required ten thousand hours of television? Was my brain completely shut down during these binge sessions, or was another part of it highly activated? TV doesn't rot my brain. TV just covers up the stench and sight of whatever rot there already is, deeply lodged inside. TV occupies my brain and prevents it from going to the dark places I want to avoid.

Doctors and nutritionists say that binge eating is destructive to a person's health. Doctors of psychology, sociology, and media studies today question the binge viewing phenomenon that streaming has made more universal from a similarly anxious hypothesis. I learned in therapy that when I zone out in front of the TV and binge eat, I am in a state of self-abandon. This observation was quite shocking to me, and I grew emotional at this realization because my constant complaint has been my trauma around abandonment and neglect. On his Hulu series *The Choe Show* (2021), Korean American artist David Choe discusses his eternal sense of abandonment and feeling of insufficiency because, as the middle child of three boys, he was selected to be sent away to live with his grandparents in Korea at age four while his two brothers and parents stayed behind in LA where he was born. Their excuse for sending him away was financial hardship, and this resonated with me because I endured the same trauma as a toddler. It was very common for Korean parents to send one child away to live with relatives temporarily because of financial distress, but it takes a major toll on that child's self-esteem and self-worth.

When I asked my mother why she kept ditching me at other people's houses when I was four and five years old, she grew defensive, saying she didn't "ditch" anyone. Regardless of her denial, I felt ditched. When a kid is left in the care of other people, she will never receive the care and attention that she needs from her own parents. Bad things happen to neglected kids. Predators can detect a neglected kid, and they can detect a grown woman who was once a neglected kid. While the intensity of this pain from childhood has diminished over the years, it hasn't completely gone away. It lingers and haunts. It shows its ugly face to me if I do not practice adequate self-care. In that way, my body is a living barometer. The more I treat my mind/body with kindness, gentleness, and love, the stronger I am.

Once I learned that binge watching while eating cheese-covered ttŏk-pokki, fried mandu, soondae, and ramyun with a six-pack of Hite is self-abandonment—and not "treating" myself to "decompress" as our consumer culture dictates—I wept because I didn't realize I was reinflicting the same trauma of abandonment onto myself with food and screen addiction. That's how trauma functions, though. A child learns to cope with their trauma by making friends with it. That's what I see when I watch mukbang videos made by petite Korean chicks in their late teens and early twenties who eat an entire table full of spicy noodles. Mukbang is an exhibition of a flagrant eating disorder and past fiscal hauntings. It projects a nation's coping mechanism while suppressing intergenerational grief that stems from the collective memory of hunger.

But a hunger for what? Is it only food? No. It's also a hunger for security, support, and care—essentially, love. That's why addictions are visible around the globe. We all need the same thing. It's no wonder that K-drama fans binge watch these shows that replay the same love stories in different ideations forever. Dr. Ham hypothesizes that overachievement is a proxy for seeking love, but as it turns out, self-destruction by trying to disappear into food and TV shares the same aperture.

South Korea's excessive stylization—be it through fashion, media, makeup, food, booze, or hyper-aurality of ASMR videos—is an indicator of its new-money status as well as its self-destructive clinging to past traumas that have gone unaddressed. Although South Koreans generally do not starve today, anorexic and bulimic entertainers reiterate the nation's memory around starvation through self-induced hunger to have a career, while gluttonous mukbang stars are overeating on YouTube for the same exact reason. Korea's past, filled with physical injuries from the ruthlessness of war, is echoed in acts of self-mutilation as entertainers undergo plastic surgery to change their physical appearance for the camera. All that Korean consumption you witness on your screens is more than just PPL to fuel the machine that brings you visual entertainment and expands globalized consumerism and American franchise imperialism via Subway. All that eating and drinking is more than just global advertisement to enhance South Korea's tourism and international marketing. These are over-the-top, excessively layered ways of exposing South Korea's anxiety, wondering when all this decadence might disappear again through killing, dying, and famine due to civil war, foreign invasion, or economic meltdown requiring another international financial bailout.

Anyway, I personally don't like Subway sandwiches. If I ever crave deli, I wander into any bodega in Manhattan and ask for turkey on a Kaiser roll with mayo, lettuce, and tomato. A bag of salty chips and a fizzy soda to pair are a must.

LESSON 7:

#METOOKOREA AND RESILIENCE IN *SOMETHING IN THE RAIN* AND *ONE SPRING NIGHT*

WAS A LATCHKEY KID SINCE KINDERGARTEN. I RECALL BEING HOME alone in our apartment and sitting in the closet with the laundry basket because I felt so lonely. Sometimes I was with a sitter.

A fellow Korean woman in our Brooklyn neighborhood was briefly my babysitter when I was six. Her husband dry humped me while she stepped out to run an errand. When I was eleven, my parents took me to a Korean Protestant church in New Jersey, and the youth pastor took me alone into a room and rubbed my thighs with his hands while chastising me for being hyperactive. I was frozen into terrified silence in my shorts as my jaws clenched and ripped a frigid smile across my face. I hoped that he would stop as long as I kept smiling in discomfort as he touched my thighs while lecturing me on how to behave more "ladylike." A friend my age accidentally walked in and saw the pastor touching my thighs. In her state of shock, she could only muster, "Oh, oops," before closing the door and leaving me alone with this man again. After our talk was over, I ran out of the room to catch up with that friend. I expressed my uneasiness about what had happened, and she expressed the same at having witnessed it. When I told my parents about the pastor touching me, they both chuckled and said that he was probably unaware of what he was doing and that I shouldn't take it so personally. My parents minimized my complaints of abuse from other adults in our Korean community so often that I never told them about my most traumatic molestation memory from age five that surfaced when I was thirteen. Van der Kolk writes, "Children sense—even if they are not explicitly threatened—that if they talked about their beatings or molestation to teachers they would be punished."[53] The way the church condemned any form of sexuality was even more horrifying to me, filling me with helpless fear and shame. I thought I was permanently damned and broken. I blamed my five-year-old self for being a stupid sinner.

I began exploring my sexual traumas at age twenty in the safety of a therapist's office after an emotional breakdown in college when I couldn't stop crying on campus. Thank goodness for my breakdown. Thank goodness for whatever discourse I was exposed to at the time that enabled me to reach out for psychiatric help. I took myself into my university counselor's office on my own accord. Thank goodness for my eighteen-year-old self who chose to leave my abusive church and home environments the moment I graduated high school. Thank goodness for my twenty-year-old self who walked into that therapist's office and bravely began unearthing her traumas. Once I named the shameful secrets that had festered inside me for years, I realized that none of what happened to me was shameful because I had done nothing wrong. I recognized my strength and survival, and I still give myself that recognition daily. As Herman writes, "Remembering and telling the truth about terrible events are prerequisites both for the restoration of the social order and for the healing of individual victims."[54]

---

53   Van der Kolk, *The Body Keeps the Score*, 133.

54   Herman, *Trauma and Recovery*, 51.

MY BODY TOO

Affect, according to communications scholar Zizi Papachrissi, is an emotion and feeling tied to the potential for action and emergence—"the sum of all possibilities."[55] In simple terms, *affect* refers to emotions and feelings. The reason why #MeToo emerged as a massive movement is because affect preceded it; there was a shared affective community among betrayed women who felt that their complaints of sexual harassment, gender discrimination, and oppression went unheard, not believed, unaddressed, and unresolved by their justice system, work environments, and social spheres. Digital hashtag activism was the result.

Following the #MeToo movement in the States, #MeTooKorea began trending in South Korea in January 2018 after prosecutor Seo Ji-hyun spoke up about her sexual assault at work. In a complete transcript of the JTBC interview, Seo notes how infuriated she was when her colleagues who had witnessed the groping ignored it and never followed up to check in on her.[56] Following this newsbreak, a trend in outing male celebrities for victimizing and assaulting women in the entertainment industry snowballed quickly in Korea.

On March 5, 2018, news broke of politician Ahn Hee-jung's rape scandal. On March 11, 2018, former K-pop boy group Big Bang member Seungri resigned from the entertainment industry after reports connected him to crimes of sex trafficking, gambling, and embezzlement at his club Burning Sun. Given the high level of alert among civilians at the time, a show like *Something in the Rain* takes on a political dimension to address the sociocultural affect of Korean women who experienced sexual assault in the workplace but were made to feel alone in their grief.

Something in the Rain aired from March 30 through May 19, 2018, written by Kim Eun and directed by Ahn Pan-seok. The show's themes overlap with the timing of #MeTooKorea. Yoon Jin-a is a woman in her midthirties who works at a corporate coffee franchise in middle management, but her boundaries are

---

55 Zizi Papachrissi, *Affective Publics: Sentiment, Technology, and Politics* (Oxford: Oxford University Press, 2015), 13.

56 Youjin Lee, "The Prosecutor Who Exploded #MeToo in Korea: The JTBC Interview with Seo Ji-hyun," *April Magazine*, February 6, 2018, www.aprilmag.com/2018/02/06/the-prosecutor-who-exploded-metoo-in-korea-the-jtbc-interview-with-seo-ji-hyun/.

regularly violated at her workplace. Her supervisor, deputy chief Gong Cheol-goo, takes food from her plate without asking and publicly berates Jin-a and the other female staff as if they're children whenever he's unhappy with their behavior. Gong makes comments like how Jin-a should get married already and how it's not good for a woman to stay single when she's older. These are all very familiar experiences to Korean women.

Whenever I visit Korea, my male relatives make two consistent remarks: "You got fat. Are you married yet?" In 2019 I was determined to make it clear to my uncles that these comments are not welcome. First, no one has the right to make comments about my body. I have reasons for why my body is the way that it is, and they are deeply personal to me, just as it is a very personal choice as to why I remain single and childless. Second, sexual trauma victims are far more likely to have physical ailments and weight gain. In *Hunger*, Roxanne Gay documents her obesity history after she was gang-raped by her male peers, and she explores how this assault wreaked havoc on her interpersonal relationships and self-image: "When I was twelve years old I was raped and then I ate and ate and ate to build my body into a fortress." Given the high correlation between sexual abuse and obesity, everyone should stop to think twice before they judge people's bodies or make flippant comments about them. How a person chooses to live inside their bodies is no one else's business but their own.

I was at a restaurant in Ulsan with my eldest maternal uncle and his three daughters when he immediately cracked the two dreaded phrases: "You put on weight. Are you married yet?" I replied, "The two phrases women hate hearing the most are comments about their weight and marital status." My uncle took a moment to let this sink in and said, "And I just said those things to you." I said, "Yes." My uncle didn't say anything else after this. We just proceeded to eat our meal to move on from the subject, but my actions and words were chosen deliberately in this setting. I wanted my baby cousins to see and hear this. It was for their sake as well as mine. Not his. I wanted my three cousins—each in middle school, high school, and college—to know that as girls and women, we do not need to tolerate anything that makes us upset or uncomfortable, even from family. Furthermore, I wanted them to see that we have a voice to speak up and set our boundaries with, and even after we do, the world does not end. It remains intact. The family is still a family. We can go on eating, talking, and laughing just the same, but at least my message was heard.

I recall innumerable times when my dad made disparaging comments toward my depressed mom about her body, telling her to lose weight, exercise, and stop being lazy. Those words turned into a severe eating disorder that haunted me from my teen years into my thirties, as I cycled through anorexia, binge-eating, and bulimia. I hated my body for as long as I can remember having one. I compared it to everyone else's. My eating disorder represented more than just discomfort in my own body. I hated everything about myself inside and out. In my adulthood, I dated and befriended people who made offensive comments about my body and mistreated it. I also criticized my body and mistreated it. It's interesting to see my mother shed weight at an alarmingly rapid rate these last couple of years as my father's egregious comments about her body have now morphed into troubled words of concern.

When I look at my body now, I see my mother's body and my maternal grandmother's body. I never really knew my paternal grandmother, but I sometimes find her in my gestures that people tell me scare them, and this makes me laugh hysterically. The only memory I have of my paternal grandmother is how she used to sit on the floor at her farmhouse in Goseong with her left knee propped up, the other leg folded lotus style as her left forearm casually rested on her raised knee while her right hand stretched toward the floor where her thumb pressed into the tobacco bowl of her gombangdae—a long metal pipe. She would drink makkŏlli out of a white ceramic bowl all day in her room while smoking in that position—a timeless image of infinite bad-assery that I have pinned up in my mind's altar. If I ever need to put up walls of defense to protect myself, I channel her energy until I feel safe. I don't tolerate anyone speaking negatively about my body or mistreat it because that insults the women I love—me, my mother, my aunts, my cousins, and my grandmothers. I love my body now just as much as I love the women in my family.

KOREA'S MISOGYNISTIC COFFEE HISTORY

Coffee Bay is the coffee franchise featured in *Something in the Rain,* and it doubles not only as embedded corporate marketing but also as the workplace setting for characters to convene. Kim Eun's choice to set Jin-a's workplace as the headquarters of a coffee franchise allegorizes how pervasive workplace sexual assault and gender discrimination are in South Korean society, just as coffee is highly pervasive in all urban societies where people are constantly on the go. Tolerating workplace harassment out of fear of backlash, losing job security, and being passed over for promotions and pay raises are as common as people drinking coffee to force their bodies to remain awake enough to labor and maintain the gears of a capitalist system. Coffee never agreed with me physically. I'd become jittery, and it worsened my insomnia. The only agreeable thing about coffee for me is the smell, and yet I forced my body to adjust to these unpleasant physical reactions just to assimilate, stay awake, and overwork for years.

I don't really drink coffee anymore. I'll have a decaf Americano every now and then, but I mostly stick to ceremonial matcha and gyokuro. I never set foot inside a Starbucks. If I ever do, it's because I need to use their Wi-Fi and their bathroom. I don't even know why Starbucks bothers selling beverages. Just take my dollar and give me your bathroom code. I'm not there for any of your drinks. I'm only there because I have a bathroom emergency. Starbucks has developed a trashy reputation in recent years as the world's toilet. Call me bougie (I am), but there are so many nicer coffeehouses with better coffee. But there was a time when Starbucks had an upscale vibe.

Expensive coffee brands have a fascinating contemporary history in relation to economics and gender politics in Korea. Coffeehouses known as 다방/ *tabang* were all over Korea since the colonial era, where they served coffee and alcohol. In the 1970s and 1980s the tabang became a gathering space for intellectuals, artists, and activists to meet for coffee, booze, and cigarettes.[57] Now that coffee franchises have replaced this trend, the tabang has been relegated

---

57 Bonnie Tilland, "Baker Kings, Rice Liquor Princesses, and the Coffee Elite: Food Nationalism and Youth Creativity in the Construction of Korean 'Taste' in Late 2000s and Early 2010s Television Dramas," *Acta Koreana* 24, no. 1 (2021): 77–104.

in contemporary culture to a place commonly associated with prostitution. I recall seeing a few tabangs back in 2009 when I lived in the Mapo District prior to its latest phase of gentrification. Even back then, those businesses had changed their products to primarily fried chicken and beer because locals could find better coffee elsewhere.

Starbucks first entered the South Korean market in 1999—just two years after the nation's economy collapsed due to the IMF crisis—and quickly became the go-to spot for overpriced American coffee. Korean Starbucks goers were associated with high-end spending. As more Starbucks cafés cropped up across Korean cities between 2005 and 2006, the sexist term 된장녀/*toenjangnyŏ* appeared in the Korean discourse via internet trolls in comment sections and blog posts.[58] Toenjangnyŏ literally translates as "soybean paste girl," and it is a sexist slur that criticizes Korean women who seek luxury products from the West, originating as a critique of women who buy Starbucks coffee that costs more than a full meal with toenjang jjigae in the late nineties. As scholar Jee Eun Regina Song puts it, this sexist term turned these women into "gold diggers of Western goods and lifestyles."[59]

Moral panic over Korean women's consumer taste for modern trends is not new. In the late phase of the colonial era, Korean women's shopping habits were just as over-scrutinized and policed by the Japanese imperial government as it entered World War II. The colonizers expected any money Korean women had to spare for consumption, be it fashion or entertainment, to be put toward war efforts: "Female aspirations for expensive Western dresses, hair perms, and heavy makeup were now considered 'indulgent' and 'disgraceful' proclivities that had to be 'rooted out at once.'"[60] When Koreans made collective efforts toward independence, women were expected to donate their jewelry to the cause. Colonial and local patriarchy treated Korean women like children by dictating how they should spend. But contemporary K-dramas

58 Soo Ah Kim, "Misogynistic Cyber Hate Speech in Korea," *Feminism Research* 2 (2015): 279–317.

59 Jee Eun Regina Song, "The Soybean Paste Girl: The Cultural and Gender Politics of Coffee Consumption in Contemporary South Korea," *Journal of Korean Studies* 19, no. 2 (2014): 429–448, 444.

60 Shin-ae Ha, trans. Kyunghee Eo, "The Wartime System and the Symptomacity of Female Same-Sex Love," in *Queer Korea*, ed. Todd A. Henry (Durham, NC: Duke University Press, 2020), 152.

demonstrate the consumption power that South Korean women have over their local economy while setting global trends and influence.

Korean women's fandom gives cultural currency to male Korean stars on K-dramas. (See *Record of Youth* [2020].) Over 80 percent of K-drama fandom is made up of cis-women. The success of a male actor often hinges on his reception among K-drama fans based on his desirability exhibited through female fantasies written by women. Meanwhile, Korean male frustration stemming from feelings of ineptitude and emasculation under the shadow of America's hegemonic masculinity contribute to the materialization of sexist terms like toenjangnyŏ, which is associated with Starbucks.[61] The term toenjangnyŏ indicates Korean men's insecurities when confronted by Western economy in the aftermath of the IMF crisis, and the target of their attack are fellow Korean women. Interestingly, Coffee Bay—as seen in *Something in the Rain*—is a domestic coffee franchise. Two decades after Korean women were labeled as toenjangnyŏ for spending their hard-earned money at Starbucks, Coffee Bay is now just one of numerous Korean coffee chains, along with Angel-in-Us, A Twosome Place, and Dal.komm. These coffee houses dominate Korean (and global) airwaves and streaming platforms with their sponsorships, and are inescapably commonplace, selling beverages that cost more than a cup of Starbucks coffee in 1999.

It's ironic how the trend that "toenjangnyŏ" women set has become a source of enormous profit for South Korea today. The nation's coffee import rose over 45 percent in 2022 and is valued at over a billion dollars.[62] Overpriced coffee consumption is equated with luxurious living, and thanks to early trendsetters who took the cultural bullet for being spendthrifts, South Korea's now teeming with more than fifty thousand coffeehouses and millions of coffee drinkers running around frantically trying to make a living just so they can buy more expensive coffee to guzzle and keep them going.

---

61 Hegemonic masculinity "embodies the currently accepted answer to the problem of the legitimacy of patriarchy, which guarantees (or is taken to guarantee) the dominant position of men and the subordination of women." R. W. Connell, *Masculinities* (Berkeley: University of California Press, 1995, 2005), 77.

62 Yonhap, "S. Korea's Coffee Imports Jump 45.1% in 2022," *Korea Herald*, January 9, 2023, www.koreaherald.com/view.php?ud=20230109000140#:~:text=The%20value%20of%20the%20country's,imports%20have%20exceeded%20%241%20billion.

Don't mistake coffeehouse sponsorships on your K-drama to be a simple corporate plug. That coffeehouse is packed with political, cultural, and socio-economic meaning. It is gesturing to the globe that South Korea is a nation that can afford to drink lots of high-quality coffee so that it can work lots of hours and make lots of money. It is televising the country's developed status, elevating itself within the ladder of global hierarchy. It is a means for corporate South Korea to project onto the world that the nation is, indeed, economically flourishing. It is, however, selectively forgetful of how misogynists mistreated expensive-coffee drinkers. In that case, Kim Eun's choice to use Coffee Bay as a backdrop to Jin-a's abusive workplace is fertile with political meaning.

FEMALE SUBJECTIVITY AND OFFICE SEXUAL ASSAULT

Something in the Rain contains a political vigor beneath its dry realist aesthetic that illustrates the casual sexism women are exposed to regularly. Deputy Gong and his supervisor, Vice President Nam Ho-gyun, force their female subordinates to drink, sing, and dance with them at 회식/*hoesik*, aka work dinners. They make sexually suggestive comments toward women and ignore their body language communicating discomfort. The men know that these women cannot stand up to them, given the corporate hierarchy and social patriarchy. The male characters in *Something in the Rain* demonstrate how there is no mutual respect and professional decorum recognizing female colleagues as fellow adults. As cultural anthropologist Jesook Song writes in *Living on Your Own*, it is common for men in Korean white-collar settings to treat single women like children as a tactic to condescend and reinforce patriarchy while simultaneously demonstrating its fragility.[63] When Jin-a finally speaks up on her workplace sexual assault, the corporation retaliates by calling the male executives victims of libel. Jin-a is ultimately transferred to Paju—a city far from Seoul.

Sex scandals in Korean show business have always existed, but the press typically misrepresents women as blackmailers rather than victims.[64]

---

63 Jesook Song, *Living on Your Own: Single Women, Rental Housing, and Post-Revolutionary Affect in Contemporary Korea* (Albany: SUNY Press, 2014), 33.

64 Jinsook Kim, "After the Disclosures: A Year of #sexual_violence_in_the_film_industry in South Korea," *Feminist Media Studies* 18, no. 3 (2018): 505–508.

Victims were unable to speak up because they were scarred from their personal traumas and then retraumatized by victim-blaming rhetoric in the news. Recent exposés revealed that many entertainment industry journalists were themselves sexual predators of young up-and-coming stars. Young K-pop stars, models, and actors starting out in the industry are commonly exploited, groomed, and abused by executives, managers, journalists, and other celebrities who have more power. Chairwoman Lee Mi-kyung of the Korea Sexual Violence Relief Center stated in January 2018, "The Korean media outlets, the prosecution and businesses are all linked, and female actresses and artists are often pressured to trade sexual favors for career advancement."[65] Suicide rates among Korean entertainers are high due to their restricted environment. Stars who have met premature deaths by suicide include Goo Hara, Jong Hyun, Sulli, Lee Eun-ju, Choi Jin-sil, Jung Da-bin, Jang Ja-yeon, Park Yong-ha, and Jeon Tae-soo, just to name a few.

As media and psychology researchers Chandell Goose and Jacquelyn Burkell write, "Although the ethical standards on how to report on incidents of sexual assault have been formalized in guidelines, journalists often ignore or compromise these guidelines for the sake of attracting public attention."[66] Perhaps this is also why so many Korean women I've known minimized sexual assault.

When I was nineteen I got shit-faced drunk and called my parents to tell them that I had been molested by a stranger at age five after they left me at my paternal aunt's house in Korea. Upon hearing this, my mother told me that when she was a young woman, she was also sexually harassed by a drunken male colleague in a cab. Her take was that this was normal—suck it up. But my father cried and apologized to me. He said if he were in Korea now, he'd track that bastard down and kill him. I believed him, and it was a rare moment when his rage felt supportive as it was channeled toward a protective fight for justice and love for me. This empathy my dad showed stays with

---

65 Jo He-rim, "Korean Celebrities Find It Difficult to Break Silence on Sexual Exploitation," *Korea Herald*, January 29, 2018, www.koreaherald.com/view.php?ud=20180129001049.

66 Sooah Kim, "The #MeToo Movement and Korean Journalism," *Journal of Asian Sociology* 49, no. 4 (2020): 399–424, 406.

me. Whenever I feel incensed with helpless injustice due to my rape traumas, I turn to this remark and find a warm comfort in my father's words to remind myself that I am loved and not alone. Support for survivors from their loved ones and community is vital.

In recent years many Korean workers—primarily women—spoke out against the entertainment industry's normalized practices of misogyny. This eventually led to indictments and investigations of K-pop stars like Jung Joon-hyung, but even people like him, while easily vilified by the press and society, are also victims of dehumanization by the entertainment industry system. I don't agree with his choices, but I don't judge him or any sexual predator as simply a villain. Abusive labor conditions in the K-pop industry are common knowledge. K-pop trainees get recruited when they are as young as grade schoolers. They are exposed to the industry's dark demands, such as forced dieting, sexual exploitation, financial exploitation via disadvantageous contracts, and kinship with abusive industry bosses and seniors who are acclimated to abuse.

The historical reality in Korean working women's collective memory and present-day experience overlap to give *Something in the Rain* a feminist significance. Gender and cultural studies scholar Ruth Barraclough highlights documented events from the colonial period, during which Korean female workers from the 1920s went on strike to demand a safer work environment free of assault from their supervisors.[67] Whether it's blue-, pink-, or white-collar work, the feminine reality of workplace assault by male supervisors is consistent alongside female rebellion through complaint. (I recommend queer and gender studies scholar Sara Ahmed's monograph *Complaint!*) *Something in the Rain* utilizes Jin-a's subjectivity and the steady transformation of her character to didactically illustrate how a woman who rejects abuse gains self-worth by breaking out of social expectations and embracing freedom. As Jin-a develops confidence through Jun-hui's loving support, she learns to stand up for herself and not withstand harassment.

---

67   Ruth Barraclough, *Factory Girl Literature: Sexuality, Violence, and Representation in Industrializing Korea* (Berkeley: University of California Press, 2016), 33.

ONE SPRING NIGHT AND DOMESTIC VIOLENCE

Writer Kim Eun reunited with director Ahn Pan-seok after their success with *Something in the Rain* and gathered pretty much the same ensemble cast for their collaboration on *One Spring Night*. Our beloved Jung Hae-in reappears as the male lead in *One Spring Night*, but the female lead is now played by Han Ji-min, who I felt grossly lacked chemistry with Jung. *One Spring Night* deals with South Korean society's more insidious forms of sexism, as well as domestic violence and marital rape. The show also points to a larger problem of standardized cultural heteronormativity that affects single-parent families.

Jung-in is a headstrong librarian in her thirties with an older sister, Seo-in, a younger sister, Jae-in, and a boyfriend, Gi-seok, who works at a bank. Jung-in's father, Tae-hak, is the principal at a school and is set to retire within the year and feels highly insecure about the prospect of having no income or a sense of purpose. Jung-in's mother, Hyeong-seon, is very supportive of her daughters but also highly cautious, avoiding anything that might trigger her husband's rage.

Drama ensues when Jung-in leaves Gi-seok to date Ji-ho, a pharmacist and single dad to a five-year-old boy named Eun-u. Throughout the show Gi-seok persistently tries to shame Ji-ho for being a single father. Meanwhile Seo-in is in the midst of trying to get a divorce from her abusive husband, Si-hoon, who not only beat her but also committed spousal rape and impregnated her. Herman writes in *Trauma and Recovery*, "When the rapist is a husband or lover, the traumatized person is the most vulnerable of all, for the person to whom she might ordinarily turn for safety and protection is precisely the source of danger."[68] (This conundrum is shared by victims of child abuse at the hands of their caretakers.)

Herman's book includes a historiography of American women voicing grievances in their psychologist's office in the 1950s through the 1970s. During this time women were having nervous breakdowns and receiving analysis because they were unhappy at home. They confided in their doctors

---

68 Herman, *Trauma and Recovery*, 62–63.

about their marital rape trauma. The US law changed for women's rights and reproductive health because brave survivors honestly shared their stories and worked toward change through grassroots activism. As of today, marital rape is illegal in all fifty states of America, but prior to the 1970s, when a husband forced himself onto his wife, the law did not recognize married women's right to feel safe. The law in South Korea still does not recognize spousal rape, but in 2013 the Supreme Court upheld that it is a crime to rape one's spousal partner and could result in a prison sentence.

The shame that women feel around domestic violence is culturally tied to the general fabric of misogynistic culture in South Korea. Domestic violence is between spouses or partners in a single home, but if and when that home includes children, those children are also victims of domestic violence. Although my father did not hit my mother regularly, I did see him hit her inside our Brooklyn apartment when I was six years old. I saw my mom fall down face-first onto a desk corner. When she lifted her head back up, my mom's left eye was dark. My mom fainted after this, and I watched my dad pick up her limp body to carry her to bed. I don't recall anything after that. All I remember is crying hysterically and being shocked out of my mind. My mom's eye ballooned up into the size of a golf ball. When my mom and I visited a Korean neighbor of ours, the aunty jokingly teased my mom in front of me: "So your mom gets whooped by your dad, huh? Pathetic, isn't it?" The aunty brushed the event off casually and insensitively, like it was just another common marital row in any household. I found her tone and choice of words to be about as offensive as the violence itself. Why was everyone putting up with it like it was all okay? And what the hell could I do about it as a six-year-old? I felt completely helpless. As an adult, whenever I find myself seeking justice for minor offenses, I notice my effort to claw out of that same trapped helplessness I felt then.

My dad exhibited domestic violence in a myriad of ways. When I was eight he threw my mom's jewelry box across the room, barking at her for spending money on "useless crap." When I was eleven, my dad screamed at my mom in the kitchen for being a slob. I watched from behind a wall as he grabbed frozen food from the freezer and smashed it across the floor while screaming at her for keeping expired foods for so long. Hoarding and messiness are symptoms of depression that I've seen in my maternal relatives' lifestyles. After I heard my dad slam the door and storm out, I walked into the kitchen, sidestepping the frozen food, and went to my mother, who stared out of the window while tears ran down her face. Tears streamed down my own face as I hugged my crying mother from behind, and she clutched onto my arms. Because in such moments, there is nothing else to do but to hold one another and cry. What was my mother expressing by clutching onto my arms like that? To show what? Appreciation? Apology? Support? Rage? Grief? Desperation? Help? All the above. If you meet my elderly parents today, walking around holding hands while jabbering about mundane shit like flowers and dried fruit, you'd never imagine them as a couple who was once so deeply entrenched in domestic upheavals.

In *One Spring Night* the protagonist's older sister, Seo-in, is a renowned broadcast anchor with a successful career. She is married to a dentist named Si-hoon, who also appears on television and has his own practice, but he beats and rapes her behind closed doors. Seo-in, however, is active. She keeps evidence of his beatings through photographs of her bruises that she maintains in a safe. I believe the mise-en-scène deliberately captures Seo-in's actions here to demonstrate steps that a battered and raped woman can take if she is trapped in an abusive relationship. When Seo-in breaks down while admitting this to her mother and younger sisters, she repeatedly apologizes tearfully to the women who break down beside her, sharing a communal grief that is well understood among women. When Seo-in first shows her mother the photos of her bruised body, Hyeong-seon sobs over her daughter's plight.

When Seo-in's impulsive and unruly younger sister, Jae-in, catches Si-hoon raising his hand at her eldest sister, Jae-in reacts with fury and then tearful wails, pained by the sight of a brother-in-law she never liked from the get-go mistreating her older sister. Later, when Jung-in finally finds out the truth behind why Seo-in is leaving Si-hoon, Jung-in cries while hugging her older sister silently. Because what is there to say or do in such moments except cry? Herman recognizes the great importance for a domestic and/or sexual assault survivor to have community support from those closest to her after experiencing a tragedy, which "can have a strong healing influence."[69]

Domestic violence isn't something to brush off casually. It's not something to laugh about with children who witness it in their homes. It violates that person's core and hurts everyone who loves her. Watching Seo-in and her family members sob with pain, rage, and grief over the brutality she suffered becomes a space of therapeutic healing for people like me. When I watch shows like *One Spring Night* or Noh Hee-kyung's *Dear My Friends*, which is rife with instances of domestic abuse, I sob. I don't sob while watching the actual affliction take place. I'm pretty numb to those scenes. I sob when I watch other women surrounding the domestic abuse victim cry from heartbreak. I think back to the times when my dad hit my mom. I think back to the times when my parents hit me. There is nothing to say or do in such moments except cry and hold.

We love a show like *One Spring Night* because it gives us space to process the injustices that women suffer time and time again. How many women had a *choice* in who to partner with or to leave that partner if the marriage was abusive? How many women had a *choice* to become a mother? If South Korea's Supreme Court did not recognize spousal rape until only 2013, how many domestic partnerships honored consent prior to copulation? Furthermore, abortion in South Korea was not officially legal until 2021. Prior to this, women did get abortions, but the fact that it was illegal cast shame over anyone who got it; it was also too expensive for those with fiscal limitations because insurance did not cover it. Furthermore, divorce in South Korea still requires both parties in the marriage to agree to it. It is not possible to get divorced without this mutual agreement, leaving domestic abuse victims like Seo-in trapped even though she wants to leave her husband.

When Seo-in tells her father, Tae-hak, that she is divorcing Si-hoon, Tae-hak tries to force Seo-in to remain in the abusive marriage with her abuser. Tae-hak is no different from Si-hoon in that they are both obsessed with

---

69 Ibid., 63.

their image and maintaining status quo. This reveals the great irony to sexist expressions like toenjangnyŏ, which was conjured to shame women who plastered themselves with luxury goods to uphold an image, while men like Si-hoon and Tae-hak have similar dimensions of image obsession that they maintain through patriarchal power and control.

There's a pattern in K-dramas with domestic violence in which many learned men tend to be the biggest aggressors. In *Dear My Friends* there is a tenured professor who beats his wife. In *Avengers Social Club* (2017) yet another tenured professor beats his wife. In *Green Mothers' Club* (2022) a doctor abuses his wife and ruins the family's finances with his gambling addiction. This K-drama trend of educated men with violent tendencies shows how much effort toxic men put into building a praiseworthy reputation and public admiration to ward off any questions: *How could such an accomplished man possibly be a wife-beater or rapist?* The same question could be asked of church pastors and high-ranking professionals. Perpetrators consciously build an airtight reputation for themselves to make their victims less believable while simultaneously expecting victims never to speak of their shame. Van der Kolk says, "When your reality is not allowed to be seen and to be known, that is the trauma."[70]

AWAKENING AND HEALING BY DEVIATION

Herman notes that in rape cases, the offender is typically someone the victim knows within her own social circle. In my own lifetime, I've been sexually assaulted numerous times by people I knew and trusted. I never felt like I had agency over my body or the right to voice my own pleasure and discomforts to enforce my safety and boundaries. This is the long-term consequence of the countless times people in my social sphere committed physical, emotional, and sexual violations against me.

I've felt pressured since childhood to never speak of my sexual assault survival because people are often insensitive in how they manage themselves around me after learning of it. I've heard people around me state, "Abuse is

---

70   Michelle Esrick, *Cracked Up: The Long Arm of Childhood Trauma* (Ripple Effect Films, 2018).

hard, but it can be overcome except if you were molested." When I would reply that I am a survivor of molestation, they would clam up and avoid eye contact. They would behave as if my reveal was inappropriate and offensive. There is hardly any cultural breathing room for survivors of childhood sexual assault in this world, and this paragraph is my contribution in changing that here and now. If you're a survivor of sexual assault from childhood and/or adulthood, I see you. You are not broken or defective. You are not to blame. You have the right to safety, pleasure, and freedom in your own body *no matter what.*

Herman notes a social pattern of male perpetrators having higher social status than their female victims, which causes those closest to the victim to exile her. Society frequently sides with the perpetrator to avoid any messiness that arises from the transgressions of a man in power. This is precisely what happens in *Anna* (2022), starring K-pop star Bae Suzy. A high school teacher grooms and dates Yumi when she is still a teen. When the teacher gets caught, Yumi is expelled and then forced to leave town at the crack of dawn while the teacher retains his position. Such instances are the norm rather than the exception among girls and young women. This is why Seo-in decides to quit her job as a newscaster and turns down an opportunity to host her own TV show. Seo-in withdraws from society, knowing that her perpetrator will create a scandal that won't frame her in a sympathetic light, no matter her status as a rape and domestic violence victim. Herman, however, repeatedly contends that a trauma victim's shattered sense of self can be rehabilitated through loving emotional support from her family and community.[71]

Healing is very evident in *One Spring Night* through art. Art pieces together a woman's broken sense of self by giving her freedom of expression and agency through creativity. Jung-in—well aware of how repressed her mother is after living decades with a violent man—gets Hyeong-seon to join a calligraphy class to build self-esteem. Hyeong-seon uses her calligraphy talent to write Seo-in a card, congratulating her on her pregnancy

---

71 Herman, *Trauma and Recovery*, 61.

after she chooses to keep her baby, telling her that Seo-in is already a successful parent. Herman emphasizes the importance of a survivor's need for supporters to help her rebuild "a positive view of the self."[72] Hyeong-seon expresses that support for Seo-in's choice to be a single mother—a radical decision for a South Korean woman living in a highly heteronormative society that shuns families that deviate from said heteronormativity and rejects unwed women. This deviation is also evident in how Jung-in chooses to be with Ji-ho, despite him being a single father.

One Spring Night critiques heteronormativity through toxic male characters who reduce marriage to power ploys while ignoring female autonomy. This emphasis on heteronormativity, however, hurts men like Ji-ho, for he is an unwed single father to a little boy whose mother abandoned them both. The supporting characters to the protagonists correct this ignorance. Hye-jung is Ji-ho's boss and friend at the pharmacy. She speaks to him with a sturdy voice of loving reason whenever he gets tripped up in his own insecurities as a single dad. Jung-in offends Ji-ho at the library by asking him to rush Eun-u out the back exit because her ex-boyfriend is on his way in. Jung-in despairs over the hurt she caused by casting shame on Eun-u. Ji-ho explains his anguish to Hye-jung, saying he's not sure if he can continue seeing Jung-in for the sake of his son. Hye-jung tells Ji-ho that he is using his son as an excuse not to see Jung-in and that no child likes to see parents compromise their joys: "Children hate hearing their parents say, 'I gave up everything and sacrificed just for you.'" Hye-jung's comment echoes the literal phrase that helicopter parents scream at their children in K-dramas about schools, even though their children never asked for such sacrifices. Ji-ho believes he is unworthy of love because of his status as a single father.

We love One Spring Night because it exhibits a powerful message about recovering one's self-worth and love in the aftermath of their afflictions. The show offers hope for everyone, including Seo-in, as she is about to embark on a journey ahead as a new mom, turning a family like Eun-u and Ji-ho into a beacon of hope. Just as Something in the Rain shows how patriarchal standards

---

72 Ibid., 63.

hurt men, *One Spring Night* shows how misogyny and oppressive heteronormativity hurt single parents and children. Heteronormativity doesn't just marginalize queer folx; it marginalizes anyone who is outside of a blood-related family order. We love K-dramas like *Something in the Rain* and *One Spring Night* because they connect urgent feminist concerns to the well-being of the individual and society overall. Feminist concerns are not just women's issues; they are everyone's, as they concern human rights.

RECOVERING FROM TOXIC MASCULINITY AND THE CYCLE OF ABUSE

What is toxic masculinity? It's when a man's definition of the ideal man conflicts with his own actions. That's when toxicity emerges. You can ask yourself, "Would I behave this way toward my most beloved and cherished person?" If the answer is no, and you do it anyway, that is when toxicity arises.

One Spring Night is chock-full of toxic men. At the center of this male social interconnectedness is an innocent little boy named Eun-u. The showrunner deliberately chose to make Ji-ho's child a boy. This choice is significant and speaks volumes on how to heal from traumatic afflictions as a result of toxic masculinity.

The show reminds viewers that toxic men—regardless of their shortcomings—were all at one point a beloved little boy. Eun-u represents that past identity—one who is loving, generous, forgiving, and adorable. Who and what that boy will grow up into depends on his environment, history, and caretakers' attention. That history is being written before us as Jung-in joins the father-and-son family by invitation as their chosen wife and mother and as Jung-in accepts that invitation by choosing Ji-ho and Eun-u as her husband and son.

When I was eighteen I was raped by a Korean American man eight years my senior. He had a high reputation as a medical school student and Sunday school teacher at the Korean church I attended. I called him "oppa," and the other boys my age called him "hyung." This man groomed me since I was seventeen. As soon as I turned eighteen he began continuously pressuring me into being physical with him, despite my repeated rejection because I was not comfortable. He used all kinds of manipulative words, but my mind was fixed on not giving in to him. I had only been physical once prior to this with my high school boyfriend, who was my equal and someone I trusted and felt safe around. But this older man was not my equal.

One late spring night, after my high school graduation, he invited me to his Brooklyn apartment to celebrate over dinner. While eating, he kept pouring me white wine until I blacked out. When I woke up the next morning, I realized that he'd had sex with me. I felt shocked, ashamed, and afraid. I didn't know what to do. He had violated me when I was immobilized, despite all the times I said no. To add insult to injury, he was already aware of my molestation trauma because I had been vulnerable with him about it, given that he was a trusted church representative I was encouraged to seek counsel from. I had sought his counsel by opening up about my past, and instead of helping me, he took advantage of my vulnerability and raped me on the day of my high school graduation—the same day I had lunch with my parents and friends who congratulated me. This man kept me locked in a severely toxic and abusive relationship for nearly two years, then very suddenly ghosted me on Christmas. It took me years to process this trauma.

At one point dangerous men were abused boys. Given my empathetic capacity from trauma, I understand that my abusers were once victims too. This man who raped me, for instance, told me that his male cousin raped him when he was in grade school. He told me this the night before he ghosted me. Looking back on it now, I can tell he told me this to end our relationship abruptly and to not feel guilty. Perhaps he thought he could rationalize trapping and abusing me for two years because of what he went through as a child. Of course, as his victim, I do not accept any of this. However, I do understand how the cycle of abuse comes to be.

In episode eleven of the *Road to Resilience* podcast, Dr. Jacob Ham sits down with comedian Darrell Hammond and filmmaker Michelle Esrick. Hammond mentions a major step in his recovery when he felt a moment of compassion for his abusive mother by seeing her as a helpless little girl. In response to this, Esrick says that she wanted her film *Cracked Up* to convey the cycle of abuse—that abusers were at one point abused:

> *It doesn't mean we exonerate the perpetrator but if we vilify, we are never going to break the cycle. . . . And I believe that we are so afraid to feel any kind of compassion for a perpetrator because we think it means excuse and exonerate. And it doesn't mean that. But how are we going to break the cycle after cycle after cycle after cycle?*[73]

The #MeToo movement isn't about men versus women. It's about an entire system of abuse that harms everybody. People who are dehumanized and disconnected from themselves can't help but dehumanize others. It doesn't take just one or two people to create a social malaise. It takes an entire culture and system that accept misogynistic, inhumane, and predatory practices as the norm. That's why I applaud anyone who stands up and refuses to tolerate abuse.

Although I do not exonerate my perpetrators, I have the wherewithal to know that they were or might have been victims of abuse themselves. This expanded awareness gives me breathing room to help me process my traumas without getting stuck in helpless indignation. Getting stuck in blame is not healing, although recognition of injustice is an important step on the longer road to recovery.

Something in the Rain and *One Spring Night* illustrate how militaristic, hypermasculine power structures and politics destroy lives while also exhibiting exemplary acts of social support that enable individuals to find strength and leave their abusive partner or job, no matter what losses may come, and walk toward a path of self-preservation and self-love.

We love *Something in the Rain* because it shows a woman in her thirties transition from a state of learned helplessness to embodying agency and empowerment without losing respect for herself and those around her. We

---

73 Darrell Hammond, Michelle Esrick, and Jacob Ham, "The Long Arm of Childhood Trauma," *Road to Resilience*, April 24, 2019.

love *One Spring Night* because it instructs us to follow *feelings of safety* to be our navigational guide rather than merits from academia, tenure, and financial security. See past the bells and whistles of such illusions of safety and reach for palpable humanity. Children like Eun-u are perfect teachers in how they follow affect as a compass to seek safety. It's a vibe—a feeling—and it doesn't recognize or care if someone is a board member, principal, dentist, SNU alum, and so on. Eun-u teaches us that if someone is gentle, kind, and loving, they are safe. And that is enough.

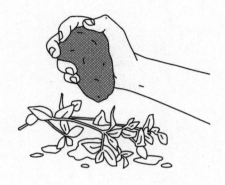

LESSON 8:
GO MASH SOMETHING

THAT WAS SOME HEAVY STUFF, SO LET'S TAKE A BREAK AND HAVE some play time. Go make farting noises or play with a cat, dog, or hamster. Watch TV. Eat some candy or drink a smoothie. Splay out on your couch and stare at the ceiling for an hour. Or do some yoga to realign your chakras with Nico Marie. Or go outside, find a rock, and smash some chickweed into a paste. I used to do this for hours whenever I played outside between ages five and seven, as though it were a very important task. It helped me find equilibrium because it was meditative. I stopped one day after I bashed the rock over my left middle finger by accident, causing the nail to fall off. But I still think about going back to it because it was not only supremely relaxing but also felt productive. Toward what end? Who knows? Who cares? If you want to understand the meaning of life and why we're here, go outside, find a flat rock and some pulpy weeds, and mash away—but don't injure yourselves. Just do it for fun. Five- to seven-year-old Grace recommends it with five stars and nine fingernails.

LESSON 9:
THE CYCLE OF MILITARY, CHILD ABUSE, AND BULLYING IN *DP*

WHILE WATCHING SHOWS LIKE *THE GLORY* OR *SUMMER STRIKE* (2022), which include egregious acts of school bullying and violence among teens, I wonder why the kids are so abusive toward one another. Neither show explores what the bullies are subject to, so this question never gets answered. In *Juvenile Justice*, however, there is a girl named Yeong-na living at a youth reformation center who bullies the other girls into submission. Yeong-na is brusque and expresses rebellion with cigarettes and radical hairstyles. Although Yeong-na terrorizes her peers, the show offers a sympathetic glimpse into her family situation when she runs away to find her mom. Once Yeong-na tracks her mother down, however, her mother shuts the door in her face. Yeong-na reacts with feral rage at this abandonment and thrashes against the door until her mother's boyfriend steps out and beats her. Yeong-na's rough demeanor reflects a deeper pain of neglect. While school bullying is common in K-dramas, it is not separate from larger issues like family dysfunction, corporal punishment, systemic poverty, and militarism.

In *Twenty-Five Twenty-One* there's a scene of a high school boy named Ji-woong getting beaten by his teacher Mr. Seo. Mr. Seo hits Ji-woong's face while berating him: "Bastards like you don't wake up unless you get beaten to death." In reaction to this, Ji-woong's peer Seung-wan screams at the teacher to stop: "When are you going to stop beating kids? You could just use your words, but why do you use your hands first? Corporal punishment is illegal now. Don't you know?" Mr. Seo tells Seung-wan to go ahead and report him to the cops, so Seung-wan does exactly that. But when the police arrive, they defer to the school principal's decision, stating that this is a school matter and not a state matter. Children's rights are not protected in South Korea, where the stick used to beat kids is ridiculously nicknamed "the cane of love."[74]

In 1990 South Korea signed the United Nations Convention on the Rights of the Child, indicating that the government will take appropriate measures to protect children from physical and mental violence by maintaining their "human dignity" during disciplining. In 1998 the Korean government banned corporal punishment in all schools but then rescinded it a year later due to educators' complaints that maintaining discipline became unmanageable.[75] Thus, the rules around corporal punishment between teachers and students in Korea remain vague. Authority figures using a stick to beat kids into submission dates to as early as tenth-century Korea. The normalization of physical abuse from authority figures toward children and subordinates is saturated into the nation's consciousness.

Seung-wan's questions to her teacher, however, stay with me: "When are you going to stop beating kids? You could just use your words, but why do you use your hands first?" These are good questions. Why is violence tolerated? Where does it stem from? Why does it persist?

When I was six my dad hit me for the first time to discipline me. He also enforced military methods like holding in a plank position or holding my

---

74 Ko Jun-tae, "Controversy over Corporal Punishment Rekindled," *Korea Herald*, June 28, 2020, www.koreaherald.com/view.php?ud=20200628000197.

75 Ben Brown, "Perceptions of Student Misconduct, Perceived Respect for Teachers, and Support for Corporal Punishment Among School Teachers in South Korea: An Exploratory Case Study," *Educational Research for Policy and Practice* 8 (2009): 3–22.

arms up straight toward the sky while balling my hands into fists for extended periods of time. If I ever loosened my position, I'd be screamed at and hit. These same methods were applied to me in preschool in Busan. I had already been taking beatings since age four from my preschool teachers and mother, but my dad had never hit me before, so it was shocking when it first happened. I cried and begged for him to stop, but he beat me anyway. Afterward he said, "Do you have any idea how painful it is for me to hit you?" The question was framed as if I had been the one to cause my own affliction. These kinds of reinforcements were almost always made after my authority figures abused me, because they never apologized or attempted to repair our relationship thereafter. They just left me with the feeling that I *deserved* abuse as I sat alone with the open wounds of my injury while shame, blame, confusion, and resentment built. At the time of hearing this rhetorical question, I wondered in silent ire: *If it hurts you so much, then why do you do it?* Over time this pondering turned into self-directed injuries with alcohol, cigarettes, eating disorders, negative self-talk, and abusive relationships with friends, partners, colleagues, and bosses, compounded by my infernal feeling of worthlessness. That's what child abuse does to a person. It makes them feel worthless and estranged from themselves.

NORMALIZATION OF HIGH-STRESS ENVIRONMENT

The foundation of South Korea's television industry is militarism. Television networks were very much a part of the militarized economy that Park Chung-hee envisioned for the country in the 1960s, which carried into the 1980s with Chun Doo-hwan, integrating military service with the labor force. This involved making military service a prerequisite during recruitment, allowing it to be recognized as prior work experience, and offering benefits or advantages at job interviews and exams to those who've completed their military duties—essentially men.[76] Such policies excluded women from finding employment at major corporations with high wages and benefits. These sexist policies exacerbated cronyism and nepotism

---

76 Seungsook Moon, *Militarized Modernity and Gendered Citizenship in South Korea* (Durham, NC: Duke University Press, 2005), Kindle 744–755/4595.

among men. Although some of these policies have been abolished due to women's rights activism in the late nineties, military culture still dominates corporate environments today.

As political and cultural sociologist Seungsook Moon writes in *Militarized Modernity and Gendered Citizenship in Korea*, "Corporate culture in major business firms was characterized by rigid hierarchy based on rank, the command mode of one-way communication, and a collective ethos used to justify individual sacrifice. These aspects of corporate culture underlay interactions among workers and managers in offices and on shop floors."[77] That's why the first episode of *Live* (2018) by Noh Hee-kyung includes a scene of Jung-oh at a job-fair panel interview with two male interviewees. The male recruiter asks the male candidates which university they attended and whether they served in the military—questions that would not be asked of Jung-oh because she is neither a college graduate nor a former military service person. Ultimately, one of the two men gets hired. Militaristic hierarchy in working relationships among women is also visible in *Record of Youth* at the beauty salon when the assistant makeup artist, Jung-ah, is harangued by her supervisor for not knowing her place and developing rapport with her boss's clients.

The Korean television industry is also militarized and hierarchical, with junior staff paying respects to those with seniority. This militant culture is present on production sets in both Korea and Hollywood. As John Caldwell puts it, the production industry's strict adherence to these top-down processes demonstrates their "military-identity complex."[78] This military-identity complex within a Korean set gets reflected and parodied in *The Producers* (2015), where a seasoned floor director (FD) advises a rookie PD, Baek Seung-chan, on what to expect on the set of the variety show *2 Days & 1 Night* (2007–present): "When you step onto the set of *2 Days & 1 Night*, do so with the mentality of entering a battlefield. So dress and pack appropriately. . . . You won't have time to eat, so you won't have time to brush your

---

77 Ibid., Kindle 802/4595.

78 Caldwell, *Production Culture: Industrial Reflexivity and Critical Practice in Film and Television* (Durham, NC: Duke University Press, 2008), 131.

teeth. . . . You won't be able to brush your teeth so washing your hair is out of the question. When you're in a car, you're going to sleep no matter what because you won't be able to sleep otherwise." The FD's description of a production set mirrors a military environment and echoes Moon's commentary about upholding the collective goal to justify an individual's compromised well-being.

Worlds Within (2008), starring Song Hye-kyo and Hyun Bin, dramatizes a K-drama set and its taxing work conditions. In the opening sequence of the first episode, a production crew races against the sun to complete the final shot, then rushes the tape over to the network for editing right before airing it on time as Vivaldi's "Winter" grippingly plays over the sequence. There are images of crew members suffering injuries on a rushed set, PDs sweating, and chief producers (CP) cursing, slapping, and kicking their subordinates for the delays—the same kind of behavior found in a Korean military environment. This behavior is also found in organized gangs, offices, families, schools—just about anywhere. Part of the reason why K-drama productions are so high-pressure has a lot to do with the standard of "last-minute live filming," which prioritizes ratings and lowers production costs.[79] These work conditions are exacerbated by the militant on-set environment maintained by the military-identity complex, which mirrors the nation's actual military.

Shows like *The Producers* and *Worlds Within* are the K-drama industry's Calvinist love letters from producers to consumers, demonstrating the staff's extreme labor to deliver entertaining content to the viewing public— a self-martyrdom that begs viewers' sympathy. In this way, crew members rationalize the harsh work conditions and their boss's violence as a means toward a higher purpose—television as a public service. There's also a queasy pride associated with overcoming such harshness.

In scholar Youjeong Oh's research, a crewmember on a K-drama set claims, "Not sleeping is required practice in this field. We are so used to

79   Youjeong Oh, "The Interactive Nature of Korean TV Dramas," in *Hallyu 2.0: The Korea Wave in the Age of Social Media*, ed. Sangjoon Lee and Abé Mark Nornes (Ann Arbor: University of Michigan Press, 2015), 135.

it. Nevertheless, drama [*sic*] should be broadcast. It is a promise with the public."[80] The crewmember's belief that the show must be broadcast no matter what the cost contains a militarized logic. The issue of public interest—a national cause for the greater good—is used to validate violence imposed onto industry workers that call human rights into question.

In recent years there have been death reports on the sets of Netflix original K-drama productions such as *Kingdom* (2019–2020) and *Arthal Chronicles* (2019). These stories are just what's been publicized in the media. In the grapevine among industry workers, however, I've heard far more harrowing stories of abuse, misconduct, and negligence that bring lasting injury and death on sets. Violence is not only accepted in Korean culture through the military-identity complex but also legitimized as an acceptable part of life in its capitalistic and neoliberal society, as it is visible everywhere such as homes, schools, and work spheres. An industry union that is separate from networks, agencies, attorneys, and management companies to protect workers' rights with fair wages, safe environments, and ample time to rest must be developed to combat these issues. What I see throughout these spaces is a problematic militarized culture that perpetuates the cycle of violence, causing affliction in every direction.

MILITARY SERVICE AND PTSD

The Korean War never ended. This war invades my dreams, bringing gripping peril in my sleep.

My dad was born in 1957, four years after the cease-fire. This was the same year that South Korea officially implemented a mandatory military conscription duty for all male citizens between the ages of eighteen and thirty-five. This means that the fate of any cis-male child born in South Korea is already predetermined to serve. There's no choice or say in the matter. Every able-bodied South Korean man is required to serve in the ROK Army, Navy, Air Force, or Marines. That's why you all cried when your BTS oppas and male K-dramas actors like Jang Ki-yong disappeared from the media for a couple

---

80   Ibid., 137.

of years to fulfill their conscription. Anyone who refuses to serve is labeled a deserter to the state and arrested, tried, and punished.

My father served in the ROK Marine Corps in the late seventies. The trauma from this service stays with him to this day, and he suffers from night terrors. My mom complains about how awful it is to share the same bed as him because of his screaming and flailing. My dad is just one of millions of Korean fathers who is haunted by night terrors due to the brutality he suffered during his service in South Korea.

My dad never knew his father. He was the youngest born to my grandmother when she was in her forties, and she became a widow when he was barely two years old. When I asked my dad how his father died, he said he didn't know: "Most men back then died in their forties. It wasn't so unusual. So, our village was full of widows. But I think my father died of a heart attack." The absence of a father is a deep wound for my dad that made him feel abandoned by a man he didn't even know but was supposed to have. My paternal grandfather is someone who never existed in his life and therefore did not protect or guide him. My dad told me that on the last day of his military service, he watched his peers get picked up by their fathers to go have a drink so they can instruct their sons on what to do next in life. Because my dad did not have a father to pick him up and take him out for a drink, my dad cooped himself up in a room somewhere and drank soju alone with a picture of my paternal grandfather tacked up on the wall while shouting at it in a booze-fueled agony. He felt lost.

My dad grew up with three older brothers who were all significantly older and two older sisters. My dad's eldest brother was twenty-five years older than my dad and took on the role of a surrogate father figure. This uncle terrorized my dad all throughout his childhood. My dad told me, "Your uncle used to be a really gentle guy. But he served as a Korean marine in the fifties, and when he came back, he was a madman. He would grab a sickle blade and run around town, terrorizing people, threatening to kill them. He used to beat me relentlessly when I was a kid. He scared me so much, and I hated him when I was a boy."

South Korean veterans of the Korean War like my uncle were the first to experience mass militarized mobilization, like being subject to extreme bodily discipline that turned them into weapons of destruction against individuals who looked no different from themselves—people they were told to kill for reasons that made no sense to them. Class inequity caused further injury to my family. Men who came from economic stability were sent to college to avoid the draft in the fifties, but my paternal and maternal roots are in farming. Our family's skin is darker—a sign of having toiled in the sun and denoting hard labor, lack of education, low class, and poverty. Neither of my parents went to college. None of my paternal uncles or aunts went to college. Military service was a duty imposed upon my uncle, and he served reluctantly without knowing what to expect and returned completely unhinged.

My eldest uncle returned with PTSD as a war trauma survivor, but he received no psychological support. No one did. There is no telling what unspeakable horrors my uncle witnessed and participated in as a marine. I can only catch glimpses of these horrors documented in Korean War history books written by academics, and even while they are written with an arid distance, the details are utterly grim. In my uncle's case, there is the identifiable person that he once was before the war trauma—a gentle farmer—and then the deranged, violent man who returned and regularly beat my dad.

My dad told me a story:

> I was about eight years old when this happened. My mother was busy that day, and she forgot to bring my big brother his 중참/chungch'am while he was working in the field.[81] This pissed him off, and he flew into a rage at the house. I was just coming home from school at that moment. Right as I was about to open the gate, my brother threw a sharp farm tool at the door in anger. The force of the impact flung the door into my face and my forehead started to bleed. If it hadn't been for that door, that blade would've gone straight through my head and I would be dead. I remember seeing the tool embedded against the door because he threw it so hard.

---

81 중참 /chungch'am is a midday meal that farm workers indulge in while working in the fields to take a break, replenish, and rest, typically accompanied by makkŏlli. It is also referred to as 새참/saech'am.

This is just one of the very few stories my dad shared with me in which he experienced a life-threatening moment as a child in his home due to his mentally ill older brother.

When my dad returned home after his military service in his twenties, my uncle threw his arms around him and sobbed hysterically. My uncle cried, "You served in the marines, boy! I know how much you've suffered! *I* was a marine! I know *exactly* what you've been through, you poor thing. I know! I know!" My father had never witnessed such humanity or flood of emotions from his big brother before. It shocked him. Before this moment my dad's perception of his brother was that of a nightmare. The man had been an unpredictable, alcoholic tyrant—a feral tiger in his house—whom my dad simply had to learn how to survive around. This big scary man was now broken down before him, expressing unbridled sorrow and vulnerability that my father did not realize he was capable of. For the first time my uncle was humanized before my dad. My uncle cried that day, not because he felt bad that his baby brother suffered the same horrors as he did but because my uncle finally felt like his own military trauma was *seen* by a family member who also served in the marines. My dad told me, "After he held me like that and wept, all my hatred and fear for him disappeared. I said, 'It's okay, *hyung-nim*. I'm okay.'"

DP AND CONTEMPORARY MILITARY CONSCRIPTION TRAUMA IN SOUTH KOREA

DP is a Netflix original production based on a webtoon written and illustrated by Kim Bo-tong. The script is cowritten and directed by filmmaker Han Jun-hee and stars Jung Hae-in. The opening credits' video montage is very telling of the show's ethos. It shows a boy's lifespan from infancy to the recruitment ceremony where families and loved ones watch the young men assemble just prior to their military entrance. The final shot is an extreme close-up of the show's protagonist, An Jun-ho, who turns to look at the camera, breaking the fourth wall with a despondent look that carries a cold detachment and a hint of depression mixed with helplessness in his eyes. The opening credits remind viewers that all soldiers were at one point innocent babies, born defenselessly into this world with an obligation. Conscription is not an option. There is no luxury of choice. The footage of the soldiers' past as young boys pointedly targets my affective response, eliciting empathy, compassion, and sadness at their lot.

From the start of *DP*, it's apparent why a dark shadow is cast over Jun-ho's face. Once he starts boot camp, he is immediately thrown into hell. His commanding officer tells him and the other trainees that if they take more than a minute to get dressed, they're not a soldier but a "good-for-nothing" civilian. The trainees are told to eat within three minutes flat. They are forced to remove their masks and stand while inhaling tear gas. They are in hell.

The acronym "DP" stands for "deserter pursuit." Jun-ho gets selected as the rookie DP to assist Corporal Han Ho-yeol. The DP soldiers' task is to leave the army base in search of deserters. It's more than apparent that new recruits are unhappy with their environment. As Moon states, South Korean men generally do not wish to serve in the military because they lose valuable time in their youth, are forced to put their economic responsibility to the family on hold, and constantly face their "fear of death."[82] This fear of death among soldiers is rooted in the potential of real battle with North Korea, but it is also the violence of the training itself, which is rife with hazing in the barracks that sometimes results in death. The fear of death is also linked to the possibility of suicide.

My Korean American friend Hyoung served in the ROK Army in the nineties and told me that when the first recruits arrive, they are required to always move in pairs because new recruits have a high suicide risk. Because the men are never allowed to be alone—even when they go to the toilet—none of them have privacy to masturbate. Hyoung told me that wet dreams were common in the barracks during the first couple of months due to this physical restriction. Hyoung chuckled his way through this story, but the painful humiliation and discomfort of these men were evident. One's human rights and dignities go out the window in the liminal space of state service.

In *DP*, as Jun-ho and Ho-yeol are tasked with a new deserter case, each deserter's backstory gets pieced together, a process that is reminiscent of

---

82   Seungsook Moon, *Militarized Modernity and Gendered Citizenship in South Korea: Politics, History, and Culture* (Durham, NC: Duke University Press, 2005), 68.

trauma processing in therapy, in which survivors piece back events and weave a story to make sense of their lives. Jun-ho and Ho-yeol are not only tasked with finding the runaway soldier and bringing him back to the base where he will be tried and punished for desertion, but they are also giving the runaway soldier recognition of his pain, acknowledging why he left in the first place. As Van der Kolk writes, "Trauma stories lessen the isolation of trauma, and they provide an explanation for why people suffer the way they do."[83]

DP functions as a creatively cathartic witness, offering all conscripts acknowledgment of having withstood and survived similar pains and injustices during their mandatory duty. In this regard, TV is not dissimilar from what my uncle gave and received from my father when they clutched each other at the house as brothers who shared a hardship as marines. TV becomes a ritual for processing, catharsis, and healing.

In the first episode, a soldier named Shin Woo-suk deserts because of the assault he endured in the barracks. The mise-en-scène reveals Woo-suk's grief as the camera closes in on the back of his head while a male patron hits his skull repeatedly and spews profanity. The scene jump cuts to another close-up shot of the back of Woo-suk's head in a military helmet as another officer shoves and berates him. The parallel montage continues as a male patron pours water over Woo-suk's head to demean him, followed by a jump cut to a soldier hitting Woo-suk's head with his helmet. These shots are dramatized with slow motion, jumping around a slow close-up of Woo-suk's profile as he sobs alone in a dark motel room while inhaling the fumes of a lit coal briquette to end his life. Militarized violence is found off-base in capitalist environments where arrogant patrons mistreat service workers. Classism dictated by capital is just as inhumane as the rigidity of the military complex. Systemic inequity is exposed through characters like Park Sung-woo, who comes from money and power; he lists the ways that socioeconomically privileged men can avoid their draft through loopholes. This is in stark contrast to Jun-ho, who comes from a lower economic background and has no nepotistic advantage.

---

83   Van der Kolk, *The Body Keeps the Score*, 237.

HAZING IN THE MILITARY

Another deserter in DP named Jun-mok escapes from the base because he can't withstand the bullying. Jun-mok suffers from sleep apnea and snores a lot. In response to this, the other soldiers put a gas mask over Jun-mok's face and fill it with water while he's asleep, waking Jun-mok up to being waterboarded—a military tactic that we Americans are familiar with because we read about it in the papers when our country's military used it against Al-Qaeda forces during the Bush administration.

The most heartbreaking character in DP, however, is Suk-bong, who is regularly assaulted by his seniors Jang-soo and Yi-kang. Suk-bong has a gentle demeanor and is an anime enthusiast and artist. Suk-bong used to be a judo athlete but gave it up to become an art teacher. When asked why Suk-bong stopped judo in middle school despite competing nationally, he replies, "I just didn't like hitting people." But Jang-soo is different from Suk-bong, as he takes sadistic delight in victimizing others.

Jang-soo regularly harasses Suk-bong for being an anime enthusiast, calling him "otaku." Yi-kang sexually harasses Suk-bong by forcing him to masturbate in front of him. Jang-soo engages in similarly demented cruelties by forcing Suk-bong to stand still while naked from the waist down as Jang-soo burns off Suk-bong's pubic hair with a lighter. Jang-soo not only beats Suk-bong but also forces Suk-bong to beat up the trembling new recruits when they first arrive. When Jun-ho notices Suk-bong hitting younger officers, he is shocked because it's in such sharp contrast to how Suk-bong was in the beginning, offering benevolent comments like, "Let's be good to our juniors."

Abusive men like Jang-soo and Yi-kang represent the inevitable manifestation within an environment like the military base, where men are subject to regular physical, mental, and emotional torment under the guise of "discipline" and "national service" to perform their roles as "men" and devote their loyalty to the state as soldiers. Meanwhile, they are not engaging in any combat with a real enemy. So, where does all that heated aggression go?

That overheated energy needs to go *somewhere*, and it lands on victims like Suk-bong, Jun-mok, and Woo-suk—fellow allies who eat and sleep in the same barracks as their abusers. *DP* alerts us to the danger of pent-up combative energy that young men sit with in a highly restrictive environment that brings out the absolute worst in them and results in the demise of innocent soldiers.

CHILD ABUSE AND STATE VIOLENCE

I began kindergarten at a public elementary school in Brooklyn. School was extremely difficult because of my language barrier and cultural clashes from what I was accustomed to at my Korean nursery school. Not being able to communicate my needs was torture. I didn't know how to ask to go to the bathroom, so I would hold it in until I burst into tears from pain. I didn't know how to explain myself or ask questions. Not having a voice was hell.

My mother barely spoke and understood English. My kindergarten teacher told my mom about the time I cried because I didn't know how to say that I needed to use the bathroom and notified her of the time that I was accidentally hit in the face by a wooden block because a classmate was swinging it around during play time. My mother somehow interpreted this as me "throwing toys in class" and "spitting." I have no idea why or how this transcoded into her brain. My mother took me home that humid afternoon right before summer break, sat me down in a chair, put a sad face sticker on my forest-green Fila T-shirt, demanding to know why I threw toys and spit in school. I adamantly denied these accusations because they had never occurred. But she continued to interrogate me and insist that this is what went down. My six-year-old brain was confused and terrified as she grilled me: "Are you calling your teacher a liar? Should we go back to school and ask why she lied?" The thought of a conflict between my teacher and mom was unbearable, just as it was unbearable watching my parents fight at home regularly. My mother wore me down with these persistent false claims until I grew exhausted and gave in, hoping that my feigned admission would end the haranguing: "Fine. I did it."

My mother stood up and went to the horizontal blinds on the windows and unhooked the long plastic tilt wand. She said, "I am going to hit you a hundred times for your bad behavior in school."

Fear shot through my whole body. She had me get on my knees and stretch out my palms face up—the same way I had been instructed to endure my beatings in nursery school in Busan.

"I want you to count out loud each time I hit you until we reach one hundred."

After the first whack, I pulled my hands back and screamed in pain while crying. My mother flatly said, "Since you pulled back, we're going to start over. Count up from one again."

I put my hands out. She landed three hard whacks as I screamed, "One, two, three," then pulled my hands back in pain again. This went on for what felt like hours. My whole body from my head down to my feet was drenched in sweat. When I was unable to count anymore due to the sobbing, my mother beat me all over my body randomly with the stick—my thighs, legs, back, and arms. I remember screaming for my dad, who could not hear me because he was out. I eventually blacked out. I did not faint. I just blacked out. My memory cuts off from there because my brain was rescuing me from further trauma.

A couple of days later I was sitting on the floor, leaning against the wall of the living room where I had been beaten and noticed a splatter of blood on the white paint. I noted silently to myself with complete dissociative numbness: *That is my blood.* I wonder if my father felt the same way when he looked at that sharp object embedded against the gate of his childhood home as blood fell from his forehead.

About a year after this incident, when my family and I were sitting on our living room floor, eating dinner on our coffee table, I said to my dad, "Umma hit me because she misunderstood what the teacher told her in English. The teacher was telling her that I cried because I couldn't say that I needed to go to the bathroom in English, and that I got hit in the face with a toy. But umma beat me with a stick until I bled." My dad apologized to me on her behalf and said that he was heartbroken over what I told him. He then told my mom to apologize to me too. I felt my father's empathy in that moment, but my mother's verbal apology did not fit the scale of the abuse I suffered, just as the beating I received that day did not match the "crime."

The beatings from my parents did not stop after this talk. They carried on for years until I was older and big enough to fight back. But this particular memory is my most painful one because it filled my six-year-old body with utter humiliation, betrayal, and helplessness caused by the person I relied on for my survival.

Dr. Ham says, "What's really screwed up is that, as a baby, the only way to deal with fear and terror is to run toward your caregivers. They're supposed to protect you. You scream out hoping that they'll come to your rescue. But if they're the ones who are hurting you, then it puts you in a terrifying loop where you want to run from them but at the same time, your body tells you to go find them. And then you spend the rest of your days trying to resolve that paradox."[84]

I spent my life inhaling book after book, searching for a way to resolve this paradox, wondering why I kept surrounding myself with people who regularly undermined, shamed, and abused me. I spend my days constantly mastering the English language as a writer and stand-up comedian to give my younger self what she desperately needed during times of abuse—a voice. Many of the people I dated were also my assailants. My closest friends exhibited narcissistic tendencies like my father or borderline personality disorder symptoms like my mother. But I never felt I could speak up to assert my boundaries because I was beaten into never trusting my own physical responses to my pain while constantly fearing that my loved ones would abandon me if I ever dared to ask for my needs to be met.

Violence moves swiftly and effortlessly as a water snake in the sea. Korean men get drafted into a military duty they do not wish to perform, during which they learn the most perverse forms of violence in their training. Some of those men bring that military violence into their homes and spread it among their families as domestic violence. Others become bosses and spread it in the workplace. Some of those men spread that military violence inside schools as teachers toward students. Then that same military violence spreads from student to student in the form of bullying.

---

84 Dan Harris and Jacob Ham, "453: An Ace Therapist Gives Dan a Run for His Money/Dr. Jacob Ham," *Ten Percent Happier with Dan Harris*, May 25, 2022.

Pent-up and overheated energy is constantly on the move. An energy like that is always looking for a place to land with forceful impact. The buck doesn't stop on its own. This energy had been whirring inside my mother's body too. Perhaps my father placed it there when he abused her, or when fellow Korean immigrants alienated her, or when her adoptive country rejected her, or when her bosses abused her at jobs she worked since she was a teenager, or when her own mother hit her and sent her away. Heated energies like anger, aggression, and violence move from body to body. This energy spreads from parent to child the same way it moves from bully to victim or from state to individual. It becomes a cycle that tumbles throughout society and across generations.

BLIND SUBMISSION

Another danger *DP* alerts us to is that of blind and unquestioned submission to top-down authority. As Seungsook Moon mentions, "While military culture in a given (national) society is internally differentiated among various groups of soldiers divided by tasks and stratified by rank, the masses of recruits, especially conscripted privates, are exposed to the cult of tough and aggressive masculinity, which also emphasizes obedience to military authorities."[85] Unquestioning subordination maintains the corruption, but *DP* questions the system of top-down order that holds the military complex together.

In episode five Yi-kang harasses Suk-bong again, but this time Suk-bong retaliates by beating Yi-kang unconscious and then deserts the base in search of his other bully, Jang-soo, who had been recently released from service. Jang-soo's situation back out in society is far from glamorous, as he lives in a cramped apartment while working as a convenience store clerk. Based on the severity of Yi-kang's beating, it's apparent to everyone that Suk-bong plans to injure Jang-soo just as badly, if not worse. Provost Marshal Chun sits down with Sergeant First Class Park Bum-gu and Captain Lim Ji-sup, asking what the game plan is. Park replies that a full-scale search is necessary. Chun then

---

85 Seungsook Moon, *Militarized Modernity and Gendered Citizenship in South Korea: Politics, History, and Culture* (Durham, NC: Duke University Press, 2005), 72.

asks Lim what he thinks. Lim replies that he agrees with Park. Chun asks Lim again, "Really? Are you sure?" Lim takes a pause to read the room while the camera captures a close-up of his slightly angled profile. Lim's eyes shift downward as he makes slight movements indicating his nervousness. Chun asks again, "Your marshal's asking if you agree." Lim adjusts his answer and replies, "A full-scale search is a good idea too, but having more men doesn't necessarily guarantee results so it could be a good call to move quietly on this." Chun strategically bounces his questions between Park and Lim until an answer he prefers emerges. This way, Chun leaves the onus of responsibility on Lim, although it was his preferred call. Disciplining a man into an unquestioning obedient soldier is the purpose of military training, but *DP* reveals the arbitrary nature of these orders by higher ranking officers and the damage it causes to the lives of men below.

The pursuit of Suk-bong, however, goes awry when Suk-bong takes Jang-soo captive at gunpoint. Suk-bong is an example of what sociologist Trent Baxter calls in his book *Bullying and Violence in South Korea* the "bully-victim"—those who were once victims of bullying and who later become bullies themselves. Bully victims, according to Baxter, "tend to be more troubled than 'pure bullies,' tend to bully more severely, and are more likely to commit major acts of violence against other[s]."[86] In response to this, Chun puts out an order for his unit's military police to arm themselves with guns and pursue Suk-bong. The young men, suited up in their police garb, fidget and ask around nervously if they really need to shoot Suk-bong. In these moments, the soldiers' humanity penetrates through their gear, helmets, and guns. Despite all the hazing they participated in or stood by witnessing, the men are reluctant to shoot a fellow soldier. When Chun orders the men to get live ammunition, the men react with shock. When Lim questions Chun's orders to treat this mission as an act of domestic terrorism, he gets fired. While Jun-ho and Ho-yeol are in the midst of successfully de-escalating Suk-bong as he holds Jang-soo hostage, Chun sends the troops in. When Suk-bong sees that he is surrounded, his threat trigger goes back

---

86 Trent Bax, *Bullying and Violence in South Korea: From Home to School and Beyond* (New York: Springer, 2017), 9.

up. Suk-bong shoots himself in the throat and falls to the ground, bleeding on fresh-fallen snow while helplessly muttering the same refrain: "Umma . . . Umma . . ."

The scene gut-wrenchingly brings us back to the opening credits of the show, where we see these men as innocent young boys who want nothing more than to be with the figure who represents protection, safety, and security from their first source of love—*umma*.

VIOLENCE AND INTERGENERATIONAL TRAUMA

When I was in middle school I had an unforgettably vivid nightmare. I was a man in his twenties dressed in a military uniform with a rifle slung across my back in the pouring rain at night. I was slumped inside a dugout as rainwater flooded below me. Despite the rain, millions of mosquitoes surrounded me. They swarmed my legs like a blanket and tore away with ferocious tenacity. I was in agony. Suddenly, I was beneath a covering that hung low over my head. Under a small light, I read a letter from a woman who felt like my mother or older sister. As I read this letter, I felt such immense longing to be near her again and to be comforted by her. I missed her so much, and the ache from this deep longing made me feel pitiful as I wept hysterically. When I woke up, this pain continued to linger inside my throat and chest, and I heard myself whimpering as I opened my eyes to the daylight of my bedroom in New York.

I walked to the breakfast table where my dad was eating, and I told him the details of this dream. My dad stopped chewing and looked at me in quiet disbelief. He said, "That's my exact experience when I was in the military." We didn't linger on the topic for long and eventually forgot about it, although the dream stays with me. I mentioned this dream to a Korean shaman, who interpreted the dream as a flashback to one of my past lives. Maybe. I believe in this possibility, but I feel more strongly that I accessed my father's memory through my dream.

Over twenty years later, when I repeated this dream to my dad, I asked him if there really were that many mosquitoes when it rained and flooded. He looked at me dead in the eye and said,

You would not believe how many mosquitoes there were. One sum-mer I was on night duty by the demilitarized zone on the south side of the river. The north was just across from us. It was pouring rain because of the monsoon season, and these mosquitoes would not let up. My uniform had a covering made of porous leather material about a millimeter thick. These mosquitoes would puncture through the leather! And I couldn't even scratch the bites because I had to keep running through the rain to get to our destination. We would eventually hole up inside a cave. There was a small opening there, and we'd hold our guns out through that space, pointing it north across the water. I was miserable. I would cry at times.

Studies in epigenetics show that animals and human beings transfer their traumas onto the next generation to prepare them for survival of the same threat they experienced. I have never served in the military in either the States or the ROK, but mosquitoes have plagued me all my life. I'm one of those people—the one who will sit with a group and get bitten in twenty different places while everyone else is left unscathed. It's as if mosquitoes recognize who I am: "You're that fella's daughter, aren't you? You've seen us in your dreams." When I get bitten, I develop horrendous welts. Even if I don't scratch the bites, my skin bubbles up into a painful rash. I later learned that I have Skeeter syndrome—an allergy to mosquito saliva. Gross.

My dad, just like myself, is a victim of developmental trauma. His big T is one long echo reverberating from the brutality of war and militarism stemming from his eldest brother's PTSD flashbacks that rippled through my dad's body in the form of violent beatings. As a marine, my dad suffered grueling torment of sleepless nights, running multiple kilometers every day and withstanding unrelenting elements, the rigid military hierarchy, and the threat of death from enemy soldiers, as well as violence and torture that broke his spirit and robbed him of his light. These physical experiences are like a hot prod burned into his psyche. As a result, an anxious paranoia always keeps him hypervigilant of imaginary threats.

I've experienced and witnessed many violent moments stemming from my dad's outbursts. Many children of Korean fathers have. I live with the memory of a raging appa who hit me, hit my mother, threw things, drank, and screamed, alongside the same appa who bought me art supplies and toys, taught me the Korean names of flowers, trees, and animals, sang me Korean folk songs, read me books, took me to the movies, held me close, laughed at my jokes, carried me on his shoulder through hikes in the woods, played with me with loving tenderness and joy, and acknowledged my wounds when I asked to be seen. Unbearable pain emerges when I try to fold these two appas into one inside my traumatized heart that harbors both love and hatred for him. My work in recovery is to allow myself to accept him for all that he is in my knowing and understanding of where and what he comes from, while simultaneously honoring all my feelings wholly and honestly. This is hard. That's why I cry daily.

When I told this story to Dr. Ham on my podcast, he wondered aloud why I would dream my father's military experience and said, "It must be such a yearning love to reach him." As soon as Dr. Ham said this, I felt a surge of emotion erupt through me. I heard myself immediately minimize the moment and the dream to avoid further emotional vulnerability, but Dr. Ham didn't let me squirm away:

> But did you hear your story? You started with this chapter about his own older brother being in the marines and hugging him and being human in that moment when they shared a common experience. I think that's why I viewed this dream as your attempt to reach your dad. Like the only way your dad was able to reach his brother was by going through the same experience he did. And you took it upon yourself to tell him the same story again when you saw him recently.

Isn't it a marvel how these cycles of intergenerational trauma tumble through generation after generation, from brother to brother to daughter and niece? After hearing Dr. Ham frame my stories this way, it became impossible for me to deny the love I hold for my father. It allowed me to access the compassion in me safely, which I had cut myself from for so long. I had been denying myself of the love for my parents, given our fraught history that makes love—any kind of love from anyone—feel like the threat of death.

I doused my memories of my parents in gasoline and lit them on fire, letting all the bad burn with the good because extreme circumstances call for extreme measures. Right after I graduated college, I stopped going to church because of the abuse I suffered from that institution. This was unacceptable to my devout Christian dad, so he slapped me until I fell on the floor and then grabbed me by the hair and smashed my skull against the hard basement tiles. I finally did what I always wanted to do since I was a little kid: I called the cops. But the police chief and my mother pummeled me with guilt and shame, telling me not to press charges. "He's your father," they said. The police chief handed me a document to sign, which stated that I was not physically harmed and did not need medical assistance even though everything about the situation warranted the opposite.

After suffering a whole month of vertigo and nausea, I was finally taken to a Korean physician I'd been seeing since childhood. My mother sat beside me the entire time to monitor and censor me from speaking up about how I was injured. My doctor sensed that there was something wrong, so he repeatedly asked me how I got my concussion. After lying the first few times, I eventually broke down and tearfully whispered, "I fought with my dad." Even as I wept, I couldn't speak my whole truth and specify how. My doctor scolded me for fighting with my parents. He gave me nothing to treat my concussion. No referral. No X-ray. No scans to see how bad my injury was. He just told me to drink water and stay away from screens for a month.

My mother did everything to protect my dad from incrimination. This took priority over my health and well-being. The concussion I suffered caused symptoms of vertigo that lasted for years thereafter. Not only did my family let me down that day, but so did the entire system—both law and medicine. The common denominator across all three groups is rock-solid patriarchy that protects toxic men while shaming victims of domestic violence and ignoring their injuries.

The strength and support I needed during this period did not come from my family. It came from my former college professor Dr. Karla Jay—a feminist queer and disability rights activist who participated in the Stonewall Revolution and Lavender Menace. She advised me to get distance from my family for the sake of my life and to regain my strength. Years later, after I passed my comprehensive exams for my PhD, I visited home for the first time in a few years, but my family, once again, subjected me to further violence and mistreatment. I had only gone home to celebrate a milestone, but my family brought me down to such a low place that I saw myself making a very detailed suicide plan in the most matter-of-fact and emotionally detached way while on the plane flying back to LA from New York. I knew this wasn't normal, but I also had no strength left inside of me to care. So I asked myself what I wanted to do and a response came: *I want to move to Berlin.*

There are no coincidences. Around this time I got an email from Dr. Jay, retired by then, who asked me a question about Han Kang's *The Vegetarian*, which she was reading in her book club. I replied to her question, but I also sought her support, given my recent decision to sever contact with my family and temporarily move to Berlin and recuperate while escaping the fraught politics in America. I sought her advice because my decision to cut ties with my parents felt so scary and wrong. I was raised to constantly override my own thoughts and feelings to accommodate others, which broke my emotional, mental, and physical well-being. I was looking for a way to survive. Dr. Jay had been a strong emotional support to me when I was twenty-two, and she was there for me again at thirty-one. She told me, "I had a really dysfunctional family and just had to walk away and not look back for a number of years. At a certain point, you realize that you are not going to change them and vice versa. You need to think about your life—you have so much ahead of you. Berlin sounds perfect."

Had it not been for Dr. Jay's words and my own inner spirit's demand— *Enough*—I would not be here today, as I had been completely resigned to just killing myself. But angels do not only live in the light. They also reside in the darkest spaces just in case we fall into the pits. I also witnessed my own inner being's clarity. She knew exactly what she wanted without the fog of other people's voices or agenda to distract. I put all my belongings and car into storage and was officially houseless for a year, living in Airbnbs all over Europe and Korea. There were a couple of times I had to stay at a hotel or a friend's couch, but I didn't care. I was free to move as I pleased and create distance from the people and places I needed space from.

I read world-renowned artist Yayoi Kusama's autobiography *Infinity Net* years later, in which she details the severe child abuse she suffered at the hands of her parents, causing extreme psychological ailments. Kusama's only escape was art. She painted nonstop to keep from losing herself to regular psychic hallucinations. Psychiatrist Dr. Shiho Nishimura advised Kusama to get away from her mother and that house for the sake of her sanity, so she did. Kusama went to New York and made a name for herself around the globe. Reading her example offered me peace over the years of guilt I felt for setting my boundaries from my family. Today, I make better efforts to prioritize my own safety and well-being above all else. I still struggle with intermittent inner conflict, but whenever I do, my angelic support system immediately comes to my aid as if they know exactly what I need. Cosmic interventions have repeatedly saved my life.

Berlin became my haven to recover my voice during this dark period. I spent my days regaining my strength, self-esteem, and health in the company of good friends, great beer, dönner, Vietnamese food, and undistracted free-flowing creativity. I performed stand-up every single night and was revitalized. Berlin is now my angel city. It is as dear to me as New York, Busan, and Seoul. As it turns out, Berlin and Los Angeles are sister cities. It's no wonder I was drawn to it in the first place.

WITNESS, RECOVERY, GROUND, AND DISSENT

Thirty years after the unjust beating I endured from my mom that afternoon as a six-year-old, I called her while looking at hail fall outside my LA apartment window to ask her a question: "Did halmŏni hit you as a kid?"

"Yes," my mom replied. "She disciplined all of us with a stick." Then my mom started to make light of it: "But all the elders hit kids back then. Everybody hit kids. It was normal."

As I heard my mom minimize child abuse so casually in her tone, I felt my trigger switch flip, and I angrily confronted her about that day in Brooklyn in 1993—an incident I never confronted her about as an adult. I was enraged as I yelled, "Just because it's normal doesn't make it right. It's absolutely *wrong* to hit kids!" I raged tearfully, demanding an explanation for why she beat me so horrifically that day.

My mother's tone shifted. I heard her grow small with shame on the other line as she whispered, "I remember that day. That day keeps me up at night. It haunts me. I wake up in the middle of the night, and I can't sleep till dawn because of that memory. I assumed you'd forgotten it. I'm so sorry. I can't even go to that neighborhood in Brooklyn because I'm afraid of seeing that building. It makes me sick knowing what I did to you that day." Then my mother started to blame other people who drove her to do this, but I did not let her squirm away. The fire and thunder in my voice held her accountable for her own actions. She apologized.

"I'm so sorry. I was completely out of my mind with unhappiness, so I took it out on you. I'm really, really sorry. It was wrong of me. You were just a little kid. I was insane at the time." My mother wept as she apologized. I was filled with agonizing guilt for confronting her. My entire neck, shoulders, and upper back were painfully stiff for the next three weeks. But I was also relieved to know that what I endured that day wasn't just my own distorted hallucination. It was a real trauma confirmed to me by my mother— my sole witness and participant in my abuse. Her apology brought such a natural urge in me to quell her pain. I told my mother that I forgave her. What was there to even forgive? This was the past. She is still my mother. But the hypervigilant six-year-old in me who never lets me sleep at night needed to hear these words from her. The ritual of apology and forgiveness exists for not just the victim but also the perpetrator, who is also a victim of a much larger wheel of suffering. I apologized for yelling and told her, "Please sleep easily from now on. Don't worry about me anymore. I am fine. I'm all right."

I did not know that my mother suffered from insomnia for thirty years just as I have. While I thought I had called my mom that day to ask a simple question, it transformed into a mission to get to the bottom of why she beat me until I lost consciousness that strange afternoon. I realized it was to break this curse of insomnia that she and I had been living with for thirty years. While I still struggle with insomnia, I have more support from my doctors now, and this horrific, torturous memory does not attack me anymore in the night.

When it comes to child abuse, sexual assault, bullying, and military trauma, all of them have a common denominator of humiliation. Herman states that humiliation occurs when the subject loses control of their "basic bodily integrity."[87] She writes, "The body is invaded, injured, defiled. Control over bodily functions is often lost; in the folklore of combat and rape, this loss of control is often recounted as the most humiliating aspect of the trauma."[88] When I suffered sexual assault and corporal punishment as a child, losing agency of my body to my abusers caused deep shame and self-hatred. When my mother made me vocally count the number of times she hit my body and forced me not to pull my hands away despite the pain I felt, humiliation erupted in me, as I was made to do things that were unnatural to my bodily impulses. The damage from this incident was evident in my adult life through my harmful choices of food, beverage, and relationships. This humiliation still plagues me, which is why somatic exercises and meditation are part of my daily routine. Staying grounded in my mind/body is a necessity, because otherwise I am completely lost from myself.

Military training does the same to a body. In *Reply 1994* there's a scene where Haitai returns from his service and can't stop responding like a soldier while sitting at the breakfast table with his homestay family. He reacts with embarrassment every time he compulsively replies like a soldier to simple questions because of what his mind/body had been disciplined to do.

Trauma needs bearing witness. It requires the subject's attention and a healer's support. Ignoring it never works. Ignoring it makes it worse. Therapist and author Mark Wolynn discusses epigenetics and intergenerational trauma in *It Didn't Start with You*, stating that we "inherit and 'relive' aspects of a family trauma."[89] Trauma doesn't disappear because we ignore,

---

87 Herman, *Trauma and Recovery*, 53.

88 Ibid.

89 Mark Wolynn, *It Didn't Start with You: How Inherited Family Trauma Shapes Who We Are and How to End the Cycle* (New York: Penguin, 2016), 44.

forget, or deny it out of shame. It repeats itself until it gets acknowledged, recognized, and processed by the person who decides to end it. My psychologist helped me greatly in facing my shadows and loneliness by reassuring me. She said, "The antidote to shameful secrets is putting it out into the light of day. We process it by talking about it."

The buck of trauma only stops when the subject decides that it stops with them. Contemporary studies in psychology and neurology show the healing effects that psychedelics have on the brain in treating trauma. LSD, psilocybin, and DMT have been greatly beneficial in my own trauma treatment by affording me an inner neutrality that I was never able to reach. Psychedelic medicine gives me a window to see my life from a bird's-eye view with love and compassion. Trauma has made my brain's default pathway an eternal downward spiral into the darkest places filled with fear, blame, rage, pity, sorrow, grief, and doubt. Psychedelics removed the plaque buildup in my other brain pathways, clearing passages toward appreciation, understanding, and equanimity. These medicines broadened my perspective and broke me out of myopic hell. They helped me see the silver linings I had been blinded to by lifting the veil and showing me that it is safe to look up and trust life. I come from severe family dysfunction that put me on a rampage of self-harm, negative thought patterns, awful feelings, and mangled interpersonal relationships, but I remember declaring aloud while on my first medicinal LSD trip: "All of that ends with me."

It's not just talk therapy that helped me. I don't believe only talking about one's trauma is the cure, just as I don't believe psychedelics alone are a cure-all. I've come to find that my own alchemy of talk therapy, somatic therapies, alternative medicine, exercise, meditation, journaling, affirmations, mindful eating, prayer to my ancestors, and my daily commitment to these rituals is what works for me. The road to recovery is unique to each individual. I found my combination, and it's always in flux. Participating in that flux brings me joy because I know I am finally being attentive, caring, and loving to myself. My mind/body, heart center, and soul, which had been unplugged from one another, are now reconnected and realigned, thanks to my inner work.

Change for the intention of healing happens as soon as the subject consciously decides to make different choices with their mind/body on how to live and then to voice what they do not agree with—like when Captain Lim questions his boss's overtly violent tactics, like when Sergeant Park questions his boss's abuse of power, and like in the second-to-last scene of season one of *DP*, when Jun-ho doesn't follow the group of soldiers who take orders to run right and he alone runs left. That scene reminds me of the last episode in *SKY Castle*, when Gi-joon openly questions his teacher's abusive words, states his own feelings, and then walks out.

Standing up to any establishment or institution takes bravery, whether it be the school, the church, the family, the government, the military, the company, the hospital, the law, or the loved one who doesn't know how to love in a healthy way. The absurdity of what is socially and culturally normalized, despite their great harm, comes to light in moments of questioning, rebellion, and insubordination. I use my fire to fight for my safety and freedom while celebrating fellow dissenters, rebels, protestors, and deserters who choose their own happiness and mind/body autonomy over what the Man tells them to do.

TOP TEN GREATEST K-DRAMAS OF ALL TIME ACCORDING TO DR. GRACE JUNG, PHD IN CINEMA AND MEDIA STUDIES FROM THE UNIVERSITY OF CALIFORNIA, LOS ANGELES, SCHOOL OF THEATER, FILM AND TELEVISION AND FORMER FULBRIGHT SCHOLAR

Make your own list, man. There's no such thing as a "top ten." Hierarchies are not real!

LESSON 11:

AMNESIAC QUEENS, ZOMBIES, AND GHOSTS OF A FORGOTTEN WAR

Y FORAY INTO K-DRAMA AMNESIA BEGAN WITH *TRUTH* (2000). Ja-young is an economically disadvantaged girl living in the basement of a house that belongs to a rich brat named Shin-hee. Ja-young's dad is Shin-hee's family driver, while Ja-young's mom works as their housekeeper. Ja-young and Shin-hee war for several years due to class differences, rivalry, and jealousy. Ultimately, Ja-young wins the affections of Shin-hee's crush, Hyun-woo, a handsome and gentle young man who comes from a well-off background. Then oopsie. Shin-hee gets behind the wheel of a car after drinking with Hyun-woo and Ja-young, and she crashes into another driver, causing a severe accident. When Shin-hee wakes up, she moves Ja-young's unconscious body to the driver's seat to pin the blame on her, assuming that Ja-young is dead. Shin-hee's accident kills the other driver, puts Hyun-woo in a coma, and leaves Ja-young in the ICU, but Ja-young eventually wakes up and her memory is lucid. Shin-hee is the one who drove that night, but no one believes Ja-young, as Shin-hee digs in her heels and insists that it was Ja-young who drove. Fuck!

Weeks pass with no signs of improvement in Hyun-woo's comatose condition, but Ja-young endures by his bedside. She believes—no, she knows!—that he will make it out of the woods. Sure enough, Hyun-woo finally awakens. Ja-young rushes over and calls out his name. The camera closes in on Hyun-woo as he turns around and says blankly, "Who are you?" OMFG. Then the episode ends with music and credits. 😩

I was filled with despair for a whole week until the next VHS arrived, and I saw Hyun-woo recover his memory after Ja-young wraps a scarf around his neck. This action triggers his sensory memory, and everything comes flooding back to him, as he screams her name with familiarity, "Ja-young, *ah*!" And the knot in my stomach finally released. Oooooooh. *So* good.

Then Hyun-woo exposes the truth! Hence the title! *Truth*! He remembers it all. It was that bitch Shin-hee who drove while intoxicated that night, not Ja-young! Shin-hee framed this poor, innocent girl that Hyun-woo loves! I can only dream of K-dramas today to be as beautifully tacky, hack, and convoluted as *Truth*.

Amnesia is a powerful storytelling device found in Hollywood cinemas like Alfred Hitchcock's *Spellbound* (1945). It takes on whole new camp levels in soap operas like *Guiding Light* (1952–2009) and *Days of Our Lives* (1965–present) on American television. Then K-dramas turn amnesia into Sriracha sauce—it goes on everything everywhere all the time.

Amnesia is an engaging device used to drive a romantic narrative because it raises the stakes and adds mystery. While before the amnesia the whole purpose was to get the lovers to finally become a couple, despite family disapproval or a jealous saboteur, *after* the amnesia a whole new purpose appears on the horizon. The one who lost their memory must recover it so their love may be whole again. Gooooood shit. I am in. Let's go.

A nice juicy K-drama frequently has a character with amnesia, but not all amnesias are the same. There's the classic amnesia, in which a character suffers a head trauma and loses memory, like Ja-young. In *All About Eve* (2000) the show's diabolical antagonist attempts suicide by drowning but survives without any memory of who she is or where she comes from. In *Winter Sonata* Jun-sang gets hit by a car, forgets who he is, and returns with a new identity. The exact same thing happens again to characters in *Land of Wine* (2003) and *Stairway to Heaven*.

Then there's amnesia among ghosts who died a traumatic death. In *Oh My Ghostess* (2015), the ghost Soon-ae can't recall who killed her or how she died. Some forms of amnesia protect the ghost from their own past life's sins, like the grim reaper in *Goblin*, who killed his wife and brother-in-law but doesn't remember. In the same show Eun-tak has temporary amnesia and forgets who her boyfriend Kim Shin is after he disappears for ten years. In *Unkind Women* the father loses his memory and disappears, conveniently forgetting that he'd been unfaithful to his wife. Short-term amnesia also plagues the father in *My Unfamiliar Family* (2020), who was emotionally abusive toward his wife for decades but forgets why. There is also dementia and Alzheimer's among elderly characters in *Navillera* (2021), *The Light in Your Eyes*, and *Dear My Friends*.

In the Korean context, amnesia is an apt metaphor for what the nation has survived and what dwells in its collective memory on both a surface and a repressed level. These characters don't lose their memory out of sheer nothing. There was a cause. As such, there are causes for why amnesia is such a hackneyed device in K-dramas that we can dig up by analyzing the nation's forgotten histories.

CULTURAL AMNESIA

Amnesia during Japanese-occupied Korea (1910–1945) was induced in the form of erasure. The Japanese imperial government imposed its colonial rule through forced assimilation. Koreans were required to speak Japanese and convert their Korean names to Japanese. Japanese colonizers assumed that once Koreans assimilated, they would forget their identity and live as Japanese. This logic is as bonkers as K-drama characters who hit their heads and wake up with no memory of their names, who they are, or where they come from.

The Koreans most closely affiliated with the Japanese during colonial rule were the elite. This national betrayal by the upper echelons of Korean society and the shame stemming from it are complicated matters that haunt South Korea to this day. In *Mr. Sunshine* the character Lee Wan-ik is a Japanese sympathizer who profits by giving up Korean insurgents to the Japanese police.

Sociologist John Lie uses the term "cultural amnesia" to describe how South Korea recollects the colonial period. Cultural amnesia is when societies forget certain histories that belong to their collective past. The most triggering World War II memory for South Koreans is when Japanese soldiers stood in long lines outside of tents to take turns raping hundreds of thousands of kidnapped and enslaved Korean girls and women. This is the one cultural memory that South Koreans and the Korean diaspora express a great deal of outrage and grief over. Lie, however, contends that this grief overpowers the cultural benefits that Chosŏn gained during the colonial era that the nation forgot.

Japan's colonial oppression was severe. They imposed strict censorship laws that prevented Korean dissenters from speaking up for their rights (not that they didn't—especially the comedians). But it is also true that Chosŏn was enriched by cultural modernity and industrialization via Japanese influence, given its long relationship with another expert colonizer, Great Britain.

Korean society began to change radically during the colonial era. As Lie writes, "Mass schooling, the military and its destructive weaponry, the Western bureaucracy with its discourses and uniforms, capitalist factories and department stores—all these and much more entered Korea in a rapid and compressed manner in the first half of the colonial period."[90] New ideas in the form of art, architecture, and literature entered the Korean consciousness through Japanese translations of European ideas. Lie notes that colonized Koreans begrudgingly or even avidly embraced "the colonial masters and their civilization" in a capitulating fashion.[91] There were influential writers like Yi Kwang-su—arguably the first Korean novelist (albeit not my cup of tea)—who claimed that Koreans ought to give in to Japan and co-prosper in their East

---

90 John Lie, *K-Pop: Popular Music, Cultural Amnesia, and Economic Innovation in South Korea* (Berkeley: University of California Press, 2015), 71.

91 Ibid.

Asian relations. Lie also cites Korean youths during the colonial period who strived to become kamikaze pilots and fight for Japan's imperial war cause. Lie writes, "It's no wonder that most South Koreans today see colonial rule as an era of unremitting darkness: cultural amnesia as contemporary convenience."[92]

Trauma occurs during the actual affliction, but its effects can remain dormant until much later, as I know from experience. Even if Korean civilians did emulate their colonizer's lifestyle, language, education, and modernity, were they operating with a sense of autonomy, agency, and choice? Capitulation does not mean consent with intention. It means to cease resisting the opponent. It implies a learned helplessness, which occurs when a trapped person or animal is repeatedly abused until they stop fighting their abuser. Van der Kolk writes, "Scared animals return home, regardless of whether home is safe or frightening. I thought about my patients with abusive families who kept going back to be hurt again. Are traumatized people condemned to seek refuge in what is familiar?"[93]

Perhaps this amnesia that causes South Koreans to forget the cultural, economic, and social benefits present during colonial occupation is not just a convenience but rather a necessity for survival. As mentioned in chapter 1, a child feels the threat of death without their caretaker's love. I wonder if a civilian feels the same threat without national sovereignty promising to protect them. Hope of co-prosperity between Korea and Japan was fundamentally flawed because Japan annexed Korea and dissolved its monarchy.[94] Reading about Korean elites who buttered up and sat beside Japanese colonizers while enjoying the fat of colonization reminds me why I read subordinate women who "consent" to sex with their supervisors as nonconsensual. When such a strong power disparity is at play, it's hard to call it consent. Coercion is not an agreement. Surviving is not living.

As sociologist R. W. Connell recognizes, "Violence is part of a system of domination, but is at the same time a measure of its imperfection."[95]

---

92 Ibid., 73.

93 Van der Kolk, *The Body Keeps the Score*, 31.

94 S. Lone, "The Japanese Annexation of Korea 1910: The Failure of East Asian Co-prosperity," *Modern Asian Studies* 25, no. 1 (1991): 143–173.

95 Connell, *Masculinities*, 84.

The moment coercion through weapons, violence, and manipulation comes into play, the playing field is no longer level, and ideals of consent or co-prosperity disappear.

THE KOREAN WAR: AMERICA'S FORGOTTEN WAR

In *Stairway to Heaven* Jung-suh is the daughter of a well-off single dad, widower, and professor named Su-ha. Jung-suh's close friend is a slightly older boy, Song-joo, who is a chaebol.[96] Su-ha marries a film actress named Mira, who moves in with him and Jung-suh. Mira is initially very loving toward Jung-suh, but she has two teenaged children of her own, Tae-hwa and Yuri, from her previous marriage. After Mira's kids move into the house with Jung-suh and her dad, Mira reveals the dark side to her split personality.

Whenever Mira feels a competitive rivalry against Jung-suh through her daughter Yuri, she physically and emotionally abuses Jung-suh. Mira also separates Jung-suh and Song-joo so her daughter Yuri can date him and become a chaebol's wife.

When the kids grow older, Yuri runs Jung-suh over with her car out of jealousy. Jung-suh's head trauma from the accident causes amnesia, and Yuri lies to her family and Song-joo, telling them that Jung-suh died in a fire. But Jung-suh's stepbrother Tae-hwa, who had been in love with Jung-suh since high school, takes advantage of Jung-suh's amnesic state and starts living with her after implanting a fictionalized memory in her consciousness. Oy vey.

The kidnapper's act of implanting a new story in Ji-soo's consciousness reminds me of how Lie describes Japan's cultural imperialization of Chosŏn: "The general trend of colonial rule was assimilation, at once expunging things Korean and implanting things Japanese."[97] Implanting a new narrative also reminds me of how the Korean War and its multitude of grievous stories went erased, denied, and locked away in the classified files until historians and the Truth and Reconciliation Commission began to unearth them in the 1990s and early 2000s.

---

96 "Chaebol" refers to a family or an individual who controls an entire conglomerate. Think Disney and Samsung.

97 Lie, *K-Pop*, 13.

When it comes to the Korean War, the whole world suffers from amnesia. The Korean War is nicknamed "The Forgotten War." But historian Tessa Morris-Suzuki writes, "The term 'Forgotten War' . . . refers largely to an American amnesia."[98] While the US chose to forget that the Korean War was ever part of its history, American soldiers returned home with the brutality they endured, witnessed, and participated in during service. "Secondary trauma" is when a person witnesses another person being traumatized through attack while participating in the attack itself or being there to offer aid. America dropped more bombs on the Korean peninsula during the Korean War than it did in the entirety of World War II. When the American government treats the Korean War as though it never happened, it is not only an offense to the millions of Koreans who died but also to the US service personnel stationed in Korea, both past and present.

Culturally speaking, mainstream America did not have a grasp of where and what Korea was for a long time. When I first moved to the States, I did not have the words to offer the US cultural imaginary an explanation of what I was. Telling Americans that I was Korean was no different from telling them that I was an alien, as most people had no clue where Korea was on a map, even though their taxes have been funding the US military occupation in South Korea since the 1940s.

After World War II, US forces occupied enemy countries like Germany and Japan. The American military presence in South Korea, however, is a confused matter, as South Korea was never a US enemy. The US began to station hundreds of military bases around the globe in this manner after the Korean War.[99] The beginning of America's experimentation with "containment" policy—meaning containing or limiting the spread of communism—began with the Korean War and was fanned by the flames of US McCarthyism. This precedent of attempting containment and failing in Korea is the reason why the US tried to do it again during the Vietnam War until Vietnam kicked the US military out. Cumings cites that the Korean War gave the US

---

98 Tessa Morris-Suzuki, "Remembering the Unfinished Conflict: Museums and the Contested Memory of the Korean War," *Asia-Pacific Journal* 7, issue 29, no. 4 (2009): 1–24, 1.

99 Cumings, *The Korean War*, 207.

government a reason to enhance its military budget to four times what it had been during World War II, and it hasn't gone down since.[100] Ever since the Korean War became America's excuse to increase its defense budget toward containment by fighting against communism, the same logic has applied to America's fight against terrorism through wars in the Middle East.

RACISM FROM WAR

The all-white high school I attended in Rockland County, New York, had very few minorities. I once heard a white teenaged boy describe another Asian kid in our school as "a stupid gook" while the other white kids laughed. American GIs used words like "gook" to dehumanize Koreans and mentally enable themselves to rape, kill, mutilate, and torture civilian victims. Now, a kid at my high school was using this word to disgrace a fellow Asian American student. He said it so casually and confidently within earshot of me. This happened over twenty years ago, but I remember it because it erupted fear, insecurity, and sadness in me. I wonder how many of my own relatives felt the same way when American GIs treated them like a doormat. The origin of racism is found in war.

During the Korean War, American soldiers were trained to hate "gooks." Cumings documents quotes from soldiers stating that their "dearest wish was to kill a Korean" or get themselves "a gook" because, otherwise, these American men, who were also capable of kindness and generosity, "would not have been able to kill [Koreans] indiscriminately or smash up homes and poor belongings."[101] The derogatory term "gook" exists in the English rhetoric because US soldiers used it to rationalize killing Koreans. As therapist and author Resmaa Menakem writes in *My Grandmother's Hands*, "White-body supremacy comes at a great cost to white people."[102] White supremacy hurts everyone, just as war hurts both civilians and soldiers and misogyny hurts all genders. In the face of a violent affront, no one goes unscathed, which is why

---

100 Ibid., 197.

101 Ibid., 170.

102 Resmaa Menakem, *My Grandmother's Hands: Racialized Trauma and the Pathway to Mending Our Hearts and Bodies* (Las Vegas: Central Recovery Press, 2017), 105.

clear delineations between *perpetrator* and *victim* are suspect. As Menakem suggests, secondary or vicarious trauma is still a trauma that causes injury to the participant, aka the "perpetrator."

America never "won" the "cold" war as history presumes. America's war involvement in Korea and in Vietnam did not result in any wins. Terms like "cold war" and concepts like "winning" or "losing" must be questioned if we are to imagine a world free of war.

REMEMBERING THE FORGOTTEN

My antiwar sentiment stems from the personal. I want my humanity recognized and seen. If the atrocities of the Korean War continue to go unrecognized, then where does that leave the nation and its people who still live with these traumas in their minds/bodies and pass them down? Korean American artist Deb JJ Lee writes in their book *In Limbo*, "But what is a fate worse than being even more invisible to others?"[103]

Amnesia is not just another hackneyed trope in K-dramas; it draws constant attention to what was forgotten. In the instance between Korean and US relations, the amnesia trope is a wake-up call coming from the mist of a midcentury war that went overlooked. America's cultural amnesia of its atrocities during the Korean War explains why South Korea is such a global overachiever as a nation; Koreans overwork and overexert to the point of illness and death so they can become the best at everything—and they now have the world's attention. Although it may not be a pointed question, there's something sinister and ironic in South Korea's excessive use of pastel colors and glittery charm in K-pop branding and the sweet to melodramatic music that plays after Eun-tak finally remembers who Kim Shin is after forgetting him for one whole episode. All of it is asking, "Do you know what you've forgotten?"

Willed amnesia is denial. Just because a war is nicknamed "forgotten" doesn't mean that it is so. This very act of naming, processing, registering, and acknowledging that I do here is the opposite of forgetting. While I question

---

103 Deb JJ Lee, *In Limbo* (New York: First Second, 2023), 215.

the relevance of school today given the myriad of problems in our higher education system—such as overcharging anxious students for basic education while outsourcing course work to adjuncts who are severely underpaid, overworked, unprotected, and burnt out—I see the need for continued research by scholars. Piecing together and restoring past events through archival research is an act of acknowledging forgotten injustices. To that end, I give my work meaning by treating it as a ritual of recognition of past afflictions that my ancestors experienced. My work honors past grievances that were forcibly shut down and ignored. It appeases the ghosts of my broader past. I give them my witness through scholarship with the intention to appease, liberate, and restore peace.

ZOMBIES AND THE REPRESSION OF "ILLEGAL" MEMORIES

I'm not into zombies, but I've always wondered why zombies are so vicious. Like, what are you so angry about, guy? Why are you chasing, snarling, and eating people?

Zombies do not have any capacity to think or reason. They blindly rampage toward destruction. They are all lizard brain with no rationale or awareness. Zombies are technically not alive. They run, attack, and feast while dead. They embody a human form, and yet they are not human. They are separated from their humanity and have no mind/body autonomy. Zombies have no memories. They just bum rush and bite a living person's flesh with an insatiable appetite for more flesh.

In Kim Eun-hee's *Kingdom*—a mash-up of political thriller, historical period piece, and zombie horror—a group of wealthy elites of the yangban class decide to save their one-percent asses while leaving the peasants behind to fend for themselves on land as the zombie contagion spreads across Chosŏn. An old woman has an aristocratic son who died after a zombie attack. Even though they are prohibited from taking any infected bodies onto the boat, she sneaks her dead son's body onboard anyhow. Of course, the dead son rises as a zombie and attacks his mother, spreading the infection. The scene clearly shows that zombies have zero selectivity or bias when attacking people.

The most applicable theory in Korean studies that I've come across to describe Korean zombies and amnesia is from cultural anthropologist Heonik Kwon's body of work, which gives insight into why Korean media is obsessed with undead memories. In his essay "Korean War Mass Graves," Kwon writes about the massacres that locals witnessed in the midcentury: "South Koreans were not able to recall this reality publicly until recently, while continuing to live in a self-consciously anticommunist political society."[104] It's not that Koreans did not have the memory—they were *forbidden* to recall such a memory. This suggests a willed forgetting and denial of the past to survive.

Kwon details in *After the Korean War* that both the South and North "committed preemptive violence on a massive scale" toward any potential sympathizers of the "enemy" before the official war date, June 25, 1950.[105] Even prior to this date, any civilian "accused of anti-state sympathies became a critical liability for the entire surviving family."[106] Thus, it was not just an individual or personal matter to sympathize with the "other" side. Sympathizers and collaborators put their entire family's lives at risk, and loved ones could be "deemed guilty by association" just because they were related to politicized individuals.[107] In many cases, there wasn't even evidence that the accused was an enemy sympathizer. Any accusation or suspicion was enough to condemn that person and their whole family to death. Both the South and North regimes enacted these preemptive massacres to terrorize people into their war effort.

Once the Korean War's cease-fire was declared, having any knowledge or memory of events from the war became taboo. Kwon writes, "South Koreans were not able to publicly share their experiences of the politics of collective culpability until recently, while living in a self-consciously anticommunist political society."[108] South Koreans' amnesia in the aftermath of the Korean War was willed for survival, because if they testified as a witness to the grand atrocities,

---

104 Heonik Kwon, "Korean War Mass Graves," in *Necropolitics: Mass Graves and Exhumations in the Age of Human Rights*, ed. Richard Wilson (2015): 76–91, 79.

105 Heonik Kwon, *After the Korean War: An Intimate History* (Cambridge: Cambridge University Press, 2020), 5–6.

106 Ibid., 6.

107 Ibid.

108 Ibid.

they were risking death by their own government. This is an induced amnesia based in fear of one's own memory. The same rule applied in the North. Kwon states that approximately two hundred thousand lives were taken at the start of the Korean War due to state violence against their own civilians, although the exact number of the death toll remains unknowable, as many of these bodies disappeared into mass graves or the ocean: "The violence committed by one side radicalized the intensity and scale of the violence committed by the opposite side, and this vicious cycle of terror perpetrated against the civilian population devastated countless local communities to the extreme."[109]

On July 28, 1960, two thousand people gathered at a public square in Daegu. Women in white hanbok—worn to grieve the dead—read letters to their missing family members. The crowd wailed in loud lamentation over the deceased who had gone unmourned. The South Korean government since banned such rituals and labeled them a national security threat until very recently.[110] The cultural amnesia of civilian deaths from war isn't exactly memory loss but rather memory repression, similar to the cultural amnesia Koreans have about their colonizers.

But it was not only their own governments that betrayed Koreans; relatives, friends, and neighbors also turned their backs against one another over ideological differences in the face of threat. As Kwon notes, the same people who used to share food and childhood games together in their village later sold one another out to cops and pimps or killed one another. The trauma of betrayal runs deeply when trusted individuals are the ones who bring on the affliction. There are numerous instances of internal conflicts, finger pointing, betrayal, and sacrifice in the teen zombie K-drama *All of Us Are Dead* (2022), where high school students stuck in classrooms battle their way through a zombie outbreak, making difficult choices about whether to let a student in or out over fear of contagion.

The two Korean governments made open discussion of such war atrocities illegal because of their own shameful history of civilian massacres. On

---

109 Ibid., 23.
110 Ibid., 22.

July 8, 1950, South Korea declared a national state of emergency so the military police could arrest large numbers of people on charges of collaboration and execute them without due process. The US military government implemented similar emergency measures in South Korea from September 1945 through August 1948, specifically to weed out communist sympathizers. This "state of emergency" politics and martial law in South Korea had no existing framework to justify their existence, forcing Korean lawmakers to turn to their former colonial occupier's Meiji constitution to institute the emergency clause over the nation.[111] These colonial laws became the basis of the martial law that dictators like Park Chung-hee and Chun Doo-hwan later used to justify political violence against their own people. The US also hid shameful war secrets, such as the Nogun-ri massacre, which became public knowledge only in the 1990s. The Nogun-ri massacre took place from July 26 through 29, 1950, when US warplanes opened fire on four hundred unarmed South Korean war refugees for three days, leaving only ten survivors.

Throughout *Kingdom* and *All of Us Are Dead* there are countless visuals of hundreds of zombies piling on top of one another as they rush toward the living to tear and eat their flesh. Such images point to the innumerable dead who died without knowing the cause of their own deaths and being thrown into a pit left to be forgotten, as well as their memories among grieving loved ones that were rendered illegal by the state. Therein lies the long reverberating wail that echoes intergenerationally throughout domestic and diasporic Koreans to this day. The wailing overcompensates for the suppressed sounds of grief forbidden by dictators.

In Heonik Kwon's book *The Other Cold War* he utilizes the term "decomposition" to describe the literal and figurative decay of Koreans' memories of massacres from before, during, and after the Korean War. Kwon also acknowledges the frustration over the living's inability to mourn the dead due to laws that declared such acts to be treason. The illegal status of memory demonstrates the invasiveness of the political and ideological state agenda by attempting to control a person's most private quarters—the psyche. Kwon

---

111 Ibid., 28.

writes that "'the decomposition of the cold war' has a more literal meaning, which is to relocate the human casualties of the bipolar conflicts (and the actions concerning their decomposing bodies and troubled memories) from the invisible margins to a vital center in the history of the global cold war."[112] Contemporary K-dramas process this history by moving the invisibility of these decomposing bodies from the margins to the center via globalized TV. Piles of rotting dead bodies fill the world's screens. The gasping, gagging, and screeching of these zombie bodies are allegoric of the neglected dead who seek reprieve after local and foreign governments betrayed them in their greed for power. They're asking: *Do you know what you've forgotten?*

◇◇◇◇◇◇◇◇◇◇◇◇◇

I read zombies as a conjuring of an ugly past that I wish to lay to rest. Past woes, indignation, and despair that orbit a point of injustice keep rising back up as flashbacks—my undead memories and my undead past lives. These memories felt "illegal" to me because I knew what happened to me was wrong, but I could not name them for the sake of protecting my abusers. When my zombies get triggered into motion, they spread like contagion in the form of a bad mood if I let myself get carried away into my decomposition. Nothing spreads faster than a shitty mood. The only way to avoid such contagion is finely attuned, moment-by-moment self-care.

I know that when I meet my needs, I am more likely to be calm and centered as I navigate the world and get through my day. I also don't pretend that my zombies are not real. If they ever surface, I acknowledge them and remain curious as to why they're here. I also reassure myself that what's past (dead) is past (dead), and if it walks around and starts terrorizing the world, I know it's not a real threat but rather just a memory that could easily be put to rest by inquiring of it: *Like, what are you so angry about, guy?*

---

112 Heonik Kwon, *The Other Cold War* (New York: Columbia University Press, 2010), 14.

THE VIETNAM WAR: SOUTH KOREA'S FORGOTTEN WAR

Our globe has a hierarchy dictated by political economy and race. Expressions like "first world" and "global north" are broadly used in reference to North America and Western Europe, while "third world" and "global south" are used to denote countries in South America, Asia, and Africa. In South Korean history, for example, US interventions and influence during and after the war are examples of neocolonial paternalism. South Korea and the US both suffer from yet another kind of amnesia: Korean participation in the Vietnam War (1955–1975), which began only two years after the Korean War cease-fire.

As South Korea slowly reconstructed with the majority of the nation living in poverty, the US government offered the ROK government money in exchange for Korean soldiers to fight in Vietnam. South Koreans fought American battles again in the twenty-first century; during Roh Moo-hyun's administration, South Korea sent the third-largest number of troops to Iraq, with Great Britain being second and the US sending the most.

Between 1964 through 1973 Park Chung-hee sent over three hundred thousand Korean mercenary soldiers to aid America in Vietnam. Most of these men were from working-class or rural backgrounds. These cost-efficient Korean recruits made a fraction of what their American comrades made in the Vietnam War. In exchange, the South Korean government made a billion dollars from the US government, which became seed money for South Korea to build its economy into what it is today.[113]

In *Little Women* (2022) the middle sister, In-kyung, is a reporter who recovers a journal written by General Won Gi-seon, the patriarch of the wealthy Won family. General Won documented how he and his troops' mission was to destroy a spy camp in North Vietnam and kill its Laotian and Thai agents—an assignment from the Americans. The Korean soldiers were left in the jungle to die after they completed their mission. The Korean government was aware of this plan from the get-go and collected a million dollars as compensation. Won's journal states, "In a way, our motherland

---

113 Paul D. Hutchcroft, "Reflections on a Reverse Image: South Korea Under Park Chung Hee and the Philippines Under Ferdinand Marcos," in *The Park Chung Hee Era: The Transformation of Korea*, ed. Byung-kook Kim and Ezra F. Vogel (Cambridge, MA: Harvard University Press, 2011), 542–572, 556.

exchanged our lives for money." Won's experience as a Korean mercenary soldier in Vietnam is one of abandonment from his motherland. This scene, however, does not address the war trauma that the Korean military inflicted onto Vietnamese civilians.

Modern Korean studies scholar Jin-kyung Lee writes, "Koreans' demand for redress of the historical injustices committed during Japan's colonization of Korea must be accompanied by South Koreans' need to seek Vietnamese forgiveness."[114] Lee catalogues offenses such as the Korean military's use of the US chemical weapon Agent Orange against Vietnamese civilians and the babies that Korean soldiers abandoned in Vietnam after fraternizing with local women. Lee critiques the Korean cultural industries that have economic domination in the Vietnamese market to reify South Korea's "subimperialist status over Vietnam."[115]

South Korea's amnesia of its war atrocities afflicted against Vietnam is another repressed memory along with its own war traumas. Just as Korea's economy benefited from the Vietnam War, it continues to benefit today by designing cultural products for the world to buy that are now built by under-paid and mistreated Vietnamese laborers working in Korean-owned factories. K-dramas reflect South Korea's cultural amnesia by utilizing storytelling for productive trauma processing, but they restrict this to the Korean experience, despite many overlapping experiences across cultures that share the same injuries.

WHEN MEMORIES RETURN

It's very satisfying to see an amnesic K-drama character's memory return. In *Moon Embracing the Sun* (2012) Yeon-woo sits down with the Queen Dowager who tried to kill her and confronts her simply by raising her head to look the queen directly in the eyes while dramatic nondiegetic music blasts over the scene to indicate that justice is about to be served. In K-dramas, wrongs always get righted.

---

114 Jin-kyung Lee, *Service Economies: Militarism, Sex Work, and Migrant Labor in South Korea* (Minneapolis: University of Minnesota Press, 2010), 76.

115 Ibid.

The best memory return for me is in *Stairway to Heaven*, when the sweet and ever-so-polite Jung-suh finally loses her shit. Once Jung-suh recovers her memory of the accident that Yuri caused and realizes that Tae-hwa kidnapped and lied to her for five years, Jung-suh goes ape-shit on everyone's asses. She screams hysterically at Tae-hwa and smacks his backside while telling him to take responsibility for ruining her life. Jung-suh confronts Mira on an elevator by grabbing Mira's wrist when she raises it to slap her and wrangling her into a corner, saying, "You haven't changed one bit." Mira looks at Jung-suh with fright while Jung-suh glares back with no fear—only righteous fury. Jung-suh calmly says, "I remember everything you did to me. I'm going to do to you exactly as you did to me."

Fucking finally. Speak your truth, mama.

But that's not all. As it turns out, Jung-suh is slowly going blind because her retinas were damaged after Yuri hit her with a car. So Jung-suh goes home and beats the shit out of Yuri with a pillow while screaming, "Do you know what you've done to me?!" It's camp, cathartic, and feels as good as cracking open a can of Chilsung cider.

Choi Ji-woo's enraged performance on *Stairway to Heaven* was satisfying because I ached my way through her passive performance on *Beautiful Days* just two years earlier, when her character, Yeon-soo, the morally upright good girl, gets leukemia but never throws a fit. Suppressed anger turns into depression, and Yeon-soo is *super* depressed. À la Freud, Van der Kolk reminds us that problems cannot go ignored, for trauma is like "a splinter that causes an infection" and will continue to demand the mind/body's attention no matter how much the subject tries to forget.[116] That is why I fully appreciate Jung-suh wilding out with unbridled rage, screaming at the top of her lungs.

Contemporary K-dramas have evolved greatly over the last two decades. Strong female leads today send a radically different message about love, teaching the heroine to prioritize her own security and happiness above else. I see this trend in *The Interest of Love* (2022–2023), *King the Land* (2023), *One*

---

116 Van der Kolk, *The Body Keeps the Score*, 246.

Spring Night, My Liberation Notes (2022), *Something in the Rain*, and numerous others. The days of unconvincing passive female characters with leukemia and amnesia as self-sacrificial martyrs are over.

K-RAGE

I never understood this stereotype of Asians being demure, passive, and quiet. I witnessed so much Korean rage while growing up among Koreans in Korea as well as the diaspora in New York. The show *Beef* (2023), created by Korean American showrunner Lee Sung Jin, is an excellent exploration of K-rage through characters like Danny and Issac, whose demented episodes are as familiar to me as the back of my hand. I saw K-rage when my relatives got drunk and belligerent at reunions. I witnessed violent K-rage in my home. I witnessed K-rage in the community as nonstop complaining, gossiping, hitting, yelling, and depression. I saw K-rage in Korean parents at church when they would pray in positions that never illustrated a free soul that was at peace with god. They'd be in an agonized state of desperate pleading, with eyes squeezed and foreheads scrunched, whispering rapid words with no breaths in between and clutching their palms so tightly that they sent tension throughout their whole trembling bodies. They seemed to be imploring for rescue. I exhibit K-rage whenever my safety is threatened, and it has both gotten me out of dicey situations and into them.

Hwa-byung is a disease that is clinically diagnosed in South Korea. It translates literally as "anger illness."[117] Considering the amount of trauma and vast changes the Korean peninsula has undergone in the last century, and considering how much oppression, suppression, and repression came thereafter, illnesses borne out of anger are understandable. Meanwhile, society is quick to shame individuals for expressing anger, despite this emotion being a necessary survival trait. People rarely discuss how anger serves us.

---

117 Sung Kil Min and Shin-young Suh, "The Anger Syndrome Hwa-byung and Its Comorbidity," *Journal of Affective Disorders* 124, nos. 1–2 (2010): 211–214.

The limbic brain responds to a threat in several ways. Pete Walker, therapist and author of *Complex PTSD*, names four: fight, flight, freeze, or fawn.[118] Although my responses to threats over the years have varied across all four depending on the situation and the person(s) involved, more than half of my reactions lean toward fight.

I realized that my subconscious chooses a fight response because anger is an *active* response. Flight doesn't always feel right because it feels like cowardice: *Why should I be the one to flee when I have a right to hold space?* Freeze and fawn are not active. They are passive responses that leave me helpless to perpetrators and further harm. Fighting through the fire with rage, however, is my attempt to get shit done through an active response, so I feel productive when I engage my anger. The underlying logic is: *I am getting myself out of danger by taking action.* I use my sense of urgency by rushing myself toward *safety*—that's my finish line. I use my fight mode and adrenaline to carry me to shelter. Meanwhile, our society shames us for exhibiting anger. Repressed anger—aka depression—is an illness that grows in number every day around the world. Our rhetoric has phrases like "anger issues" and "temper tantrum," which shame and infantilize people for expressing rage, but why is anger not credited for all its uses and purposes? Why is anger not understood as an acknowledgment that there is indeed a lot to be angry about in this world and that it is as valid as our other emotions?

When I was a child, authority figures constantly punished me for being angry in the face of injustice. I used to beat myself up after getting into conflicts from a place of anger. I still do. I used to believe that my anger was something to curb, cure, or get rid of, but I view it very differently now.

As a species, we evolved while retaining anger because it serves us. When I feel anger, it tells me that something or someone violated my boundaries. Anger informs me about how to take care of myself and pushes me toward self-love.

---

118 Pete Walker, *Complex PTSD: From Surviving to Thriving: A Guide and Map for Recovering from Childhood Trauma* (Lafayette: Azure Coyote, 2013). In *My Grandmothers' Hands: Racialized Trauma and the Pathway to Mending Our Hearts and Bodies* (Burlington: Central Recovery Press, 2020), Resmaa Menakem names five: rest, fight, flee, freeze, or annihilate. Menakem states that while fight is like a punch, annihilate is like a decapitation.

Anger also demands justice. It has a bigger Self in mind—my community, peers, and kin. Are we all safe? Who harmed us? How do we correct this wrong? My fight response and anger serve me, so why the hell should I turn my back on them? All my feelings are valid, and I have my reason for feeling them. It's to keep me safe.

Natalie Gutiérrez, therapist and author of *The Pain We Carry*, writes about her own relationship with anger and her abusive past: "I had so many reasons to be rageful. I now know my rage was trying to call out for help. It needed a witness. My rage wanted the hurt to stop, from the world and in my home."[119] I empathize with Gutiérrez's remark that she had many reasons to be angry. If I start counting my reasons to be angry, I would probably die from exhaustion and stress because anger is a bottomless pit. The more I feed it, the hungrier it gets. In this regard, anger does not serve me if I dwell in it. Anger is just part of the broader emotional cycle, and as with all things, it is necessary and possible to get through it to the other side, but it first requires self-acknowledgment.

Dr. Jacob Ham encourages a self-compassionate response to trauma survivors by speaking *to* the anger and giving it space through acknowledgment and time to defuse, especially because "self-loathing is a key experience for people with trauma."[120] This self-loathing derives from the survivor's anger response in the past, whether it was raging or shutting down. Whenever I feel ashamed of my K-rage, I remind myself of the times when anger served me. My anger defends me whenever I am insulted, assaulted, or disrespected. Anger is a part of us, and it deserves space, time, and loving attention. It can be mined for tremendous intelligence to help our growth until it's ready to transmute. The key for me is patience with myself.

Dr. Ham suggests a mindful community approach toward anger responses when trauma survivors get triggered: "What I need for myself is for the people who love me to know that I have a Hulk and that he comes roaring out, and then as soon as Hulk is gone, I'm gonna be back. But please

---

119 Natalie Gutierrez, *The Pain We Carry: Healing from Complex PTSD for People of Color* (Oakland, CA: New Harbinger, 2022), 8.

120 Hammond, Esrick, and Ham, "The Long Arm of Childhood Trauma."

don't mistake me for my Hulk."[121] So the next time you feel like whipping out your phone to film someone losing their shit at the supermarket, be mindful, compassionate, and aware. That moment can happen to any one of us, and it's okay if it does because we are human. Patience, mindfulness, and compassion take practice, and the world is full of worksheets. Each moment is a new opportunity to start over. If I screw up, I can always work toward acceptance. If I notice myself judging someone harshly, then I am judging myself harshly. We all have a story. We all have unique responses to specific triggers. Please remember this the next time you feel compelled to shame a stranger on the internet for having an episode. Instead, use that moment as an opportunity to look inward to self-reflect rather than point fingers.

During one of my daily emotional flashbacks, I kept hearing myself engaging in tense dialogue with people who had violated my boundaries and made me feel used and misconstrued. My irritation during these dialogues rose to the point that I found myself screaming inside my car to break out of the negative loops inside my head, then begging my own brain to please shut the fuck up because the incessant rants that erupted in my mind were exhausting me. Then, *eureka*. I realized the reason why I was so angry at the culprits in my mind is because I now have self-worth. The moment I gave this thought recognition, the voices calmed and I was flooded with gratitude. Self-worth—this nebulous thing I always felt that I lacked—was now found inside of me like a sturdy rock. I sent the loud staff sergeant inside of me my gratitude and understanding as I watched him finally remove his helmet and put down his gun. He had a very important message that I needed to hear, and when I finally heard him, I felt peace. Anger is such a complex and intelligent emotion.

This is why stand-up comedy is a godsend for me. It's the most aggressive form of performance art I know, and it's a perfect conduit for me to safely express my rage in a productive manner. I do what it takes to respect my anger so that it doesn't hijack my system. I do what I can to befriend it.

---

121 Ibid.

I once dreamt of a reddish-brown calf with black stripes and four Rottweilers lying down on the floor in Sphinx-pose with their heads raised and alert as if waiting for a command. I kept wondering why these animals visited me. In Hollywood media Rottweilers are often vilified as monstrous. They are depicted as aggressive fighting dogs and associated with criminals. But I personally love Rottweilers. I think they're about as cute as baby calves. I love their stocky-sturdiness compared to their leaner Doberman cousins. Rottweilers are fierce protectors, loyal, and very affectionate toward their human companions. They were used for herding and guarding on farms, and they defended the army in ancient Rome. This is how I look at my K-rage. My anger is protective, loyal, intelligent, and affectionate when it serves me. I turn to it with adoration, gratitude, and love.

LESSON 12:
SEXUAL REPRESSION, QUEERNESS, AND FEMINISM IN K-DRAMAS

A WHITE AMERICAN JOURNALIST RECENTLY CONTACTED ME TO ASK questions about how queerness is represented in K-dramas historically, and I sensed this reporter's angling pierce through the email from afar, like she expected me to critique South Korea's cultural environment as necessarily intolerant of queer identities. I perceived a similar angling back when I taught an undergraduate course at UCLA on K-dramas. Several students commented that "traditional" K-dramas were more conservative with gender and sexuality politics compared to contemporary ones, such as *Itaewon Class* and *Record of Youth*, which include queer characters. These are sweeping generalizations untethered to any historical context or evidence. They come from assumption rather than research.

I need to stop and question this attitude for a second, as it contains a Western-centric and US-exceptionalist bias that projects a regressive image of South Korea when it comes to sexual and queer-gender identity politics. Are K-dramas really restrictive when it comes to these bounds?[122]

THE QUEERNESS OF KOREAN AND IMMIGRANT EXISTENCE

Korean is a queer-friendly language that does not have any pronouns. Quite a few Asian languages share this queer quality. That's not to say that gendering in Korean is not ever-present. While I grew up addressing older male friends as "oppa" and older female friends as "unni," my male peers addressed older boys as "hyung" and older girls as "noona." But even these expressions have evolved throughout the ages in Korea. There's a show called *Slave Hunters* (2010), aka *Chuno*, set sometime in the early Chosŏn dynasty, in which the male characters address older men as "unni" because back then "unni" in the male context was the norm. Now, compare that to the way my mom addresses my dad's noonas—her older sisters-in-law: she calls them "hyung-nim." Some of this also varies depending on the regional dialect in the country. My entire family is from South Gyeongsang Province, so it's common to hear women with a strong sister kinship to address their elder community sisters as "hyung-nim." The Korean language shows that gender bounds and culture are fluid and that they change depending on time and space.

◇◇◇◇◇◇◇◇◇◇◇◇

My pronouns are she/her/hers, but I also appreciate they/them/theirs because I don't always feel fem. I feel masc, fem, in-between, and neither. I also like queer-gender identification because I was harangued throughout my childhood for being gender deviant in my mannerisms and expression, and this drove adults crazy. When I got older, a couple of guys I dated scolded me for being mannish. Well, fuck that noise. I like the way I am, and the way I am depends on my mood. Nothing is fixed or constant.

When I was in first grade my dad bought me my first Halloween costume based on *Aladdin* (1992), my favorite Disney movie at the time. Did I dress

---

122 For more on queerness in Korean television, see my article "The Queer Politics of Korean Variety TV: State, Industry & Genre," *Jump Cut: A Review of Contemporary Media*, no. 60 (Spring 2021), www.ejumpcut.org/archive/jc60.2021/GraceJung-queerTV-Korea/index.html#top

like Jasmine that year? Nope. My dad straight up dressed me as Aladdin. I became an accidental drag king at age seven. Did my classmates make fun of me? Yes. Did my teacher eye me up and down strangely after complimenting the other girls who dressed like princesses? Absolutely. Was I humiliated? Of course. But am I proud of the queer chaos my dad and I created that day at my Brooklyn public elementary school? Fuck yeah.

Being an immigrant is a queer existence. I use the term "queer" here in the broadest and most malleable sense. I am queer in that I have never been fully accepted into American society. I did not speak English when I first arrived. I was undocumented for over ten years, and my paperwork called me an "alien"—a cred I've grown fond of now that aliens are a trend. 😑

The onus of proving one's American belongingness and citizenship with official documentation began with Chinese migrant workers in the late 1800s. Anti-Asian discrimination is literally the reason why the system of immigrant processing exists in this country today. Prior to Chinese migration, no one was asked to show their papers because white immigrants were "settlers" in America, while nonwhite immigrants were "aliens" who needed to prove their worth in order to stay. So the Chinese built American railroads, which are used to this day for all your mobile devices' wireless connectivity and cloud storage (see Tung-Hui Hu's A Prehistory of the Cloud).

My queerness showed in my poverty too. I wore hand-me-downs from older kids of all genders that fit me awkwardly from childhood into my teens. I never felt quite like a girl or a boy when I was a kid. I enjoyed roughhousing and running with boys just as much as I liked playing a make-believe lady in distress, but I also didn't mind playing a make-believe soldier, cow, or turtle. But adults around me were constantly reinforcing gender norms, telling me not to run, shout, or move freely because it wasn't "lady-like" to run in a skirt.

Gender and sexuality are not rigid or categorically constant as society keeps suggesting (see Judith Butler's Gender Trouble). This fluid movement is the space of queerness I hold for myself, and it offers me a freedom I wish I had in my youth whenever people shamed me for flashing my underwear. In reaction to the shaming I endured from uptight and boring grown-ups, I feel zero shame today when I drop my pants on stage and moon hecklers at a show, telling them to kiss my ass.

SEXUAL REPRESSION IN SOUTH KOREA AND AMERICA

Sexual repression in South Korea is about as real as it is in America. A Korean comedian I befriended in Seoul named Jung-yoon worked as a visiting sex education instructor for girls in high school because proper sex ed is grossly overlooked in the country. Jung-yoon told me stories of grievances she received from alarmist parents who took issue with her teaching girls how to protect themselves from pregnancy and STDs, accusing her of encouraging sexual activity. Fellow Korean immigrant friends from the 1980s and 1990s whom I've known in the States told me that they didn't learn anything about sex until they moved overseas and learned about it at their private high schools. Others didn't learn about it until they walked into a clinic in college after contracting an STD.

I grew up in a sexually repressed Korean American community and Korean immigrant household where sex was treated as this very private ritual meant solely for procreation between a man and a woman within the bounds of marriage. Beyond this, no mention of sex or sexuality was ever permitted. This is also the reason why I struggled to voice my sexual assault experiences from childhood because a conversation remotely related to sex seemed intolerable among adults. When I was at Yonsei University during my Fulbright year, I heard an American professor theorize that the reason why South Korea is so sexually repressed is not because Korea is and has always been so; rather, it is because the Christian influence trickled in from the US at the turn of the twentieth century through missionaries and war aid. Premodern Korean history was the exact opposite, with an emphasis on feeding the male sexual appetite with kisaengs and mistresses, although female chastity and monogamy were hyper-emphasized due to patriarchal values stemming from Confucianism. I still see aspects of this on Korean TV, where there's always space made for male desire, but female desire remains sanitized or infantilized. Although this is slowly changing with radical shows like *Somebody* (2022) and *Mask Girl* (2023), sexual repression in Korean television is still evident, and as a millennial Korean American raised on sanitized Korean and American media, I do feel it.

When I was in Europe I was shocked to realize how uptight I am. I was at the movies in Berlin with my then boyfriend to see Spike Lee's *BlacKkKlansman* (2018), and I could not believe the amount of cock, tits, and ass I saw in trailers prior to the feature film. I literally held my breath in astonishment. When I explained this culture shock to my German boyfriend, he laughed and said it's because I'm American. In *The Producers* Seung-chan compares the incestuous free romance he witnesses at his workplace to Hollywood's sexual freedom. This is a huge misconception. Hollywood has the most gratuitous history of sexual sanitation, dating back to the 1930s. Despite cable shows that push the envelope, America is still culturally limited compared to Europe when it comes to sex.

I noticed my repression again when I was at a venue in Kreuzberg to perform stand-up. I saw another performer in the line-up run around stage topless in the middle of her act. I gasped and covered my mouth, to which my Austrian comedian friend Tobias teased me relentlessly throughout the night: "They're just boobs, Grace." Someone else asked me, "Are you a prude?" I guess I am! I didn't know! I was surprised at myself to realize how rigid I can be when it comes to public nudity, even though I've been going to Korean public bath houses since I was a toddler.

The amount of sex I see in contemporary K-dramas today makes the conservative, bun-headed old lady inside me gasp. The K-dramas I grew up on would barely hit first base until twelve episodes in. But now, in shows like *One Ordinary Day* (2021), I see sex scenes with Kim Soo-hyun's tight peach butt bobbing up and down in the first episode after doing a bunch of illicit drugs with a complete stranger. It's a radically different K-drama world today, and my inner old lady is still catching up.

Korean TV is and has always been sanitized to be "family friendly" by the KCC. Anything broadcast or shown on cable is censored for nudity, profanity, smoking, gratuitous violence, excessive sex, and knives when used as a weapon. But K-dramas made for online platforms get a pass on all of this because broadcast censorship laws do not apply to online content, and now there's a proliferation of excessive smoking, fucking, drugging, and killing. My faint-of-heart reaction to them reminds me that I am of a certain time and space. The neon-blue-haired gay boy inside me, however, laughs at this and screams, "They're just tits. You have 'em too!"

I say all this to make two points. First, sexual repression is evident in both South Korea and in the US stemming from Christian ideology, and second, this sexual repression is a significant reason why homophobia is still prevalent in both countries. Queer relations question the validity of hetero-coupling and sex as merely a form of procreation (see Michel Foucault's *The History of Sexuality*). Queer relations remind us that sex is also meant for human pleasure, loving connection, and for exploring what dwells in our deeper psyches and hearts.

With all that said, I read South Korea's sexual repression as more than just an ideological issue entrenched in religious dogma. I see it rooted in a real fear of facing the enormous sexual trauma the country experienced from colonization, war, and military dictatorships when the police raped and/or killed women protestors.[123] Processing rape trauma that millions of Korean women suffered throughout the decades of its modern history is still underway.

STATE VERSUS QUEER CITIZEN

Politically speaking, being queer in South Korea is not illegal. Koreans cannot be arrested for being gay, lesbian, trans, or gender-queer. The sociocultural acceptance of open queerness in South Korea is not as widespread as, say, San Francisco, New York, or LA, but mainstream culture is rapidly changing.[124] This is also evident in K-dramas.

While hetero relationships dominate contemporary K-drama storylines, it is also true that K-dramas in the last decade increasingly include queer characters and relationships. The political climate in South Korea is tumultuous due to President Yoon Suk Yeol's policies that disregard the rights of marginalized identities, but the nation remains mindful of its national

---

123 Miriam Ching and Yoon Louie, "*Minjung* Feminism: Korean Women's Movement for Gender and Class Liberation," *Women's Studies International Forum* 18, no. 4 (1995): 417–430.

124 See queer scholarship by film theorist Ungsan Kim and anthropologist John Cho.

self-image through media as a democratic and free nation.[125] *Itaewon Class* features a trans character who finds love with a cis-man in the end. Numerous queer—albeit closeted—supporting characters appear in shows like *Reply 1997* (2012), *Reply 1994*, *Prison Playbook* (2017), and *Record of Youth*. *Dinner Mate* (2020) includes a gay male character who voices his frustration at how his society rejects him for his gayness.

Coffee Prince (2007) was long heralded as a mainstream queer K-drama, but it's no longer alone. Numerous fictionalized historical period dramas known as 사극/*sageuk* like *Sungkyunkwan Scandal* (2010), *Mr. Queen* (2020), and *The King's Affection* (2021) play with cross-gender cosplay, gender queering, and queer love openly and regularly within the bounds of hetero-romance while also pushing its boundaries. *Somebody* is a radical K-drama that includes lesbian love, female masturbation, and female pleasure. Given the queer bounty in K-dramas, I cannot say that queerness is as completely excised from Korean television, culture, and history as the anglers I mention earlier were ready to assume.

Korea's documented queer history dates back to ancient times. The *hwarang* were a group of military men who not only protected the king during the Silla Dynasty (57 BC–935 AD) but also remained sexually available to him.[126] Queerness in Korean television is hyper-present in the form of excess, camp, cross-dressing, gender-bending, and pushing the boundaries of the status quo in every direction.

I received an email from a college student who identified as a "queer gyop'o" and told me that they had read my academic article on Korean TV and queer politics repeatedly because the information was a comfort to them.[127] So this chapter is dedicated to all my fellow queer gyop'os out there who need these words to feel seen, as well as to correct any notions that privilege Western perspectives on how queer politics *ought* to be carried out in

---

125 For more on preserving a progressive national image versus the actual felt realities within the gay community, see Youngshik D. Bong, "The Gay Rights Movement in Democratizing Korea," *Korean Studies* 32 (2008): 86–103.

126 Young-Gwan Kim and Sook-Ja Hahn, "Homosexuality in Ancient and Modern Korea," *Culture, Health & Sexuality* 8, no. 1 (2006): 59–65.

127 교포 (gyop'o) refers to the Korean diaspora.

South Korea. I take issue with how we Americans reduce foreign countries' political climate for queer identities as "backward" because it ignores the steadfast history, life, and work of queer individuals of that nation, which have always existed, regardless of Western awareness. To privilege Western doubt would mean to forget and ignore the lives and activism of queer peoples who have been and continue to be.

This is not to say that I have not witnessed pain and the trauma of rejection among my fellow queer Korean Americans. Given my own queered identity as well as my trauma disorder, since childhood I could quickly detect anyone who deviates from hetero standards. I could also feel their pain even while they were locked in denial. A son of a church reverend I knew growing up was so apparently gay to me, but he remained deeply closeted for the sake of his own Christian values and his father's role as the head of an institution that did not tolerate anything that deviated from a WASP assimilation, including homosexuality. Underneath this is a very distinct verve of fear, as we are a racial minority in a country with a history of Asian suppression, exploitation, violence, and murder. Because of his own shame and his inability to be free, any sight of my own uninhibitedness maddened him, and he was verbally and physically abusive toward me.

In college and throughout my twenties in New York, I befriended many queer Korean Americans who were liberated within their chosen families but completely repressed back at home with their parents, where they ignored their parents' questions about when they were going to get married to the "opposite" gender. Out of shame, many of these queer friends turned to self-destructive habits like drug and alcohol abuse as well as unsafe sexual encounters. They felt conflicted, harboring guilt for lying to their parents for fear of rejection while also feeling imposter syndrome during Pride month because they were not out and proud with their family. Now in LA and in my thirties, I still see this pain among my queer friends who live in conflict.

A gay Korean American man in his late twenties named Tim, who was born and raised in LA, told me he resents the Westernized pressure for all queer people to be proudly out because it ignores ethnic and immigrant specificities that speak to his intersectional complexities. Tim said the pressure of white/mainstream American gay politics makes him feel like he needs to cut ties with his strictly Christian and homophobic family while also living with his elderly and sick Korean parents as their caregiver. Tim said:

> *I don't know where we're at now, but I still don't feel comfortable yet to talk to [my parents] about it. I would honestly prefer to never do it because it's like, "You know. We know. I don't have to share this with you. You've seen me wear all the dresses and dance around. Like, you know." But I do have an understanding for them now that I didn't always [have]. I was too influenced by* Glee *and American narratives. White American narratives about being queer . . . to me, in America, it's all about your individuality, and it's like, "Once you're eighteen, you get up out of your cornfield town and move to New York City and never speak to your parents again and you find your chosen family!" You know? "And maybe one day you can do makeup for an off-Broadway show and your life will be complete!" And, it's like, I don't want to lose my family. When I moved out, I was ready to do that. I was gonna go to West Hollywood, and this was gonna be my new life. And I'm kind of glad it didn't go in that direction and [my mom's] stroke forced us all to come together 'cause this is what I actually want. I want to make this work. Even if it's not perfect and it sucks, I would rather . . . like, I don't want a chosen family! I want my family, you know? I will never meet anyone out there who is not my family who I love more than my family. This is it. That's it. And I've tried! . . . I was like, "I'll find my tribe or whatever," [but] I hate everyone here! I hate everyone! They all suck!*

Tim has a subjective and agentic approach to how he integrates his queer being while navigating his familial complexities. In that regard, I see his inner work as politically activated and mindful of not just queer politics but also racial politics through his resistance to neocolonial pressures stemming from American queer rhetoric. Tim is resisting the same angling that I felt sensitive to.

QUEER FEMINISM IN SEARCH WWW

Search WWW is the queerest K-drama I've seen in recent years. Four years after *Search WWW*, the writer of the series, Kwon Do-eun, wrote *Twenty-Five Twenty-One*, which also focuses on female friendships, rivalry, and love. Both shows include strong lesbian subtexts that hardly function as subtexts because of the profoundly transparent appreciation and love between same-sex characters. They're both super gay shows, and I love them.

The queering in *Search WWW* is evident through gender-role swapping. In K-dramas male characters tend to drop honorifics toward female characters early in the relationship based on age, class, and occupation dictated by patriarchy. In *Search WWW*, however, Tami has a one-night stand with Morgan, who is ten years her junior, and she drops her honorifics while he maintains them. Tami is a career-driven woman who does not believe in marriage, while Morgan wants a family of his own. Tami wants independence, while Morgan wants someone dependable and committed. *Search WWW* turns the older K-drama trope on its head. The female protagonist here does not need a man to dig her out of a financial hole, rescue her from abusers, or give her an engagement ring. Tami is proudly single.

In 2004 the same actress, Im Soo-jung, starred in one of my lifelong favorites *I'm Sorry, I Love You* as Eun-chae. Her costar Jeon Hye-jin played Seo-kyung, a mentally disabled, poverty-stricken single mother and twin sister to the male lead. Eun-chae is immensely passive on that show, like many K-drama heroines of this era, and Seo-kyung is also written to lack agency. But these two actresses reunite over a decade later in *Search WWW* completely transformed. Tami is a highly competent marketing executive at the leading search engine company Unicon, and Song Ga-gyeong is the director. Tami and Ga-gyeong once had a close relationship as colleagues and friends, but that relationship became strained as Ga-gyeong's position rose in the ranks at Unicon after her marriage to Oh Jin-woo, the son of chairwoman Jang He-eun of the conglomerate KU Group.

Ga-gyeong's role on this show is especially interesting because, while she appears to have the wealth and status of a powerful woman, she is a political pawn between her parents and her mother-in-law. As such, Ga-gyeong is a puppet and a chaebol prostitute. Her mother-in-law, Chairwoman Jang, repeatedly calls Ga-gyeong "hers," expressing a queer obsession and hunger for Ga-gyeong. Ga-gyeong seeks agency by hiring handsome young men for her entertainment and pleasure at host bars—a concept that is typically associated with white-collar men who hire young women to pour drinks, sing, entertain, and offer intimate services. But Ga-gyeong attends a male host bar to decompress while young men pour her drinks and obey her every command, no matter how debasing.

Ga-gyeong's toxic corporate masculinity as a cis-woman offers a sympathetic perspective through a female lens as to how and why corporate structures are so patriarchal and abusive. The problems do not stem just from the individual. The individual is caught in the net of an intricate corporate web woven with its own rituals, demands, and expectations that are highly profitable and severely dehumanizing.

TRANS-QUEER ROMANCE AND OBJECTIFICATION

Tami's relationship with Morgan—albeit hetero—is a trans-queer relationship. I'm using the term *trans-queer* per Quinlan Miller's use in their book *Camp TV*, wherein they read cross-dressing comedic characters in early American variety shows as trans-gender-queer performers. Tami dominates her cis-male partner, Morgan, with sexual aggression and hesitation to commit, while Morgan responds with neediness, thus exhibiting a trans-queer relationship dynamic that veers from typical K-drama romances. When Morgan shows up at Tami's office, she looks at him with lust, undressing him with her eyes, admiring his swept hair and his low-cut shirt. To this, Morgan re-genders her by saying, "What a perverted *ajussi*." [128]

Chairwoman Jang indulges in the lustful hetero-cis-female gaze just as much as Ga-gyeong and Tami do by hiring young male models to pose nude for her while she draws them or tattoos their bodies. Men are playthings in *Search WWW*. Even when Tami asks Morgan to be her boyfriend, she does so by saying, "놀자," meaning, "Let's play." Other male characters fulfill a

---

128 아저씨/*ajussi* is used to address middle-aged Korean cis-men; it likens to "uncle" or "mister."

shallow function rather than contribute to meaningful storytelling. Men like Jun-su are deliberately written as unconvincing partners while the relationship between Tami, Scarlett, and Ga-gyeong is multilayered with complexity, pathos, and love. The final scene includes all three women driving down an endless road in a convertible with no red lights or men around to stop them. This Thelma-and-Louise-esque scene expresses female freedom and queer love. Even the "WWW" in the title suggests "woman" three times.

Search WWW queers K-drama gender expectations by putting women in the agentic place. I see so many K-dramas fueled by patriarchal determinations of what an appropriate relationship is like. The shows I grew up on always include toxic men whose actions are framed romantically through the mise-en-scène with music and special effects. Men grab women by the wrist and drag them wherever they want, force women to try on new clothes without asking, push women to get makeovers, shove women into cars, and introduce them to toxic families without asking, and are bullish when initiating physical intimacy by blindsiding women with sudden smooch attacks and zero prior consent. Many male leads would scream at female leads, calling it "love." Some shows, like *My Lovely Sam Soon* (2005), even romanticize male violence, like when Jin-heon slaps Hee-jin in the face. Shortly after this scene they're in bed together. Duuuuuude. So not cool. But these shows—mostly written by women and directed by men—are filled with choices that reify the toxic male gaze while normalizing misogyny. Tami, however, deliberately pursues sexual satisfaction by topping her male partner, making *Search WWW* a refreshingly queer feminist show.

Traditional gender roles are also reversed in *Search WWW*, where women are powerful executives in the workplace but lousy at domestic execution. Meanwhile, their male partners are adept at household chores. Tami is a slob, whereas Morgan is tidy. Ga-gyeong is a terrible cook, whereas her husband, Jin-woo, knows food preparation and how to set the table.

Tami also reverses K-drama gender roles by grabbing Morgan's wrist and dragging him away. The problematic male-to-female wrist grab is a common visual trope in K-dramas. It is violent but packaged in a romantic light through effects. I've seen it in pretty much every single K-drama rom-com in the 1990s and early 2000s. As of late, these wrist grabs and abrupt face-smash smooch scenes have diminished somewhat. *Search WWW* satirizes this trope with a female-to-female wrist grab, as Tami's colleague Scarlett rescues Tami from Ga-gyeong's abuse in a queer love triangle.

In old school South Korean lesbian culture, butch women were called "baji-ssi," which refers to pants wearers, while fem women were referred to as "chima-ssi," referring to skirt wearers. Ga-gyeong is definitely a baji-ssi, as is her tough-as-nails mother-in-law. Tami is more of a chima-ssi. Scarlett, however, is a misnomer. This makes her the queerest character of all. Scarlett's hair, makeup, accessories, and clothes are very fem, but her personality traits are highly butch. Scarlett's queerness even breaks the bounds of queer rhetoric within its local queer culture. This is the liberating thing about queerness as more than just an identity. Conceptually, queerness points to that which could never be fixed or restricted by a categorical identification. It's so beautifully freeing.

In what way are you queer? How do you express it subjectively and agentically? Where are you able to identify queerness in K-dramas? These are helpful questions for generating a productive and liberating viewing experience that resists any side-eye angling.

LESSON 13:
US–SOUTH KOREA RELATIONS AND NATIONAL SELF-PERCEPTION IN K-DRAMAS

I NEVER IMAGINED THE DAY I COULD TALK ABOUT K-DRAMAS WITH non-Koreans, but this is now happening regularly. K-pop has the world's attention for breaking records with billions of views on YouTube, and Hwang Dong-hyuk's *Squid Game* broke streaming records on Netflix.

Growing up in the 1990s, I was filled with strong misperceptions about my identity and developed an ethnic self-hatred for being Korean. Racism and microaggressions are and have been regular encounters throughout my life. It's common among millennial Korean Americans like me to feel conflicted when we encounter non-Koreans hyped up on Korean products. It's embittering. Like, *Didn't you used to bully me for that shit? Now you think it's cool? What the fuck?* I used to be ostracized in America for being Korean and for eating Korean food, listening to K-pop, and watching K-dramas and Korean films. Nowadays being Korean has suddenly become a reason for people to look my way. What this experience has taught me is that the politics of fads and cultural trends that the masses follow dictated by mainstream interests are shallow, arbitrary, and never to be trusted.

A BRIEF HISTORY OF KOREAN AMERICAN HOLLYWOOD

Whenever I'm on set working as an actor today, I find myself giving to my younger self exactly what she wanted to see as a kid—her face on-screen. I used to scour Hollywood media for figures who seemed remotely Asian. Beyond characters in K-dramas, who else looked like me? I recall Rufio from *Hook* with Filipino American actor Dante Basco and reruns of the 1970s show *Kung Fu* with David Carradine, who was white but played a hapa man in yellowface. I didn't know it at the time, but Korean American actor Philip Ahn also had a supporting role in that show.

Ahn is the first Korean American to appear in Hollywood films and TV.[129] He worked since the 1930s with Chinese American actress Anna May Wong. They were buddies. Both Asian American stars were underpaid compared to their white costars and pigeonholed into Orientalized roles, but they had each other's support.

The first American sitcom to ever star a Korean American male lead is *The Son-in-Law* with comedian Johnny Yune. Rue McClanahan played Yune's mother-in-law. The pilot aired in 1980 but never went to series because Yune quit the show after NBC overworked him to the point of burnout.[130] To keep myself busy during lockdown, I published an article on Yune's comedy career in an academic journal and made a "Drunk Korean American History" video as an homage to Comedy Central's *Drunk History* by Derek Waters to celebrate Asian American and Pacific Islander Heritage Month in 2020.[131]

---

129 Philip Ahn's father, Dosan Ahn Chang-ho, was an independence fighter and activist during the Japanese colonization in Korea prior to the war and division. The post office in Los Angeles's Koreatown is named after him. If you want to read a good book on Philip Ahn's life and work, check out *Hollywood Asian: Philip Ahn and the Politics of Cross-Ethnic Performance* by Hye-seung Chung (Philadelphia: Temple University Press, 2006).

130 Grace Jung, "Recovering the TV Career of Korean American Comedian Johnny Yune," *New Review of Film and Television Studies* 18, no. 4 (2020): 480–501.

131 Grace Jung, "Drunk Korean American History: Johnny Yune," April 25, 2020, YouTube, www.youtube.com/watch?v=sNc53IdNdkI.

The first Korean American woman to star in a network sitcom over ten years later is Margaret Cho in *All American Girl* (1994–1995) on ABC. Alas, white men produced the show, and it misrepresents Korean American family matters completely. Journalist Jeff Yang, the father of Hudson Yang from *Fresh Off the Boat* (2015–2020), wrote a scathing review of Cho's show in the *Village Voice* when it first aired.[132] I don't blame Yang for his disappointment in *All American Girl*, but many AAPIs had a lot of issues with *Fresh Off the Boat* too. As media studies scholar Bambi Haggins reminds us in *Laughing Mad*, when it comes to people of color and their appearances on major network television, there will always be compromises that accommodate the white mainstream gaze. But that is also changing quickly with groundbreaking shows like *Beef*, which explores what it is like to be human with characters who just so happen to be Asian American.

Americans today are obsessed with K-dramas, and this must be recognized as separate from albeit interrelated to the work of Korean Americans. My Korea-born Korean American identity is always in flux. My overall self-perception as a person has changed for the better through trauma treatment, and I no longer hate myself when I look in the mirror. I see similar shifts taking place for South Korea via K-dramas.

SOUTH KOREA'S SHIFTING POLITICAL AWARENESS ON TV

In *Fashion King* (2012) a small-time hustler named Young-gul runs a sweatshop with a few seamstresses in Dongdaemun. Young-gul's money-making schemes involve outwitting larger domestic brands by poaching their styles, duplicating them, and saturating the market at a much lower price for the exact same look. Ga-young, a young orphan woman, develops a crush on Young-gul and begins working for him, despite her own talents for conceiving original design ideas. The show fetishizes New York as a fashion mecca. It regards white male fashion designers' attention as validation. When Ga-young gets accepted to a New York fashion school, it gives her further

---

132 Jeff Yang, "20 Years Ago I Helped Kill the Asian-American Family Comedy—Today My Son May Help Bring the Genre Back to Life," *Quartz*, May 10, 2014, https://qz.com/208265/20-years-ago-i-helped-kill-the-asian-american-family-comedy-today-my-son-may-help-bring-the-genre-back-to-life.

credibility as a bona-fide designer in Seoul, ignoring her many years of working as a skilled seamstress with her own design ideas since childhood.

I compare this to *Now, We Are Breaking Up* (2021), which exhibits greater national confidence and stands up to international political discrimination. The show follows a talented designer named Young-eun at a high-end Korean fashion label called The One, where she heads her own line, Sono. As a Korean line, Sono struggles against the company's more popular European line Claire Mary. *Now, We Are Breaking Up* has its share of Euro-fetish.

Young-eun studied in Paris to build her portfolio as a serious designer and to stand out in the cutthroat fashion industry. Young-eun's lover, Jae-gook, did the same by starting out as a photographer in Paris. There are moments when these Korean characters unnecessarily address each other in awkward French, but the mise-en-scène is jam-packed with luxury fashion, accessories, hotel rooms, and bedrooms to suggest that they are upper-class, highly educated, cosmopolitan, globetrotting members of Korean society. Historically, Seoul and Busan are not capitals of world fashion, whereas Paris is, and this reality is revealed in how Korean fashion workers demonstrate insecurity or excessive backscratching in the presence of French designers.

Young-eun attends Korea's Fashion Week in Busan as an executive of Sono while vying for a collaboration opportunity with a white male French designer named Olivier. Olivier leads Young-eun on but ultimately signs with a different company. Olivier represents a patriarchal European prejudice that does not respect Korean women as designers but rather views them as seamstresses who execute Western design ideas. Olivier's treatment of Young-eun contains a condescending attitude that only values Koreans for their cheap labor.

Young-eun wows everyone by beating the odds and turning her brand Sono into a coveted domestic luxury brand. As a result, a top label in Paris offers her a position as their head designer. Jae-gook understands Young-eun's hesitation to accept the job because he knows that the French fashion industry will use Young-eun up and spit her out, expecting an Asian woman to work far more to prove her worth in a vain attempt to impress racist

Europeans who won't take her seriously. In *Search WWW* Morgan similarly tells Tami how he suffered discrimination growing up as a Korean adoptee in Australia and that he deliberately learned how to play the bass in a band to gain his white peers' approval—an indication that when a person is Asian in a white-dominant environment, they must provide something *extra* to gain acceptance through exceptional cultural currency. Jae-gook and Morgan— both played by Jang Ki-yong—express their frustration as Asian minorities who feel pressured to accessorize their identity to assimilate and survive in the West.

This reflexive self-awareness of marginalization in K-dramas explains the common stereotypes typically associated with Asians, like being exceptionally talented artistically, intellectually, or athletically, as well as why tiger parenting gets both fetishized and hypercriticized. Such parenting methods are stereotypically associated exclusively with Asians when, in fact, exacting standards and helicopter parenting are found in all insecure cultures keen on upward mobility.

South Korea's "tiger economy" status is referred to as the "Miracle of the Han River." Political scientist G. John Ikenberry and political economist Jongryn Mo call South Korea a "middle power": "These new middle powers are upper-income or upper-middle-income developing countries whose national interests on global governance are beginning to diverge from those of large relatively low-income developing countries due to their successful economic and political development."[133] South Korea, which was covered in the dusty rubble of war just a few decades ago, has become the tenth-largest economy in the world and the fourth-largest in Asia. Anti-Asian racism in white nations has made it challenging for the Asian diaspora who must prove their worth to get by. This racialized self-awareness and grumbling critique of anti-Asian racism are quite new in K-dramas, but they signify the changing self-perception of South Korea as it awakens to resist global white supremacy.

---

133 G. John Ikenberry and Jongryn Mo, *The Rise of Korean Leadership: Emerging Powers and Liberal International Order* (New York: Palgrave Macmillan, 2013), 3.

THE MODEL MINORITY MYTH IN AMERICA AND IN SOUTH KOREA

I was at a party talking to a British guy who worked at a nonprofit in Berlin. I was still a grad student at the time, and when he asked what I did, I told him that I research Korean television. He said, "You're gonna have a tough time finding a job because Korea's so rich now. People only care about poor countries." This comment got stuck in my craw because, one, his comment was tone-deaf, and two, he was overlooking the fact that I'm an American. A year prior, during a graduate seminar, a white cis-male student commented that educational funding should not go to Asian American studies but only to Black American studies because "Asians are rich." When I replied that white supremacists share the same logic, the professor emailed me and said I should be careful not to offend classmates by affiliating them with white supremacy. What none of the aforementioned people are privy to are a couple of stats. First, Asians in America have the highest wealth gap of any other ethnic group.[134] And second, in 2022 South Korea's wealth inequality reached the highest in its history.[135]

In the mainstream American press, Asian American success stories are used as pawns in conservative politics via the model-minority myth to exemplify America and its capitalist systems as flawlessly democratic while ignoring systemic and structural injustices that keep minorities locked in cycles of poverty, disease, poor education, and incarceration. The model-minority myth pits Asian Americans against fellow minority groups like Black and Latinx Americans. This myth also ignores the high poverty rate among Cambodian, Hmong, Laotian, and Bhutanese American war refugees.

Employment discrimination among Asian Americans is the highest in America, with African Americans ranking second. Asian Americans are

---

134 Sakshi Venkatraman, "Asian Americans Have the Biggest Wealth Gap. Here's How They're Helping One Another This Year," *NBC*, December 22, 2021, www.nbcnews.com/news/asian-america/asian-americans-biggest-wealth-gap-helping-one-another-year-rcna6465.

135 Park Jong-o, "Korea Sees Historic Wealth Gap, Worst Income Inequality Figures in Years," *Hankyoreh*, December 2, 2022, https://english.hani.co.kr/arti/english_edition/e_business/1069981 .html#:~:text=Korea's%20income%20quintile%20share%20ratio,2020%20to%205.96%20last%20year.

the largest demographic currently experiencing a decline in homeownership compared to any other racial group, with one out of five suffering from housing discrimination, while only 2 to 3 percent file complaints for this violation.[136]

Trauma and psychology literature published in the US exclude Asian diaspora experiences in their research, despite the Asian continent being consistently rife with war and colonialism. I attended an event in New York at Fotografiska where war photojournalist Maye-E Wong spoke about the ongoing Rohingya genocide in Myanmar, which she documented in 2018, detailing the plight of Muslim girls and women who were beaten and methodically gang raped by Buddhist soldiers. These impregnated women live with burden, guilt, and shame, carrying and raising sacrilegious children who remind them of their trauma.[137] This contemporary history is an extension of comparable late-nineteenth- and twentieth-century conflicts throughout Asia in the Philippines, Korea, Vietnam, Laos, Thailand, Cambodia, Malaysia, Indonesia, and more. Where is contemporary psychology's recognition of these Asian war traumas? Where's the research on AAPI addictions and mental illnesses stemming from these traumas as refugees and migrants?

When people excuse themselves with "There's not enough data about Asian demographics," I always call bullshit. I used to hear the same thing when my university wouldn't include AAPI screen texts and readings in American television or film course syllabi. The history, data, stories, figures, and media are *there*. It's just that no one bothered to look them up, ask, or wonder. It's the same old thing of making Asians invisible by pretending like we don't exist or we're not useful except as cheap labor or a glitzy cultural consumer item. It is not farfetched to say that a current or a not-too-distant war trauma has touched every Asian diaspora on the globe. If that's the case, then researchers, psychologists, therapists, and healers ought to consider the consequences of that within the people who live with those wounds. It's a

---

136 "Critical Issues Facing Asian Americans and Pacific Islanders," US White House Archives, https://obamawhitehouse.archives.gov/administration/eop/aapi/data/critical-issues.

137 Kristen Gelineau, Maye-E Wong, and Rishabh Jain, "AP: Rohingya Women Methodically Raped by Myanmar Armed Forces," *Associated Press*, December 21, 2017.

matter of even bothering to hypothesize—to *ask* and to *listen*—based on real events that occurred in our human history.

This is why the model-minority myth about Asians is a *myth*. However, just as South Korean orphans were used as America's poster children for a politicized agenda, South Korea itself is now the poster child for America's hegemonic cause through the model-minority myth on a global scale. Given South Korea's risen economy through America's war efforts, diplomacy, and grants, America now has a neocolonial Asian success story to dangle whenever it enters other nations for economic and political meddling.

Literary scholar Jin-kyung Lee writes in *Service Economies* that South Korea is a model minority to the world: "South Korean development soon became an example, serving as a model minority in the broader context of the United States' neocolonial 'under-development and impoverishment' of countries in Latin America and Africa.[138] "Neocolonialism" refers to a hegemonic nation's economic imperial influence over a country that is comparably less developed. US neocolonialism spreads its arms through cultural, political, economic, and military influences while allowing that country to retain its sovereignty only in government. For instance, while South Korea retains its sovereignty as a nation, its political economy and military were heavily reliant on the US in the aftermath of independence and war.

THE K-DRAMA OF US–KOREA RELATIONS

While the world sees the ROK today as a social butterfly, Chosŏn in the nineteenth century was called a "hermit kingdom" because it kept its gates shuttered to the rest of the world. The US pried these gates open. The first recorded encounter between Americans and Koreans is in 1866, when an American schooner aptly called the *Surprise* wrecked on the Korean coast. Korean officials were hospitable toward the American captain and crew, and escorted them to American diplomats in China. That same year another American schooner called the *General Sherman* attempted to open trade with Korea by entering Pyongyang. The crew took a Korean official hostage

---

138 Lee, *Service Economies*, 29.

onboard and opened fire at locals on shore. The crew also caused mayhem on Korean land by looting and killing seven Koreans, so the local governor, Pak Kyu-su, ordered the ship and its crew of twenty-three to be burnt to the ground.[139] Despite such pirating by American merchants in Korea, the US Navy and Marines retaliated in 1871 by demanding Chosŏn to open its doors to trade and diplomacy. When King Gojong refused, a battle ensued, and 350 Koreans were killed—a conflict that was written up insensitively in the American press as a "Little War with the Heathen."[140] In 1882 the US–Korea Amity and Trade Treaty was signed. In it, the US and Chosŏn kingdom agreed that if either of the two nations dealt with foreign oppression, the other would step in to aid. But in 1905, when Japan forced King Gojong to sign the Protectorate Treaty to begin its annexation, the US ignored Korea's plea for aid.

After the Korean War, the US maintained operational control over South Korean armed forces near the demilitarized zone at the 38th parallel that splits the peninsula in half. South Korea attempted democratic elections in 1961, and Chang Myon was officially elected prime minister; however, Park Chung-hee staged a military coup on May 16, 1961. Rather than support the democratic election by reinstating the elected regime, the US government simply accepted Park's coup as a fait accompli because Asia was already teeming with communism, and the US could not risk being at odds with Park.[141] During this time, with the support of the Soviet Union, North Korea's GNP was twice that of South Korea.

The nation struggled with poverty, political instability, and corruption for a long time, while the Republic of Korea was merely a republic in title and ruled by despots. In 1972 Park held South Korea under the Yushin Constitution, which gave him unlimited executive power and the ability to

---

139 Jinwung Kim, *A History of Korea: From "Land of the Morning Calm" to States in Conflict* (Bloomington: Indiana University Press, 2012), 282.

140 Key-Hiuk Kim, *The Last Phase of the East Asian World Order: Korea, Japan, and the Chinese Empire* (Berkeley: University of California Press, 1980), 62.

141 Taehyun Kim and Chang Jae Baik, "Taming and Tamed by the United States," in *The Park Chung Hee Era: The Transformation of South Korea*, ed. Byung-kook Kim and Ezra F. Vogel (Cambridge, MA: Harvard University Press, 2011), 58–84.

reinstate his presidency unopposed in perpetuity; this continued until he was assassinated in 1979. America did not intervene on behalf of Korean civilians who sought democracy during Park's reign.

By the 1980s anti-American sentiment among Koreans ran high. After Park's assassination, Chun Doo-hwan came into power through yet another military coup and declared martial law by using North Korean threat as an excuse. On May 15, 1980, four hundred thousand civilians protested Chun's martial law by gathering at Seoul Station, but they suffered brutal consequences at the hands of the police and military. On May 18, 1980, student protestors marched to demand political reform from the Korean government. This protest continued for ten days. Armed forces beat, killed, and/or raped thousands of people. Hundreds went missing. Over two hundred people died. Rather than support these civilians who stood up for their human rights, the US government sent troops to aid Chun's military dictatorship, and Ronald Reagan condoned Chun's actions. Chun also set up a "purification" camp to punish dissenters. Over sixty thousand Koreans were sent to the purification camp to be "re-educated." They were tortured and forced to live in horrendous conditions while conducting hard labor.[142] Nearly nine thousand Koreans, ranging from civil servants, teachers, and journalists, were fired for insubordination.

Chun enforced the Basic Press Law in 1980, giving him control of all media outlets. He ensured that media coverage of US–South Korea relations demonstrated US approval of his military regime. Despite these violations against human rights and democracy, the US did not intervene. As a result, Korean intellectuals of the mid-1980s viewed the States as another imperial power that colluded with their corrupt regime to suppress freedom, and anti-American sentiment ran high alongside Koreans' fear and suspicion of their own government.

In my research of US–Korean history, I see time and time again that whenever Korean civilians needed America's intervention the most, they

---

142 Namhee Lee, *The Making of Minjung: Democracy and the Politics of Representation* (Ithaca, NY: Cornell University Press, 2010), 44–47, 109–144.

were let down. This pain of being ignored when in dire need of aid colors the complicated relationship between South Korea and the US. History repeats itself. My Asian American community members and I were upset at how much the press ignored our pain despite anti-Asian hate crimes that sky-rocketed from 2020 onward due to racist rhetoric that continuously linked Asians with COVID-19.

After the Atlanta shootings in March 2021, a Korean American colleague shared his anger over the silence and complacency of his white friends about these deaths. Many of my Asian American friends felt ignored, afraid, and alone. But I soon saw the immense love and humanity occurring simultane-ously. I got phone calls and texts from Asian American friends who checked in, listened, and shared. My Chinese American documentarian friend Miao said, "The strongest people I've known are Asian women." My Korean American artist and therapist friend Helen told me that she finds strength in knowing what our ancestors survived. My Asian friends in Europe also reached out with kind words of empathy.

I saw Asian American activists in LA gather every Thursday in Koreatown to walk a nightly vigil to make sure that local elders and food-delivery workers were getting safely inside their buildings because so many of them were being attacked and beaten in parking lots and on the streets by strangers fueled by racial hatred. Many of these strang-ers were PoC themselves, marginalized by society while struggling with chronic mental illness and houselessness. The plight of Asian Americans is intertwined with the plight of the disadvantaged PoC community, which is why I reiterate that the model-minority myth is a myth. My queer Korean American comedian and writer friend Conner decided to make a wishing tree in Koreatown by writing messages of hopes, dreams, and wishes they had for themselves, our community, and society. We wrote our notes on ribbons and tied them onto a tree. I decided to turn my gaze toward these forms of civic space-holding and put my focus into appreciating what was *here*—so much love and equanimity.

After several years of limiting contact with my parents for my own safety and self-preservation, I reopened the line to share basic updates because I worried about their well-being, given the high number of attacks against Asian American elders. I also used the fire in my belly to finish a short documentary I began filming five years prior. It's a short profile film about a retired Japanese American auto mechanic named Joe Iwama who is now over a hundred years old.[143] Joe worked on strawberry and grape farms in Southern California with his parents before he and his family were incarcerated at an internment camp in Arcadia's Santa Anita Park racetrack during World War II. At the Santa Anita Assembly Center, 18,719 Japanese Americans were imprisoned and forced to live in converted horse stalls. Upon his release, Joe went to Chicago and learned his trade from a German auto mechanic who felt an alliance with the Japanese. Afterward Joe founded his auto shop in South Central in the 1940s, which is now run by his son Danny, who is in his sixties and my trusted mechanic to this day.

I never got around to finishing the movie due to funding issues, equipment failure, and production delays caused by my film school's administrative errors. But the wave of anti-Asian hate crimes targeting Asian elders gave my movie an urgent purpose. I needed additional funding to complete its postproduction, so I crowdfunded, and to my shocking overwhelm, I met my goal in just a couple of days. I was plagued by shame and guilt upon receiving this generosity from my friends and community due to my low self-worth that criticized me: "You don't deserve any of this." But I got over this self-criticism by witnessing how making this short film was part of the healing for me and my community.

My directorial debut *J&S Auto* (2022) screened at the Maryland Film Festival in 2022 on opening night, where one of my film heroes, John Waters, was present. After the screening he said to me, "I loved your film." I could not have imagined a greater compliment from anyone other than a cult American film icon like John Waters.

When the world I live in fucks with me, I let my inner fire stoke and roar. I then ask myself: *Who am I? What am I about? What do I fight for?* I let my creative expression answer.

---

143 Grace Jung, *J&S Auto* (2021), YouTube, December 25, 2022, https://youtu.be/zK5mPlukuWw.

ADDRESSING RACISM IN K-DRAMAS

Even up until a decade ago, when *Fashion King* was on air, Korean television placed white American masculinity on a capitalist pedestal, seeking his approval. But K-dramas today increasingly address anti-Asian racism.

In episode one of *Vincenzo*, Vincenzo Cassano—a Korean Italian consigliere and adoptee—meets with Emilio, a mafia vineyard owner. During their business meeting Emilio scorns Vincenzo with racialized insults in Italian: "Go back to your country, you arrogant yellow." Emilio follows this with a sarcastic, hand-folded bow, saying, "Arigatou, you uncivilized yellow." In a medium close-up, the camera slowly closes in on Vincenzo's smirk, repressing anger. Vincenzo gets up from his seat, turns back to Emilio, and says in Korean: "You will pay for disrespecting Asians. You savage."

In that moment Vincenzo demonstrates a diasporic Korean alliance with all Asians around the globe, despite his complicated identity as an Italian consigliere, Cassano, and a Korean adoptee to an Italian family. This moment is also a nod to Song Joong-ki and K-dramas' pan-Asian hallyu fan base who have popularized Korean media globally since the 1990s. As mentioned earlier, America's hype around Korean culture is late compared to the rest of the world. The hallyu wave did not start in Europe or the States but rather in Asia. Vietnam, the Philippines, and China each produced a remake of the international fan favorite *Descendants of the Sun*, which also stars Song Joong-ki and his ex-wife, Song Hye-kyo. Vincenzo's line here carries political weight through Song's hallyu status throughout Asia, as he defends the continent's dignity in an Asiatic alliance before a racist European mobster. Vincenzo gets his revenge by throwing a lighter onto Emilio's vineyard, which ignites in fire.

Another racialized tension between a white man and a Korean character is found in *Run On*. In episode nine a white male director of photography (DP) named Garrison is working on a Korean American indie film production and lashes out at Mi-joo, the onset interpreter between staff. Out of frustration at the lead actor's tardiness, Garrison shouts insensitive remarks at Mi-joo: "You know, this film may be just a way for you to make a living, but it's incredibly important work we're doing here, especially for Korean immigrants. Is this how you do things around here? Are you so narrow-minded because of how tiny your country is?" To emphasize tiny, Garrison makes a hand gesture with his thumb and index fingers in a diminutive motion, which contains echoes of patriarchal white supremacy's long-standing insecurity and masculinist preoccupation with size.

In the context of American television, South Korea and the US have a relationship that goes back decades. Your favorite shows like *The Simpsons*, *Family Guy*, *Bob's Burgers*, *SpongeBob SquarePants*, *Beavis and Butthead*, *Captain Planet*, *King of the Hill*, *Adventure Time*, and countless others were all hand-drawn in South Korean production studios by Korean animators.[144] Shin Neung-kyun, aka Nelson Shin, is a veteran Korean animator whose company Akom produced work for DC and Marvel franchises.[145] I love animated shows and movies, and since I was a kid, I always sat through the credits just to see the long list of dozens of Korean names who worked on these shows. As I read these names, I felt a kinship with these faceless people just by seeing familiar-sounding, three-syllable names to nurse the hunger I felt as a kid to see myself reflected in Hollywood media. These invisible minority workers continue the long trend of cheap Korean laborers executing Western ideas.

In terms of live-action original production, however, collaborations between South Korea and America are increasing due to the high demand of hallyu content worldwide. Films like *Minari* (2020) and *Past Lives* (2023), as well as shows like *Pachinko,* are some recent examples, albeit niche. More collaborations are in the works. In my own professional sphere in LA, however, white male writers and producers tell me stories criticizing South Korean producers' logics in an othering way, laughing at the "Korean way" of working and claiming that it "makes no sense." Such biases and the discriminatory belief that "the way" in the States is the only default that "makes sense" reveal that on-set tensions between people like Mi-joo and Garrison are not just made-up scenarios in K-dramas; they are based in real political and racialized

---

144 Geoffrey Cain, "South Korean Cartoonists Cry Foul Over The Simpsons," *Time*, October 30, 2010, https://content.time.com/time/world/article/0,8599,2027768,00.html.

145 Kate Torgovnick May, "A New Age of Animation," *Time*, May 20, 2016, www.theatlantic.com/entertainment/archive/2016/05/a-new-age-of-animation/483342/.

differences where the playing field is not level. Garrison's treatment of Mi-joo illustrates the bigger history of how Hollywood treats Korean laborers as invisible, cheap, and dispensable.

In *Run On* there is no pan-Asian awareness and unity standing up against white supremacist patriarchy. There is just one woman securing her job and defending herself against the insults of a culturally tone-deaf white cis-man. In comparing these two instances of racism in *Vincenzo* and *Run On*, the difference is class. Without status and wealth, one character finds it harder to stand up to an aggressor, while the other does it quite easily. K-dramas fetishize economic prosperity and make it seem as though this is the only way out of discriminatory injustice. But this is just another trap that maintains the power of illusory systems and structures.

I find Mi-joo's response far more heroic than Vincenzo's. She had everything to lose by standing up to Garrison and advocating for herself, but she did so anyway and then took responsibility for her actions. After a producer threatens to fire her, Mi-joo apologizes to Garrison and asks to finish her job, but she's able to do this only because she's never lost sight of who she is and what she is about. To me, this strong, unwavering center that Mi-joo holds is far more impressive than the destructive violence that Vincenzo uses in retaliation.

THE KOREAN DREAM

There is an increased awareness of white supremacy in K-dramas nowadays that was less apparent in the past. This is, in part, the impact of the #BlackLivesMatter movement reaching a global scale to awaken the world to white supremacy's effects as well as the global activism of Asian diasporas demanding equal rights and recognition. Such critique contains South Korea's self-awareness of its own cultural influence and a confidence to voice the silent suffering that so many Koreans endured domestically and while living abroad as immigrants. It also recognizes the national suffering due to American policies and lack of diplomacy when South Korea needed intervention. K-dramas today are conscious of anti-Asian racism resulting from increased mainstream awareness of racial and economic inequity around the globe stemming from coloniality and war. With that said, we cannot overlook South Korea's status today as a subempire.

South Korea now holds hegemonic status over South Asian countries like Vietnam and the Philippines, as well as parts of Latin America, through migrant workers who move in search of the Korean Dream. Jin-kyung Lee writes that "'the Korean Dream' recognizes Korea's new place in the global hierarchy as a semiperipheral metropole. It reveals South Korean triumphalism, subtly reflecting a Korean desire to subordinate migrants of other races and nationalities."[146] The majority of the migrant workers who flock to Korea in search of economic mobility get taken advantage of upon their arrival, and this treatment is not dissimilar from the way US employers treat migrant workers from Latin America, Africa, and Asia.

Lee contends that South Korea's subimperial status gets flexed across the globe in the form of employment and humanitarian efforts. Simultaneously, Lee documents the mistreatment of Vietnamese migrant workers at the hands of Korean factory employers, who take advantage of workers by withholding money and passports and even threatening to deport them due to their precarious status as undocumented citizens. An example is visible in *Squid Game*, in which the Pakistani character Ali goes to his Korean boss and demands his back payments. When the boss refuses, Ali retaliates and becomes a fugitive. In *Queenmaker* (2023) Indonesia-born actress Yannie Kim plays Angela, a nanny from South Asia who is unjustly fired by the temperamental Eunsung Group heiress Chaeryoung, parodying the egregious employee abuse committed by Korean Air's Cho family.[147]

Jin-kyung Lee notes that when Vietnamese workers arrive in Korea, they first learn to say things like "Please don't hit me," and "Can we have such and such things in writing?" and a host of other phrases requesting basic human courtesy from Korean employers.[148] Lee writes,

---

146 Lee, *Service Economies*, 214.

147 Jake Kwon, "Culture of Abuse and Violence at the Heart of Some of South Korea's Biggest Companies," *CNN*, February 21, 2019, www.cnn.com/2019/02/21/asia/south-korea-nut-rage-abuse-intl/index.html.

148 Lee, *Service Economies*, 215.

> *The Korean language that migrant workers in South Korea use shares certain commonalities with the English language that residents of South Korean camp towns had to pick up around the military bases, or the English South Korean immigrants must learn for their survival, or the kind of Korean language that Latino workers must acquire for their jobs at South Korean immigrant businesses in the United States.*[149]

The American Dream utilized Hollywood media to draw immigrants into the States in search of rights, liberties, and wealth while using cheap labor outsourced to Korea or hiring migrants to work undesirable jobs domestically. The Korean Dream now has a similar function, utilizing Korean media and commodities to hail migrants from developing nations into South Korea as laborers while "camouflaging the reality of institutionalized racialized labor exploitation."[150]

During a film shoot in 2012 I visited Atlanta's government housing, where Bhutanese refugees were living in poor conditions and working on chicken farms. When I was in Seoul I recall hearing my cousin complain about how South Asian immigrants were taking away job opportunities from Koreans. What she was missing, of course, is the fact that these "3-D" jobs—dirty, dangerous, and difficult jobs—went unwanted by many Koreans who seek upward mobility, but someone needs to work these jobs to keep the Korean economy afloat. These 3-D jobs are thus performed by migrant workers who seek the Korean Dream—an American Dream by proxy through South Korea's neocoloniality to the US, mirroring the same problematic institutional and structural patterns. It is thus unsurprising that nonsensical rhetoric like "immigrants taking away locals' jobs" exists in South Korea because Koreans performed numerous 3-D jobs for Americans as cheap labor, just as many refugees and immigrants are now performing them in America.

South Korea's racism against people from developing nations contains fearful disdain and an unwillingness to look at its own poverty trauma

---

149 Ibid.
150 Ibid., 214.

from a recent past. This racism is also part of the victim-bully cycle I mention earlier. Shows like *SKY Castle*, *The King: Eternal Monarch*, *World of the Married*, and *Queenmaker* employ conservative old-money WASP aesthetics of cars, guns, horses, houses, and wine in their mise-en-scène, which I read as fiscal insecurity and imposter syndrome of the nation's new-money status, burying its shadows beneath its glitz and glamor built on the backs of working-class Korean and migrant laborers who are rendered invisible, just as white supremacy and colonization have done to Asians in the West.

HOLLYWOOD-HALLYU RELATIONS

Hollywood struggles to find a fair balance in coproductions with South Korea's entertainment industry. I see microaggressive decisions made to cut out entire scenes or music cues that render certain Korean programs unwatchable, such as *Ask Us Anything* (*Knowing Bros/Men on a Mission*) or the *Reply* (*Answer Me*) series on Netflix. These executive decisions to bypass small fees or the extra effort to acquire music rights for international distribution compromise the creators' artistic integrity and content quality. Such choices exhibit a cultural disregard for Korean auteurs' artistry and original ideas. There's work to be done in Hollywood to better accommodate and respect Korean television show-runners' intentions.

Consider a show like *Penthouse*, which was broken up into three seasons with sixteen episodes each; however, for Kim Soon-ok, forty-eight episodes is modest. Given her prolific writing style and the discipline she's developed for writing over a hundred episodes per show for daily release, taking forty-eight episodes and breaking them up into three seasons becomes an easy way to sell to American markets, where seasons are part of the TV culture. Just like Korean animators, makjang drama writers' disciplined work ethic is built for Americans to easily profit from. Historically, US and European markets have always profited from fast, cheap, and efficient Asian labor. That's why AI figures and robots are commonly constructed with Asian faces. We are expected to be unfeeling, subordinate, silent, and robotically laborious for the benefit of colonial capitalism.[151]

---

151 Check out the book *Techno-Orientalism: Imagining Asia in Speculative Fiction, History, and Media*, ed. David S. Roh, Betsy Huang, and Greta A. Niu (New Brunswick, NJ: Rutgers University Press, 2015).

As mentioned, Asian American actors like Anna May Wong, Philip Ahn, and Sessue Hayakawa, who worked in Hollywood in the 1920s and 1930s, were not compensated equally as their white costars. We see this in present-day Hollywood, particularly through the lens of a globalized hierarchy that deems productions with white actors and showrunners from the US of higher value compared to productions with nonwhite actors and non-American creators. In February 2021 Netflix announced its $500 million investment in Korean content. While half of a billion dollars for production seems like a lot, when you break it down to how many shows and movies Korean production companies delivered for that amount, it's not as much as it sounds, especially when Netflix banks hundreds of millions of dollars on a single individual. Adam Sandler received a quarter of a billion dollars from Netflix, and he's just one white dude in America. Daniel Craig received $100 million from Netflix. Ryan Murphy received $300 million from Netflix. Shonda Rhimes received $100 million when she signed with Netflix. Meanwhile, how many titles does Netflix expect from South Korea's film and TV industry? And where are the names and faces of Korean stars and showrunners in the trades?

Despite America's love for K-dramas, its press still makes no attempt to spotlight and differentiate Korean creators and actors as individuals. I saw one cringe-inducing video of a white American reporter asking mega hallyu star Lee Jung-jae how he feels to be a star now, despite his three decades of show business experience and long list of hit shows and movies in his filmography. There's a myriad of Korean production companies, agencies, and talents all with their own identity, voice, and function. Why are they not named or recognized for their individuality?

In an article by *Hankyoreh*, Netflix Korea Vice President Kang Dong-han claimed that Netflix brought sixteen thousand jobs to South Korea through its investment.[152] Kang's comment frames Netflix as a white savior to Korea's economy. This is another example of neocolonialism. The entire production

---

152 Suh Jung-min, "Netflix Boasts Impact of 5.6 Trillion Won, 16,000 Jobs in S. Korea," *Hankyoreh*, September 30, 2021, https://english.hani.co.kr/arti/english_edition/e_business/1013411.html.

cost for the first nine episodes of *Squid Game* is less than $17 million. *The Crown*, however, costs $130 million a season—approximately $13 million an episode. A season of *House of Cards* cost $50 million. Compared to that, $17 million for nine episodes of a show with over a hundred cast members and high production costs for set design, production design, effects, makeup, and costume is meager. A $17 million budget is standard for a B-grade Hollywood horror flick. It's the budget of an independent film in the US. I've worked on independent film production sets, and the lower the budget, the greater the stress, agony, and lack of safety on set.

Are Korean content makers given ample time, money, and support to meet Hollywood's demands of multiple seasons? Korean television productions typically do not have seasons. Shows are usually anywhere from ten to twenty-four episodes, and once the show is wrapped, it's over. But Hollywood's appetite for K-dramas and its preferences for how to do show business are forcing the Korean television industry to adapt. *Hospital Playlist*—written by Lee Woo-jung of the *Reply/Answer Me* series—had two seasons. *Kingdom* had two seasons and a feature film as its third finale, and the show enjoyed critical acclaim and fan adoration, but there were problems that the mainstream press overlooked massively. Two staff members on *Kingdom* succumbed to death on set—one person died in a car accident while driving the prop vehicle, and the other died of an aneurysm. South Korea does not have unions that protect labor rights for cast and crew. There's no IATSE, Writers Guild, or Screen Actors Guild. These organizations in Hollywood were built out of necessity because the industry took advantage of workers to the point of long-term injuries and death.

Corporations responsible for their content must be held accountable for the work conditions they allow on their productions. In the case with *Kingdom* and *Squid Game*, it is Netflix. Netflix benefits from these K-dramas' successes, but what about the deaths, illnesses, or mistreatment of the creators and their content? These trends echo mid- to late-twentieth-century patterns as Koreans massacred one another before, during, and after the war, while American soldiers stood idly by as if they were just watching TV.

LESSON 14:
THE HUMANNESS OF DISABILITY, ADDICTION, AND "WELBING"

WHEN I WAS IN HIGH SCHOOL, RIGHT AROUND THE TIME *DAE JANG Geum*, aka *Jewel in the Palace* (2003), was on air, I kept hearing a buzz-word within the Korean immigrant community that had two Korean letters 웰빙, pronounced "welbing." I was like, *What the hell is this "welbing" business?*

I went to a Korean restaurant in Palisades Park, New Jersey, for soon-dubu jjigae and noticed small banchan additions before the main course arrived, such as a personalized bowl of steamed barley with soybean paste, pickled radish stems, and soy pulp porridge called 비지/*biji*. Healthy stuff. The ajumma told me to enjoy my "welbing" banchan. I soon realized that this was Korean for "well-being," and that these foods were for the sake of my bodily health.

Welbing is a marketing concept used in South Korea to promote healthier lifestyle choices. Welbing also branded Korean food for export and tourism, emphasizing health-conscious eating with fermented Korean products like kimchi and toenjang to diversify your gut biome, speaking to cosmopolitan kombucha-obsessed individuals to combat first-world diseases such as obesity and heart disease. Welbing was part of Korea's cultural globalizing effort in the early 2000s via food campaigns, claiming that Korean eating is better eating. In case it isn't obvious, ramyun, ttŏkpokki, fried chicken, and galbi are not welbing choices, buddy, no matter how much you want them to be.

Gender and disability studies scholar Eunjung Kim writes in *Curative Violence* that South Korea's obsession with buzzwords like *curing, healing, therapy*, and *well-being* are iterations of the nation's aspirations to be free of any disability, disease, or illness whatsoever to lay claim to its national economic prosperity and stability. This status-obsessed ideal greatly diminishes the rights of differently abled persons, and the political hang-up speaks to the nation's colonial trauma. Kim writes, "Disability has long been connected to the imaginary of the colonial Korean body politic during Japanese rule."[153] Korean literary works produced in the 1920s and 1930s include characters with disabilities that allegorize Korea's lack of sovereignty. What do characters with disabilities in K-dramas represent today?

MENTAL HEALTH, "NORMAL," AND STIGMA

Although I am open about my healing journey in mental health, my Korean family members and friends are uncomfortable with the topic. My cousin's son—my first cousin once removed—calls me 이모/*imo*, which means "aunt" in Korean. When I lived in Seoul in 2009 I saw my nephew visit a child psychologist twice a week. I didn't think anything of this and simply admired my cousin for being progressive by meeting her child's mental and emotional needs at such an early age. My cousin never told me that her son was neurodivergent. I only found out years later when I was visiting Seoul and saw him again as a teen, and it was apparent that he was on the autism spectrum. Suddenly, my cousin's routine trips with her son to the child psychologist made sense. Later that week, when I was having a drink with my cousin, she said to me with a hint of disdain, "My son is never going to lead a normal life like you."

---

153 Eunjung Kim, *Curative Violence: Rehabilitating Disability, Gender and Sexuality in Modern Korea* (Durham, NC: Duke University Press, 2017), 3.

My cousin's loaded comment comes with two assumptions: (1) that "normal" exists and (2) that I do not have a disability. The upper echelons of a civic order typically construct concepts like "normal" or "common sense," then release them as the default expectation by that hegemonic culture—the wealthiest, most educated, and most privileged elite class—causing less privileged and/or marginalized people to feel inadequate. I remember when I was a child and couldn't speak English to ask to go to the bathroom and lacked any cultural inkling of what goes on in America. My white teachers in elementary school constantly yelled at me to "have some common sense." Upon hearing this, my peers would parrot the same demand while bullying me.

Constructs like "common sense" make immigrants like me feel defective. Constructs like "normal" or "common sense" are illusions designed to create a culture of "right" versus "wrong," in or out, acceptable or intolerable. These concepts are perfect cultural weapons to otherize, ostracize, shame, and control. They are the perfect way to discriminate and cause self-doubt. The upside to having gone to grad school is that I've read Foucault and Gramsci, and their theories demonstrate the fragility of these deceptions. If anyone ever makes you feel ashamed for assuming your own version of "normal," ignore them. There's no such thing as a blanket "norm." "Common sense" does not exist. Your subjectivity matters most.

When I discussed my nephew's neurodivergence with an American friend, she commented, "Society isn't going to understand him." I wish my friend knew that by "society," she was speaking of herself, and she was casting judgment. Beneath that was her own fear that she and her family would ever be touched by such an affliction. In these interactions I see how the fear of difference, driven by the assumption of "normal" and "common sense," not only divides us within our communities but also splits us from ourselves. This fear disconnects us from our inner humanity.

RESISTING MENTAL HEALTH TREATMENT

American psychiatric history explains why people are reluctant to admit to mental or emotional distress and then to seek help. Judith Herman writes that after the First World War, men who witnessed innumerable barbarities in battle began to break down: "They screamed and wept uncontrollably. They froze and could not move. They became mute and unresponsive. They lost their memory and their capacity to feel."[154] Although the number of war veterans who had these symptoms was high, the military suppressed reports to avoid public demoralization and to maintain false images of "manly honor and glory in battle."[155] Instead of offering these psychically wounded veterans comfort, their state and doctors labeled them as "weak."

There were some military officials who said that these patients should be punished through court-martialing or dishonorable discharge for being ill. Some of these veterans were given electric shock therapy and shamed for exhibiting symptoms. They were told to have better control of themselves. At the turn of the twentieth century, when war veterans needed help the most, they were shamed and punished instead, paralleling the typical social reaction of victim-blaming rape victims. The "help" that soldiers needed came in the form of abuse for admitting to their illness or showing signs of distress. This punitive history explains people's reluctance to seek aid. Fear and suspicion of psychology is not only found in the US and South Korea; it's prevalent around the globe.

In the context of South Korea, Eunjung Kim explores US missionary history in the early 1900s intended to provide medical intervention among lepers who suffered from Hansen's disease, better known as leprosy. American missionary doctors as well as the Japanese imperial government established hospitals in Korea to justify colonial occupation on the peninsula rather than offer legitimate treatment to patients: "Forced labor, punitive confinement, forced sterilization and abortion, massacres, the state appropriation of the land reclaimed by the patients, the separation of children from their patients, and lifelong segregation in settlement villages constitute only part of the colonial and postcolonial violence experienced by people with Hansen's disease throughout the twentieth century."[156] Given this traumatic history, it makes sense why Koreans are reluctant to admit to invisible disabilities or disorders

---

154 Herman, *Trauma and Recovery*, 20.

155 Ibid.

156 Kim, *Curative Violence*, 172.

and seek help. Disability is imbued with shame in all capitalist societies where productivity is revered.

Growing up, my dad would always flip out whenever anyone said or used the word "crazy" around him. It's taken me decades to understand that when he was younger, people in his village used to bad-mouth him and his whole family for having a "crazy" person live at his house—his eldest brother and father figure. My uncle's war PTSD caused him to behave erratically, which frightened his family and neighbors. My dad's sensitivity to the word "crazy" is personal because he was judged and shamed in his youth due to my uncle's mental illness. "Crazy" is used to deliberately insult others in Korea.

In *Our Blues* Seon-ah suffers from depression. There are several sympathetic scenes from her perspective to illustrate what chronic depression feels like, such as Seon-ah waking up in bed drenched in cold water and all the lights before her disappearing. When Seon-ah's childhood love interest, Dong-seok, encourages Seon-ah to scream and curse into the air to vent her repressed rage at her ex-husband, Seon-ah repeatedly screams while facing the ocean: "You crazy bastard! Give me back my son!"

K-dramas are rife with contradictory and confused moments like this, in which a mentally ill woman uses the word *crazy* as an insult while a word like 바보/*babo*, which is equivalent to "stupid," is openly used to describe the cognitively disabled in *SKY Castle* and *The Good Bad Mother* (2023). To refer to a differently abled person as "babo" is no different from calling them "retarded." When I was a kid, I grew up around Korean adults who shamed crying children by calling them "babo." The vernacular equates disability and emoting through tears as stupidity because they associate disability and crying with weakness—and therein lies the fear of death again.

AAPIs are 1,000 percent less likely to seek help for mental health in the US compared to the white demographic, and this is tied to the fear of stigmatization. The fear of being labeled an invalid is linked to its associations with weakness and lacking use value. It's a fear tied to the need to survive—you must have purpose or you will be killed. In Asian countries, where war and despots had zero tolerance for the invalid, admitting to any illness or making any mention of a need was suicidal.

DISABILITY IN K-DRAMAS BY NOH HEE-KYUNG

K-dramas are chock-full of pathologies. I see depression, anxiety, schizophrenia, borderline personality disorder, bipolar disorder, multiple personality disorder, PTSD, codependence, dissociation, autism, alcoholism, narcissism, OCD, and so much more in every single show I've ever seen. Some K-dramas focus specifically on the topic of mental illness and disability, such as in *It's Okay Not to Be Okay* (2020), *Dinner Mate*, and *Extraordinary Attorney Woo*. But there is one K-drama showrunner whose oeuvre always includes characters with disabilities: Noh Hee-kyung.

In *That Winter the Wind Blows* (2013), Noh's adaptation of the Japanese drama *Forget Love* (2002), Oh Young is blind. In *Worlds Within* (2008) Ji-oh suffers from an eye-related illness that could potentially cause blindness, preventing him from committing to his girlfriend. In *It's Okay, That's Love* Jae-yeol suffers from a sleep disorder, OCD, and schizophrenia, while his girlfriend Hae-soo suffers from a sexual dysfunction linked to trauma. In *Dear My Friends* Wan is reluctant to be with Yeon-ha despite loving him because a car accident made him wheelchair bound. Wan's maternal uncle In-bong is also disabled after a drunken fall that affected his ability to walk. Wan sees the way her mother and grandparents treat her uncle with shame, and she struggles to accept her partner's condition. In *Live* Jung-oh lives with her mom, who struggles with anxiety and panic disorder. In all of Noh's shows, disability stands as the obstacle between lovers who try to reach each other but are disrupted by shame and fear of judgment from themselves and their families who discount a disabled person's humanity by deeming them unworthy. The characters' families represent "society" and its "norm" of ableist prejudice. The characters' internalized shame reveals their own bias. However, Noh's latest show, *Our Blues*, is a little different.

First off, the Jeju dialect on *Our Blues* slaps. Having been raised on a thick South Gyeong-sang dialect myself, hearing any sat'uri on TV is a symphony to my ears. Seeing veteran actress Go Doo-shim—a Jeju native—working in her element is as enthralling and mesmerizing as watching dolphins in the sea. While able-bodied actors performed the disabilities illustrated throughout Noh's previous shows, in *Our Blues* Young-ok's twin sister, Young-hee, is played by Jung Eun-hye, a visual artist who has tri-somy 21—a genetic disorder also known as Down syndrome. Noh audi-tioned numerous differently abled actors for the role of Young-hee but found their performances too affected. Noh cast Jung after they met at her art exhibition, and wrote many of the descriptions and lines for Young-hee based on her interactions with Jung.

Young-ok is a rookie haenyŏ in love with Park Jung-joon, the boat captain. But during the first flush of their relationship, Young-ok sud-denly shuts down. When Jung-joon first meets Young-ok's twin sister, Young-hee, he is taken aback to see a woman with an intellectual disabil-ity for the first time in his life and fumbles his words. Young-ok coldly says, "You must be shocked. She has Down syndrome." Young-hee adds to this explanation while raising the state identification card she carries around her neck during airplane travel: "It's a grade-two developmental disorder." Jung-joon continues to remain frozen in silence, confusion, and embarrassment as he looks at Young-ok, who tells him, "If you don't know what Down syndrome is, look it up on the internet," before driving away with her sister. Jung-joon immediately looks up "Down syndrome" on his phone.

When Young-ok drives Young-hee to a nearby building for her sister to use the restroom, there's a group of haenyŏ aunties and Byul, a deaf woman who sells coffee at the market, played by deaf actress Lee So-byul. The women sit in a semicircle cleaning fish, and several of them can't stop staring at Young-hee as Young-ok glances back at them defensively. One of the elders Choon-hee chides them: "Stop staring." Afterward Young-ok tries to get Young-hee back in the car, but Young-hee wanders over to the group. Another elder Ok-dong makes room for Young-hee to sit down beside her and teaches her how to clean fish. Byul sits beside Young-hee and explains that she is deaf. Young-hee immediately feels an alliance with Byul and says with a smile, "Then we are friends."

Jung-joon catches up, kneels down before Young-hee, and says, "I am Park Jung-joon. I'm dating your younger sister Young-ok. I hope we can get along," and bows his head to show respect to his girlfriend's older sister.[157] Then Jung-joon takes Young-ok aside to speak frankly with her. He says, "When I first saw Young-hee noona, I was surprised. But that's understandable. It's my first time seeing someone with Down syndrome. It could happen. I could be taken aback. If that's wrong, then I am sorry."

There's such vulnerability and courage in Jung-joon's monologue as he balances self-accountability, self-compassion, and apology in equal measure while fighting to be with Young-ok, who pushes him away by using her disabled sister as an excuse to run from love.

Young-ok's chastisement of Jung-joon reminds me of a troubling trend among educated people today, in which they equate "wokeness" or justice with calling an ignorant person out publicly to humiliate and disgrace them for mistakes or for their lack of education. Calling out to tear a person down for what they do not yet know or making honest mistakes is just as ignorant, dehumanizing, and violent, as it flaunts educational privilege. American journalist Chris Hedges states, "The politics of diversity have become advertising gimmicks, brands. . . . Identity politics and diversity busy liberals and the educated with a boutique activism at the expense of addressing systemic injustices or the scourge of permanent war. The *haves* scold the *have-nots* for their bad manners, racism, linguistic insensitivity and garishness, while ignoring the root causes of their economic distress or the suicidal despair gripping much of the country." I do not condone inconsiderate language or behavior, nor do I tolerate them when I am attacked with such. With that said, I make a concerted effort to allow myself and others to be as human as possible, because I am where I am, just like everyone else. Mistakes happen. Mistakes are allowed. Mistakes make us human, whereas perfection does not.

Noh integrates a culture of acceptance and understanding of the differently abled by including actors with disabilities in a show, generating scenes and dialogue that reflect the fear and ignorance of able-bodied and neurotypical characters as well as community elders who straighten them out with simple instructions like "Stop staring." Noh's script has inclusive acts such as making room for Young-hee to sit with the locals and clean fish. Noh also

---

157 It's common among Korean twins to be differentiated as older and younger depending on who was born first.

includes scenes where Young-hee demonstrates agency and defends herself from ableists who disrespect her.

Eunjung Kim states, "Often disability is disfigured by cure when the disabled body is forced at all costs to approximate the normal body."[158] This highlights the central argument to Kim's book *Curative Violence*, which states that to frame persons with disabilities in a text with the expectation for them to be "cured" is violent because it is tied to the violent history of colonial, racialized, misogynistic, and discriminatory practices on both national and individual levels.

Although Noh's shows address disability and feature differently abled characters, there is also a disquieting expectation from those with disabilities to overcome their illnesses and return to their community as "healed," "cured," or "better." This is apparent in *It's Okay, That's Love* when Jae-yeol and Hae-soo break up because of his schizophrenia but end up together once he recovers. It is apparent in *Dear My Friends*, when Wan tells Yeon-ha to attempt walking again as a condition to be with her. In *Our Blues* Young-hee has a history of schizophrenia but Young-ok expresses gladness when Young-hee's caregiver says that her symptoms have improved. By holding cure as the end goal in these shows, Noh reifies the curatively violent logic that characters are only capable of wholeness and happiness if and when they are no longer disabled.

Then there are shows like *Crash Course in Romance* in which disability plays a conflicted role. Haeng-seon's autistic brother, Jae-woo, is part of the family business but is also represented as a burden and a reason for Haeng-seon's ceaseless apologies to strangers who do not understand his condition. Meanwhile, their niece Hae-yi's needs as a teenager get deprioritized in the face of Jae-woo's disability. The strangest scenes on *Crash Course in Romance*, however, are when Hae-yi's class rival, Su-ah, starts having mental breakdowns and screaming fits. While the show has multiple scenes of Su-ah experiencing a psychotic break, it never gets addressed. There's no commentary on whether she gets psychological help. The show ignores her condition, then jumps into the future, depicting her as a well-adjusted college student,

---

158 Kim, *Curative Violence*, 226.

treating Su-ah's episodes as something she grows out of. While *Crash Course in Romance* addresses topics like eating disorders, insomnia, depression, suicide, child abuse, and workaholism, it does nothing to show how a character manages a psychotic break at its onset.

Extraordinary Attorney Woo, however, critiques curative violence when Young-woo's estranged mother, Soo-mi, offers to send Young-woo abroad to find treatment at American facilities. Soo-mi expresses curative violence by seeking to cure Young-woo of her autism. Soo-mi also reveals her internalized orientalist perspective that Korea is backward relative to America's treatment options. With that said, I loved the finale in season one of *Extraordinary Attorney Woo*, when Young-woo declares that she is satisfied with her life.

In the case with Counsel Woo Young-woo, she finds satisfaction in her career because she *loves* the law, just as Young-hee finds satisfaction in her artwork because she *loves* to draw. These characters demonstrate that a life with a disability is precious and purposeful nonetheless, rather than focusing solely on their disability as a burden to overcome. These shows give room to complex questions and feelings while also recognizing the vivid lives of the differently abled. They give a face and voice to disability by combatting its historical erasure onscreen and making their lives a meaningful part of the narrative that audiences invest in. As Eunjung Kim writes, "The visual presence of a disabled body emphasizes its materiality and lived experience."[159]

WELL-BEING AND BEING

Media grants us a time-space opportunity to safely indulge all our emotional responses.

When I asked Dr. Ham whether a viewing experience can be therapeutically productive, he emphasized the importance of making the viewing ritual a "reintegration of yourself":

> *Sometimes you can't cry for your own stuff because it's too vulnerable [or] your protectors won't let you. A movie or music or something*

---

159 Ibid., 109.

else can kind of come in through the side door and awaken the parts of you that are in pain that aren't allowed time in your consciousness. . . . It really depends on what they do in the moment of crying. If they say, "Stupid movie," then they're not healing. They're not taking it all the way. If they get mad at themselves or laugh at themselves and kind of make light of it, then they're not making use of that opportunity. If they see that this is awakening in them something that needed to be acknowledged, held, hugged, and then they really go through the process of, "I understand why this is meaningful to me and why I'm crying here, and I love you" to the part that's hurting, then you're making it into a healing experience.[160]

K-dramas offer me space to explore my personal pathos, process grief, and self-reflect through my emotional responses. A lot of shows are also extremely sentimental. There are innumerable cringe-making scenes and lines that give me the kind of headache I get after eating too much sugar. The fun of my own exploration is to dig through why I reject certain emotional responses. K-dramas also help me mindfully keep my projections in check. Rather than make endless intervening observations on what the characters or shows need to *fix*, as I'd been trained to do in grad school, I can just surrender to the story world with an appreciation for what's there. This becomes a great exercise in acceptance and appreciation in my day-to-day.

I went to see a naturopathic kinesiologist who checked my large intestine and said it was healthy. He asked me, "Can you guess which ethnicity of clients I worked with never had large intestinal issues?" I guessed, "Korean." He smiled in affirmation. "Do you know why?" he asked. "Kimchi," I replied. He smiled in affirmation again.

Ah, the welbing power of kimchi! It regulates our bowels and keeps our organs strong. When there's an energy (*ki* in Korean or *chi*/氣 in Chinese) blockage in the large intestine, sadness and grief get stuck in the body. Considering Korea's trauma history, it makes sense why its national food is kimchi—a spicy

---

160 Grace Jung and Jacob Ham, "Ep 112: Save Me and When Two Pisces Dream of Yin Yang Cheese with Dr. Jacob Ham," *K-Drama School*, February 20, 2023.

fermented cabbage that improves gut health and flushes out that which does not serve. This is good because I have so much I want to let go.

I was brought up on a Korean diet that was completely synchronized with health awareness. Rice gives stomachs a fullness to enrich the body with energy and confidence to take on the day. Seafood brings stamina and immunity, connecting us to our ocean ancestry. Seaweed soup improves blood health for mothers in postpartum, and Korean children eat seaweed soup every year to celebrate their birthday as a reminder of their blood connection to their mother and the blood that their mother shed during childbirth. Chicken soup (삼계탕) is eaten in the summer to restore lost energy to the heat. Eating roasted sweet potatoes in the winter keeps people warm and energized. Red meat for vitality. Beans for protein. Anchovies for calcium. Hovenia tea to treat hangovers. Bean sprout soup to treat hangovers. Haejang soup to treat hangovers. Koreans have many ways of treating hangovers because they drink so much, but the common denominator is always hot soup with rice to sweat out the toxins and fill the belly with a stabilizing carb. Part of the reason why Koreans can drink so much for long periods of time is because they always pair booze with bar food called *anju*/안주.

Korean food is also connected to cultural mysticism: Red bean to ward off evil. Sea salt to cleanse bad energy. Rice cakes for luck.

What you know to be Korean food today is hardly Korean food, friend. The deep-fried, overprocessed, sugar-packed, high-sodium options do not reflect the medicinal benefits of Korean food I've mentioned in the above but rather the Americana-franchise method of using addictive ingredients like sugar and grease to get your brain hooked on what's branded as "Korean." Why does the world love Korean barbeque? Because the marinade is full of sugar. Why does the world love Korean-style corndogs? Because they're deep-fried dough sprinkled with sugar and have cheese and salty sausage in the middle. The mindful Korean eating I was raised on—to look at all foods as medicine—is hardwired into me and keeps me strong.

After giving my kinesiologist my full medical history, he examined my body and said, "Considering what you've survived, your body is in good health. I feel honored to be in your presence. You have a lot to teach the world." I was so moved by this. Having been afraid of being "damaged" from my past, I was hearing the exact opposite.

One of my symptoms since grade school has been insomnia, but while reading sleep-medicine specialist Jade Wu's *Hello Sleep*, I've been unlearning my hypervigilant and controlling ways of forcing my body into sleep to get a full night's rest. Wu recommends patients to become friends with sleep rather than try to micromanage it. I currently practice this noncurative approach to sleep, and it makes a lot of sense. Now that I don't see my sleep as a stressful assignment every night, I feel so much more relaxed to actually let sleep happen. But that's the ironic thing about well-being: it encompasses aspiring toward betterment while also accepting the body with appreciation as it is in the present.

I feel so lucky to have reconnected to my body again. I lived with the disconnect for many years, and I finally feel like I am *in* my body. When my physician recently asked me how I feel about my quality of life, I heard myself say with full clarity, "I'm pretty happy." I felt pleased to know that I meant it.

ALCOHOLISM AND DRUG ADDICTION IN K-DRAMAS

While suicide is a problem in the Korean entertainment industry and society overall, drug and alcohol abuse among Korean entertainers is also high. Rather than ask *why* substance abuse is so widespread among entertainers, reporters shame addicts in the press. Many of these artists silently struggle with mental illness, eating disorders, trauma, and insomnia from long work hours, inconsistent sleep patterns, and abuse from the industry.

My friend and LA comedian Fu died of fentanyl poisoning back in 2021. The cocaine he purchased was cut with this highly addictive and lethal substance, and it killed him. That's bad form. It's not cool to sell a product by calling it one thing when it's actually another and deadly. Drug and alcohol addiction is rampant in show business. This is no news to anyone, but the judgment of addicts and lack of compassion for addiction as an ailment are still widespread.[161]

---

161 See Sam Quinones's books *Dreamland: The True Tale of America's Opiate Epidemic* (New York: Bloomsbury, 2019) and *The Least of Us: True Tales of America and Hope in the Time of Fentanyl and Meth* (New York: Bloomsbury, 2021).

One fond memory I have of Fu is when I was in Hollywood on Melrose hanging out with other comics. It was around 9:00 p.m., and I said I was going to take off and walk to my car, which was just a block away. Hollywood streets get dicey after nightfall, so one of my friends offered me a ride to my car, but I said I would just walk. Fu stopped me and insisted, "No. Let them drive you." It was such a small moment, but I felt a tremendous oppa warmth emanate from him.

I was on the road performing shows when I heard about Fu's death. I cried all week at multiple Airbnbs. When I returned to LA, our comedy community mourned him. But I heard one comic—a blonde who had no relationship to Fu—insensitively comment, "Well, if people take risks by doing drugs, then they deserve to die." I just let her comment hang in the air. I didn't mention how often I've seen her drive home after downing a few beers at the comedy club. But her comment is central to what most people think when it comes to drug abuse. People have this misconception that addiction is isolated to drug addicts. I even heard a psych nurse complain about drug addicts at her hospital: "Addicts are the most annoying people on earth."

There's a truth to that. Addiction can make people annoying because addicts need a fix to feel okay, and they will do anything to get that fix, including annoy, beg, reason, rationalize, steal, lie, destroy, and more. Addiction hurts the addict and everyone around them. That's because without a fix, an addict feels like they will die. This threat of death feels real, even though some people might not understand it.

A fix, however, isn't isolated to drugs, alcohol, and gambling. A fix can be anything from your phone, gossip, complaining, hot Cheetos, chocolate, news, social media, coffee, porn, sex, work, productivity, attention, sugar, and TV. If you're reading this and you think, *I'm not an addict*, I beg to differ. We are all addicted to something, my friend. Our culture scapegoats drug addicts while we stuff our self-righteous faces with lethal albeit legal products like coffee, beer, and ice cream, believing that we're not just as addicted to drugs that claim to be food when, really, fat, sugar, and booze are harmful to our health.

Intellectualizing is also addictive, and it is a widely accepted form of escapism and productivity. The hyperintellectualizing that scholars engage in is a coping mechanism. Intellectualizing brings on a high. Reading books with lofty theory and then banging out papers that rechannel other intellectuals' words into my own felt productive. It felt like *work*. It helped me escape my feelings of stupidity and worthlessness. I was confronted by my own addiction to intellectualizing at the end of my graduate career when I hit a wall. There are no more degrees to chase after a PhD. I finally admitted to myself that I kept putting myself in deeper debt to buy titles in education to combat my feelings of lack. I felt stupid and worthless, and I believed I needed to enhance my use value by gaining knowledge.

K-dramas are highly problematic in how they feature drug addicts in a hyperbolized, caricatured, and contemptuous light. In *The Glory* Sa-ra is consistently framed as pathetic, out of control, and antagonistic due to her drug problem. In *Green Mothers' Club* Chun-hui is a former nurse, doctor's wife, and mother to young kids who moonlights as an opioid administrator to private clients to maintain her lifestyle, which is in jeopardy because of her husband's gambling addiction. The drug addicts are framed one-dimensionally as bullies and blackmailers. Meanwhile, Chun-hui is framed as a victim, even though she is the drug dealer. Chun-hui's husband Ju-seok is also portrayed as a hostile adversary due to his gambling addiction. Addicts are consistently vilified in K-dramas.

Although illicit drugs are portrayed in a shameful light, alcohol is rarely problematized in K-dramas even though alcoholics and binge drinking appear in every show. One of the few shows I recall seeing alcoholism treated as a serious health issue is *Worlds Within* (2008), when former actress-turned-executive Yoon Young's hands shake because of her heavy drinking. It's a rare visual of alcoholism shown sympathetically in a K-drama. A study published in 2014 states that South Koreans drink twice as much as Russians and four times as much as Americans.[162] South Korea is a culture that greatly enables alcoholism.

---

162 Roberto A. Ferdman, "South Koreans Drink Twice as Much Liquor as Russians and More than Four Times as Much as Americans," *Quartz*, February 2, 2014, https://qz.com/171191/south-koreans-drink-twice-as-much-liquor-as-russians-and-more-than-four-times-as-much-as-americans.

I come from a long line of alcoholics. My paternal uncles drank a lot, but they also loved to chain smoke Dunhill cigarettes, which eventually killed them all through lung cancer. I used to love drinking, but I gave it up a few years ago because it stopped making sense to me. A thought kept circling inside my head as I held my glass of pinot noir: *This is a big fat waste of water.* That's all booze is to me nowadays: a huge waste of water. Living in SoCal where drought is a real threat has made me more water conscious. Whenever I drink alcohol, I get up to pee multiple times because alcohol dehydrates my body. That means I need to drink more water to replenish what I am being drained of. Every time I pee, I waste more water by flushing the toilet and washing my hands. I stopped drinking because it makes no environmental sense. I can't unsee the damage anymore—that drinking alcohol is as wasteful as producing and dropping bombs.

In South Korea, gaming addiction is a chronic problem, with approximately ten million addicts. In 2019 the World Health Organization (WHO) has officially recognized internet gaming disorder as a mental illness because chronic gaming addicts have died from depriving themselves of sleep and food for days on end. A scenario based in fact is illustrated in Noh's *Live*, in which two parents are addicted to the game world, where they find more productivity and fulfillment than they do in their unemployed and poverty-stricken life. Their addiction leads to the demise of their infant child from neglect and their subsequent arrest. Noh's script, however, does not demonize these parents. It offers a concise yet sympathetic backstory to the addicts' rationale. Noh's recognition of the addict's plight is a helpful means of adding a mindful tone for addicts in a culture that demands perfection.

WHAT DO YOU LIVE AND FIGHT FOR?

Physician Atul Gawande writes in *Being Mortal* that enabling well-being is a doctor's job and that "well-being is about the reasons one wishes to be alive."[163] What are your reasons for wishing to be alive?

---

163 Atul Gawande, *Being Mortal: Medicine and What Matters in the End* (New York: Picador, 2014), 259.

To know what one wishes to live for is as important as knowing what it is one fights for. In 2021 I took a four-week online course taught by activist and Smith College professor Loretta Ross. Ross teaches a concept known as "calling in," borrowing a term conceived by queer, disabled Asian American activist Loan Tran in 2013. Tran emphasizes respect and love over the toxic and violent practices of calling out unjust behaviors or utterances, recommending a mindful approach to injustice and ignorance over an impulsive reactivity that may lead to unnecessary conflict.[164] Tran questions what the point of the human rights movement is when the means of conducting that movement is so inhumane. Since when is trash-talking, vicious fights on social media, or criticizing one another harshly for their opinions the standards of a progressive movement? The calling-in method calls out the calling-out culture that our society increasingly engages in to feel empowered through a false sense of righteousness. Any act of elevating oneself at the expense of another's disempowerment is not in step with human rights.

I took Ross's four-week course for just $5 a class, and I saw hundreds of people registered to hear her instruction on how to distinguish social justice activism from inhumane, albeit very human behaviors, like reactivity or accusations. Ross also discusses the importance of this topic in her 2021 TED Talk.[165] Through Ross's course I learned the importance of recognizing my own personal triggers through physical mindfulness and to be attentive when listening before determining whether there is any harm. She said in class, "In doing the work, you find what you're made of. What your muscles are. What your tolerances and triggers are. You have to know your triggers so that another doesn't permanently control you. Have greater awareness and not just analysis." Ross was instructing students to return to their bodies.

As trauma literature shows, trauma *lives in the body*. My recovery journey is not just about reclaiming autonomy and agency of my body, mind, and

---

164 Ngọc Loan Trần, "Calling IN: A Less Disposable Way of Holding Each Other Accountable," *BGD*, www
.bgdblog.org/2013/12/calling-less-disposable-way-holding-accountable/.

165 Loretta Ross, "Don't Call People Out—Call Them In," *TED Talk*, www.ted.com/talks/loretta_j_ross_
don_t_call_people_out_call_them_in?language=en.

heart; it is also taking ownership of myself with loving awareness so that I can protect myself but also allow heart-to-heart connection with others.

Ross's teaching with calling in integrates self-realization and self-awareness along with bodily mindfulness—the same healing methods modern psychologists recommend. Ross's $20 course taught me to ask myself a very important question that no one ever bothered teaching me in grad school: *You're not just fighting against. Ask yourself, what are you fighting* for?

Back when I was teaching, I noticed that undergraduate students show up to class with an inclination toward kindness, empathy, and openness. My students never came to class as decided bigots. Students were never quick to jump down one another's throats as long as we took steps to foster a trusting environment that prioritized safety from the start. But I've also witnessed occasions when students would throw accusatory remarks or yell antagonistically. I've also sat through times when professors screamed at me or made racist comments.

By the spring of 2021 I had been applying to tenure-track positions at universities across North America and abroad for over a year. To prepare myself for one of the big interviews, my advisor suggested a mock interview with two other professors. One of them was a new hire at the school and someone I did not know at all. But during the mock interview I listened to this stranger interrupt me by yelling. She shouted that I was not dressed right, that I should look directly into the camera, that I was not answering any of her questions, that I did not seem to know anything about the topic at hand, and that the issues I brought up were completely irrelevant. This was an attack. I was so stunned that I did not have the wherewithal to consider that this woman was probably screaming at the horrors of her own tenure-track baggage that she collected while being in academia for so long and now projecting them onto me in a very tactless way. Perhaps she did not realize how she was humiliating me in front of my other professors on that Zoom call, who sat there silently observing. I felt alone in that meeting. It was weird watching my former teachers behave so complacently and allow this abusive tirade to occur. All I could do was get through the rest of that mock interview while holding back tears. My advisor closed by saying that if the mock interview felt terrible, then it was a success. I signed off and cried for four hours straight. The last time I cried like that was when my dog was killed in a hit-and-run. The real interview I had two days later was a disaster. I was a nervous wreck because any ounce of self-confidence I had was gutted from me. I was reeling in self-doubt after being screamed at, and I felt like an absolute zero inside and out. How dare these people call such abuse "success"? And yet this is just one tiny example of the inhumanity that goes on regularly inside the ivory tower.

When people behave reactively, I first tend to my own emotional needs. Once I am centered, I try to see their past wounds. People who antagonize viciously are simply reflecting how they were treated. I see them seeking an opportunity to take vengeance by making someone else feel like shit so that they can feel empowered. In academia, I regularly saw how ill equipped professors and TAs were at handling screamers by casting further blame or moving the onus of responsibility into a bureaucratic maze where nothing gets resolved and existing wounds are only exacerbated. But because universities charge an arm and a leg for students to attend, they feel the pressure to *fix* what cannot be fixed because of student/consumer demands for fixing. Many new students arriving in college are scared because they pay insane amounts of money to attend, and their parents are just as stressed. Out of fear, students/consumers make impossible demands from the wrong people, like adjuncts who are grossly underpaid and juggle multiple classes at several different schools at a time to barely make ends meet. Most adjunct professors are burnt out. Many of them live on state benefits. Quite a few are houseless. The money we spend on education forces us to desperately hang on to the belief that this is a monetary "investment" that will ensure profit. All of this is just another trap that leads to greater suffering.

Loretta Ross taught me not to beat myself up when I make a mistake. Therapy taught me to forgive myself for my mistakes. Dharma talks with Tara Brach taught me how to nurture my wounded heart. An honest mistake can and will happen, but it's only when we find a way to be easy on ourselves that we can be easy on others. How could I forgive others for their mistakes when my personal standards are so high? How can I not feel insecure when I call myself an idiot constantly and run from this self-criticism by swallowing book after book, seeking a way to always be "right"? How will universities, tenured professors, and administrators ever manage the guilt and shame of their systemic corruption, which leads to greater inhumanity such as debt-riddled students and adjuncts who helplessly bark and yell at one another in classrooms, meetings, social media, lawsuits, and toxic commentaries? Academia forces the scholar to cut themselves off from their blood circulation by having no emotional attachment to what they write about. The subject disappears in academic writing. It's a bizarrely dehumanizing disconnection that is required in the arts and humanities, but it's unsurprising given my experiences of tenured professors advising me to acclimate to abuse—advice that goes against everything I do now to unlearn precisely this very advice that put me in danger my whole life.

Haemin Sunim writes, "If there is only intelligence and no sensitivity, you won't know how to empathize when faced with someone's suffering."[166] This is the great irony of the arts and humanities today, which overintellectualize and remove subjectivity. As a result, the fields in this arena have become more inhumane in their practices by not letting anyone be human and by not recognizing the human behind their creative expression. Mistakes are never tolerated. Fingers get pointed quickly. There's never room for pause, breath, and greater understanding. This trend is strangling so many people today and contributes to the hazard in schools.

Well, I am not interested in fighting. I just want to make stuff, have fun, and be free. That's my way of exercising my own human rights.

Does art function as activism? Absolutely. bell hooks believed in "the transformative power of art if we are to put art on our mind in a new way."[167] So never mind the intellectuals, news, and critics. We're all part of one human community in which your creation matters, as does your ever-evolving perception.

---

166 Haemin Sunim, trans. Deborah Smith and Haemin Sunim, *Love for Imperfect Things: How to Accept Yourself in a World Striving for Perfection* (New York: Penguin, 2018), 224.

167 bell hooks, *Art on My Mind: Visual Politics* (New York: New Press, 1995), 7.

LESSON 15:
MY *LIBERATION* NOTES
AND HOW IT FEELS TO BE FREE

I REALLY LOVE NINA SIMONE'S COVER OF THE BILLY TAYLOR SONG "I Wish I Knew How It Would Feel to Be Free." I listen to it whenever my chest feels heavy.

I don't know anyone who doesn't want to be free. I know many people who wish to be free from their jobs and family. There are others who wish to be free from debt or poverty. There are those who wish to be free from constant scrutiny or judgment. What do you wish to be free from?

I wish to be free from the trappings of my own mind—the endless loop of negative voices. My brain is constantly filled with murmurs of criticism, blame, judgment, despair, rage, and grief. I want to change the channel on this nonstop television in my head.

◇◇◇◇◇◇◇◇◇◇◇◇◇

When daytime talk show host Jerry Springer died in 2023, I was reminded of the sick days I spent at home when I was in middle school watching his show, thinking, *Jesus. Is* this *what adults do while we're in school?* I remember how the commercial breaks during *The Jerry Springer Show* (1991–2018) always advertised psychics, but I never understood why until I became unemployed myself. A person will turn to anything when faced with gloomy uncertainty as unpaid bills stack up on the coffee table and walks to the mailbox cause panic attacks.

By the time I graduated from my doctoral program in 2021, I had already spent a year applying for tenure-track jobs and postdoctoral fellowships at universities. Months had gone by, and my unemployment benefits were running out. I couldn't stop binge eating Cheez-Its, which I bought on food stamps, irrationally hoping that shoveling junk food down my gullet would improve my situation. I was spiraling down a labyrinth of purposelessness, zero income, depression, anxiety, and suicidal ideations. A thought kept attacking me: *Every decision I ever made in my life up until now was a mistake.* I felt like a loser and a failure. The only meaning I could extract from my atmosphere was that none of my past achievements mattered.

Every morning I woke up to an absolute standstill. In a state of panic, I applied for office jobs I did not want. I also applied for jobs as a translator, custodian, and dishwasher because I just needed *a* job. I've been living on my own since I was eighteen and always paid my rent on time, but here I was in my thirties with unpaid rent while drowning in credit card debt. Having not worked any office jobs for six years, I was now an untouchable due to the experience gap. Having a PhD made me threatening. The Hollywood industry has always been suspicious of academics—and rightfully so, as academics only know how to critique and Hollywood is allergic to it. When I circulated my résumé among my contacts for job opportunities, one woman told me to remove "PhD" from my education because people won't hire an overeducated person. Academic institutions kept giving me the impression that I was not good enough, while nonacademic institutions saw me as overqualified and therefore useless. Go read *The Professor Is In* by Karen Kelsey to get a glimpse of what I mean. Kelsey writes, "Professional suicide is what graduate students are already committing on a daily basis as they confront the reality of a PhD that cannot be turned into meaningful work, and the looming default on what are often hundreds of thousands of dollars in loans."[168]

I'd spent my early twenties working multiple unpaid internships and volunteering at nonprofits and grassroots organizations in New York to beef up my résumé, hoping to land something that would stabilize my life. What I ended up with was an entry-level job that paid less than thirty grand a year with exploitative and abusive bosses. Graduate school in my early thirties was no different, as I wrote papers and conducted research for tenured professors who mined students' research for new ideas. Kelsey writes, "Do not wait for your advisor and department to tell you the truth about their complicity in a predatory structure that exploits graduate students. Understand for yourself that they are entirely complicit."[169]

Staring at the bottom of my barrel, clouds of suicidal thoughts gathered again, so I started writing a daily list in my notebook entitled "Things I can do today instead of killing myself" to get through each day with the most basic sense of purpose and a grim sense of humor. Here's an example of the things I would write:

- Have matcha.

- Go for a walk.

- Send out a résumé.

- Look at dog videos.

- Look up what "Boomshakalaka" means.

- Write a letter or card to a friend.

- Drive to the beach.

---

168 Karen Kelsky, *The Professor Is In: The Essential Guide to Turning Your Ph.D. into a Job* (Crown, Kindle edition), 380.

169 Ibid., 381.

Each list would include three to four items. Sometimes I would have just one or two things because that was all I could muster. I was genuine when I made these lists to amuse myself. Although this ritual was tongue-in-cheek, it was also prayerfully sincere. The best jokes are so. I started posting my list as Instagram stories, and my friends would laugh nervously. No one fully understood this activity except me. I made this list to *live*—not die. I made this list so as not to waste another day on my couch getting high, zoning out on TV, and worsening my anguish by numbly eating junk food—a trinity of habits I conducted as a form of long-term suicide.

LIKE DRIVING CATTLE

I've never had a spiritual experience while watching TV before. Psychonauts have their personal lists of psychedelic cinema and an appreciation for *Midnight Gospel* (2020), but I never had a spiritual awakening while watching a K-drama until I saw *My Liberation Notes*.

My Liberation Notes follows the Yeoms, a middle-class family living in a rural fictional town called Sanpo, which is a long way outside of Seoul near Suwon in Gyeong-gi Province. The three adult siblings—Gi-jeong, Chang-hee, and Mi-jeong—live with their parents and do farm work on the weekends while commuting to the city to their office jobs during the weekdays. It's evident why. None of these working family members can afford a home in Seoul because housing prices in Seoul doubled since 2018.[170] It's not even a *house*. I'm talking puny *apartments*. Like most American millennials, most Korean millennials cannot afford a home of their own. The wealth gap in South Korea is spiking at an alarming rate as the top 20 percent make five times the average of the bottom 20 percent, and this gap is worsening each year.[171] It's not dissimilar from patterns found in the States, where the American Dream no longer includes home ownership as a feasible goal. That is why Gi-jeong, Chang-hee, and Mi-jeong commute from their rural house in Sanpo by bus and train.

---

170 Subin Kim, "South Koreans Struggle to Climb Property Ladder as Prices Explode," *Al Jazeera*, April 28, 2022, www.aljazeera.com/economy/2022/4/28/south-koreans-struggle-to-climb-property-ladder-as-prices-soar.

171 Jung Min-kyung, "Korea's Top 20% Own Real Estate 251 Times More Valuable than Lowest," *Korea Herald*, April 4, 2022, www.koreaherald.com/view.php?ud=20220405000716.

A very close-mouthed alcoholic misanthropist who only goes by his surname Gu lives in the house next door. He drifted into town by accident and ended up staying for a year, working as an apprentice to Mr. Yeom—a carpenter with his own sink and cabinet installation business. Gu also helps the family with their farm work like picking red peppers, tilling soil, and watering crops. Gu hardly speaks. He eats meals silently with the Yeom family at their table and drinks four bottles of soju every night alone inside his house. He gets nosebleeds and suffers injuries due to his alcoholism. It is apparent to everyone including himself that his drinking is self-destructive, but he can't quit. Gu is so drenched in his suffering that he does not even express it. He remains disconnected from himself through alcohol and hard labor while avoiding human interaction as much as possible.

Gu tells Mi-jeong how much he hates people wandering around his eye line and that he despises them even more when they talk: "It's all useless talk but I have to listen to it, and then I have to respond with more useless talk. What am I supposed to say? Coming up with what to say next is laborious." Mi-jeong replies that she feels the same way: "Out of twenty-four hours in a day, I only feel okay about one or two of those hours. I don't even feel good. I'm just okay. The rest of the time, I'm just putting up with it the best I can. . . . Still, I drag myself along one tough step at a time as if I'm driving cattle."

I made my list of things I can do each day instead of killing myself to drag myself along another day like a cow in a field. What else to do but graze, chew, and wait? What else to do but to hope to catch a pretty sunset before falling back asleep and hope for a different vista tomorrow?

◇◇◇◇◇◇◇◇◇◇◇◇◇

As job rejection letters piled up, I tearfully complained to my therapist about how I had done everything "right" up until this point in my life and worked very hard to get to where I am, and it all turned out to be just a dead end. I said that, considering my qualifications, it was ridiculous that I couldn't get a job. Even while rejecting me, the universities did not offer a livable wage. I saw one arts and humanities postdoc offering $20,000 a year with no benefits or housing. Meanwhile, right below that post was a STEM postdoc that offered six figures.

Prior to grad school I was an employee at a boutique film distribution company in New York. It's the usual stuff. My supervisors were dicks. I was severely unhappy. My insomnia and depression worsened. I gained weight. My drinking got worse. I was not the only one suffering. I watched a slew of colleagues quit in just the first few months I was there because of their unhappiness with management, and I began to take on their workload. When I told my boss that I needed a raise for the additional work, he said, "You're not exactly needed at this company, Grace." This was in stark contrast to what I was told when I was first hired on a lousy starting salary—that I would be mentored and trained to become an integral part of the acquisitions team.

After hearing these words, I began to do what's now known as "quiet quitting." Every workday I sat at my desk to do the bare minimum and then spent an hour or two in the stairwell watching K-dramas on my phone or taking a nap. I stopped going to any work-related functions. I stopped socializing with colleagues. I drifted numbly through the office without speaking to anyone or giving two shits about the company's goals. I had zero pride or emotional investment in my work. Instead, I went to the Henry Birnbaum Library every day after work to study for my GREs until 11:00 p.m. I applied to a bunch of film schools across the country but settled on UCLA because I wanted to be in the SoCal sun. After finishing my master's, I stuck around and got my doctorate. After I quit that office job, I vowed never to return to an office again, and so far, I have kept that promise to myself.

My therapist once told me, "If you surround yourself with people who treat you like shit, then you're going to feel like shit." It's such a plain and obvious statement—practically a tautology—and yet I needed to hear it to break my cursed cycle of toxic interpersonal relationships that I maintained out of low self-worth. Yet here I was, facing the same abusive cycle again, banging my head against a wall, trying to force myself into universities that sent out job calls but showed through their offers and treatment of applicants that people like me were anything but wanted. Academia's message to me contained echoes of what my former boss once said: "You're not exactly needed at this company, Grace."

After my benefits and savings ran out, ending up in the streets became a very real possibility, so I purchased a tent and camped alone in the woods for three nights as a practice run in case I got evicted.

When was I gonna catch a fucking break? I was so angry and bitter. Tears brimmed as I gritted my teeth in therapy. My doctor asked me, "If it wasn't for the steady paycheck, would you want to be teaching at a university?"

I heard myself promptly reply, "No." I realized that I never wanted to teach or sit at a desk working for some douchebag, and yet I kept trying to do one or the other all my life out of fear of instability.

Dr. Jacob Ham lists a few questions that are helpful to answer when reassessing one's direction in life: "Do you live by your aspirations and your goals? Do you live by the desire for love and by your virtues? Or are you living a risk-avoidant, fear-based way of thinking?"[172]

I don't know where the saying "Beggars can't be choosers" comes from, but it's quite the opposite. If you have nothing to lose, you can demand everything and anything from this life. I didn't want any office, teaching, or menial jobs. I only ever wanted to work as a creative.

I had finally cornered myself into an impossible situation and had no excuses. My only option was to fully devote myself to art and expect to win. It's something I avoided throughout my twenties as I anxiously searched for a day job or more education to support my creative work for "security." That lie was now behind me, so I made a new list and stuck it on my wall: "My demands from a job."

- Well paid

- Pleasant and respectful colleagues

- Enhances my career as a comedian, filmmaker, and writer

- Flexible hours

---

172 Rabbi Shais Taub and Dr. Jacob Ham, "Jacob Ham, PhD: 'The Opposite of Trauma Is Presence,'" *Fresh Start Podcast*, Feb. 28, 2021.

I made this list and took a big risk. I stopped applying for jobs I did not want. I remained steadfast in my intention to work as a comedian, writer, and filmmaker. This was very daunting because it went against everything I was disciplined to do, and I had no money or fallback. I was completely alone on this journey. To keep myself occupied, I briefly became a mushroom drug lord.

I learned to become a psilocybin cultivator at home through two textbooks and a local mentor who sold me the spores and taught me the basics. After growing the shrooms, I dehydrated them in a food dehydrator, ground them up, and then packaged them as bite-sized mushroom-shaped dark chocolates, individually wrapped in foil. In a city full of wounded artists in search of ways to level up their consciousness and heal, I sold out my product every time.

People become drug dealers because drugs sell *fast*. They sell faster than anything. I made back the investment I put into the equipment, grains, and spores I purchased to start my small business and paid my rent in the fall and winter with my homegrown crops. Once spring rolled along, the heat in my Valley apartment made cultivation impossible, and I was forced to hang up my mushroom drug-lord hat for the time being. The project was fun, though. What I learned from the experience is that whenever I set off to do something creative and new, my whole body goes into flight mode because of the physical abuse I endured as a child, starting with art class. Any "mistake" brings on the threat of death, and my mind/body reacts to it. At the same time, I noticed how I was filled with anticipation, excitement, and joy throughout the growing process, and I fought through my mental resistances. Cultivating mushrooms is truly a test of patience, trust, and faith. Realizing that patience, trust, and faith are all one and the same gave me the strength to endure this choppy phase.

Around this time is when people began reaching out to me with new opportunities. A literary agent in New York cold-contacted me through my website, asking whether I had any book projects she might be interested in. A film production company reached out and asked whether I had a screenplay they might consider. Another production company reached out and asked whether I'd be interested in a writing gig for a documentary. The booker at the Hollywood Improv asked me if I wanted to headline my own comedy showcase in The Lab. These outreaches encouraged me to embrace who I am without fear and own my talents with patience, trust, and faith. They were telling me, "Your art is meaningful and you're good at what you do so stop wasting your life doing shit you hate for people who don't appreciate or deserve you."

Around that same time a comedian friend told me that he works as a freelance reader for a production company owned by an A-list comedian. I sent him my résumé, which he forwarded to the team. When an offer was made, I negotiated my fee up, telling them that my higher degrees in film school qualify me for higher pay. I got the job.

The assignments I received were easy because, as a former grad student, I was already used to reading hundreds of pages every week. Reading a whole book in a day or two is no problem. Then a talent agent saw me at a comedy gig and signed me. A couple of months after that, my short film started getting invited to film festivals. Shortly thereafter, a contact through my comedian friends invited me to audition for a television show, and I booked it. A couple of weeks later, I was on set working. Not long after that, I was hired to perform stand-up at a fundraising event for a decent check. Money was circulating in my life, and I was getting paid only to do what I loved. The list I made of my job demands came true, and they continue to get answered. I still abide by this list.

Boomshakalaka.

HOW TO LISTEN

Gu tells Mi-jeong at a street food stand: "When I first started working at a host bar, I realized I couldn't do it because all people do is complain. . . . People ought to be paid to listen to others." It's apparent that Gu fought his way to the top of the food chain in the underworld to escape the drudgery of emotional labor for strangers as a male host. Mi-jeong is on the other side of the spectrum. She's well practiced in the art of listening through the Liberation Club.

Liberation Club is Mi-jeong's idea, which she comes up with while her two office colleagues Tae-hoon and Sang-min struggle to find a club to join at work: "I want to be liberated. I don't know where I'm trapped, but I feel trapped. Nothing brings me relief. I feel stifled and suffocated. I wish to break free." The two men quietly sit with the idea, then fall in love with it. The three employees pitch the idea to the support center manager at work. When she asks what they wish to be liberated from, Sang-min replies, "Korea found liberation in 1945 but we are still not liberated."

In 1970, when the US military was still in Vietnam, a small collective of American antiwar veterans organized their own peer meetings to give voice to their war traumas. They invited psychiatrists who were sympathetic to their ailments to offer professional aid in the form of what was then called "rap groups." The concept of group therapy originates from trauma survivors who decided to actively seek inner peace. It comes from people who share and listen with the intention of healing.

Liberation Club is the same, and there are rules. Each person writes in their journal what they wish to be free from, then shares it with the group that week. Each member is given a designated amount of time to speak uninterrupted so that the floor is shared equally. The listeners are required only to listen. No one is allowed to offer advice or encouragement. Confidentiality is a contract. Liberation Club gives its members space to freely and safely be themselves with witnesses and without judgment. It offers their souls a moment's rest and recognition.

My Liberation Notes offers a productive, grassroots example of how to improve mental and emotional well-being just by writing down thoughts and feelings, thereby giving the self the recognition and acknowledgment they need, then sharing that with trustworthy allies who are willing to listen in a safe space. Liberation Club is a makeshift group therapy with a creatively inspired routine built in. All of us are a potential for this. Isn't that something to cherish? Isn't that thought liberating?

Such K-drama stories are medicine. Such stories assure us that all is well. We are in good hands. So why give up? Don't give up. It's all better than nothing.

HOW TO MAKE LOVE FEEL SAFE AGAIN

Every single K-drama I have ever seen in my lifetime includes characters shaped by trauma who feel a resistance to love. The hero's journey is always a quest for love despite finding it unsafe. It's this point of tension where the drama shoots into the sky like a geyser.

The Interest of Love, based on a novel by Lee Hyuk-jin, is a nice, chewy melodrama that follows a hetero love-square situation among four characters. Drama ensues because each character has expectations from their significant other based on their worst insecurities. Soo-young vacillates between extreme flakiness and self-destructive overcompensation because she feels unworthy of love. Sang-soo is similar and hesitates over what he wants because he doesn't feel he is worthy. Both characters get in their own way of finding love because they overthink out of fear. Soo-young and Sang-soo face drama because they want love but find it frightening.

In *My Liberation Notes*, however, Gi-jeong is a woman in her late thirties who unabashedly demands love from the world. She is wholly vulnerable, and this makes her siblings and colleagues shake their heads in embarrassment because she wears her heart on her sleeve. When Gi-jeong gets a text from Tae-hoon, who offers to buy her dinner that same evening, her colleague Jin-woo tells her, "Play hard to get. It's no fun if you agree right away. Guys get the most anxious when you play hard to get. That drives them crazy. . . . Make him anxious, Ms. Yeom. For once, make a man wait for you."

Then Gi-jeong asks in calm sincerity, "Is being anxious a good thing? Why is it good when he's anxious? . . . Isn't that a bad thing? Isn't that discomfort? When a man and a woman are dating, shouldn't they give freely till they're both full? Why give your heart away frugally like crumbs? If you serve food like that, you might get murdered. So why do I have to give my affection in such a petty way? . . . Being anxious and playing hard to get . . . aren't they all bad, not good?" This makes Jin-woo fall silent in thought.

After Gi-jeong gets up to leave and meet Tae-hoon that very night, Jin-woo wonders aloud, "Why did I think this feeling was good this whole time?" Jin-woo's belief that being petty with one's affections and playing games in relationships with armored and defensive approaches to seeking companionship have been limiting his capacity to get genuinely close to anyone, which is why he dated so many women but never settled down. Meanwhile, Gi-jeong is plain, direct, and simple in her plea for love. She does not withhold. She does not play games. She doesn't have the patience or the manipulative mind to do either. She gives wholly and fully, and eventually she bags Tae-hoon and manifests her intention to fall in love before winter.

Gi-jeong's younger sister Mi-jeong makes a similar observation when Chang-hee's friend Du-hwan says that his heart began to race as soon as he heard that his crush is single. Mi-jeong says, "I never understood when people say they like someone to the point of their heart racing. It's not that I don't know what you mean. But when my heart races, it's always during a bad moment. . . . My heart never races when I'm in love. When I really like someone, it's the opposite. My heart rate slows. And I feel like I'm free. Like, for the first time, my heart is not anxious."

Gi-jeong and Mi-jeong question the sociocultural norms of love that people are acclimated to like discomfort, defensiveness, and anxiety. They question the "serious games" of romance that men like Jin-woo participate in, as well as Hallmark maxims that frame anxiety as a sign of love. These women decide for themselves what loving is. In Mi-jeong's case, she chooses to love without expectation.

When Gi-jeong judges Mi-jeong for dating an alcoholic like Gu, Mi-jeong replies, "I've never given my all nor received another's all. I'm never doing that again. If he gets better and he wants to fly away, I'm going to let him fly away with gladness. Even if he crawls on the floor, I won't be ashamed. Even if the whole world judges him, I'm going to treat him like a human being. I'm only going to support him. Not even our parents gave us that kind of support growing up." Mi-jeong, who usually spares her words, drives stakes like these into her ground with such bravery that, by the end of her monologues, I feel emboldened. All three siblings—Gi-jeong, Mi-jeong, and Chang-hee—read like saints on this show, delivering profound messages on what it means to be free.

◇◇◇◇◇◇◇◇◇◇◇◇◇◇

When I was in first and second grade, I hated falling asleep in cars because I always woke up feeling embarrassed. In my twenties I realized this indicated my fear of vulnerability. My recurring nightmares are always of me going into a bathroom to pee or making sure that the bathroom door is securely locked before I shower but then seeing that the door doesn't have a lock or that the walls are see-through. These dreams indicate my fear of vulnerability. Having suffered at the hands of my caretakers, love and intimacy feel dangerous to me. Love, in fact, is a trigger.

Dr. Ham says that the only way to do therapy right is to cocreate an empathic connection between the therapist and patient: "Trauma is an act of violence against relational connection, against feeling human, against feeling like you deserve to be loved—that loving is a good thing, that it is a safe thing."[173] That's the most heartbreaking aspect of my trauma. It makes loving extremely painful.

I wish I could've coexisted with my parents in a household where love had a sane function, but I didn't. I never developed a healthy ability to love myself. I thought it was all right to starve myself, binge eat, purge, smoke cigarettes, black out on booze and put myself in harm's way, overwork to the point of migraines, stay in relationships with abusive partners, and give away my energy to jobs and friendships that lacked respect.

With over a decade and a half of therapy, somatic treatments, psychedelics, self-help books, creative output, and maintaining a daily ritual of exercise, yoga, meditation, prayer, rest, and play, I now have the inner capacity to love myself and give myself what I want and need. I feel strong enough to say, "I choose to love and be loved without fear." This is *my* liberation note. What is yours?

"WORSHIP ME"

Mi-jeong is a temp graphic designer at a credit card company. Her boss is abusive. Her colleagues are shallow. Her ex-boyfriend, who she cosigned a loan for, is defaulting on payments and she is about to become a delinquent

---

173 Dan Harris and Jacob Ham, "453: An Ace Therapist Gives Dan a Run for His Money/Dr. Jacob Ham," *Ten Percent Happier with Dan Harris*, May 25, 2022.

borrower. At the end of her rope, she walks up to Gu as he sits outside drinking soju alone. She asks him why he drinks all the time. He replies, "What else is there to do?" In a state of desperate dejection, embitterment, and righteous anger, Mi-jeong tells Gu: "Worship me. I've never felt whole. One asshole after another. Every guy I ever dated was an asshole. So, worship me so that I can be whole. . . . Love won't do, either. Worship me."

Sanskrit gives us the phrase "Namaste," which my YouTube yoga instructor Adriene says at the closing of each video session next to her dog, Benji. It means that the divine in me—my highest self—bows to the divine in you—your highest self. It's a very simple act of worship.

Koreans bow regularly. It's how we greet one another. The essence of bowing is tied to this simple praise of one soul acknowledging the other. Psychologists claim that trauma occurs when someone goes unseen, unheard, and unacknowledged. If that's the case, then a simple bow can be healing. Namaste. I worship you.

When Koreans bow in greeting, we ask a question: "Ahnyoung haseyo?" It is a question that asks, "Are you well?" It is a kindness. It is a checking in. It is a recognition and hope that holds heart space for your well-being. Ahnyoung haseyo? My soul sees yours. Namaste. The divine in me bows to the divine in you.

When I was in elementary school my dad was triggered by something or other, as he often was, and he barked on and on about how important it is that I bow to greet adults. He said, "Koreans bow to show one another the backs of our neck as a sign of trust because back in the day, anyone could go and chop a person's head off with a sword." Albeit extreme, my father was trying to communicate that the custom of bowing among Koreans is at the heart a sign of humility and trust. Ahnyoung haseyo? I am humbled by your divine presence. You have my trust.

In life we struggle with whatever burdens weigh on our heads, straining our necks and shoulders with tormenting thoughts that ignite past wounds, replaying the same narrative of personal and broader systemic injustices. It's heavy as lead, and the weight makes turning our heads in other directions to switch perspectives challenging. That's why it's easy to call people out and disagree or demand apologies from everyone all the time. That's why it's so easy to forget the essence of who we are—a divine soul. A high presence. It's in all of us. Call it a higher consciousness. Call it a prefrontal cortex. Call it a spirit. Call it whatever you like. But it's always here. When I meditate or repeat my affirmations and prayers in search of freedom from my suffering, I direct them to my higher self. The quiet centering I gain from this daily practice grants me a modicum of peace. If I choose to see every sentient being as a dwelling space for a divine soul, then they all have my praise, because we crawl on this earth and suffer. My worship is reserved for the divine in me who bows to the divine in you. Namaste. Ahnyoung haseyo? I worship you.

Arts and humanities today focus on training students to critique, teaching them how to problematize and pick apart the world for all of its unfairness, then we let them loose out into the world, where they comment online all day every day, rampaging toxicity, reading the news, fueling their fears, growing more anxious, dousing that anxiety with more coffee, and running around on the same hamster wheel until they burn out and grow depressed. Consumerism becomes the drug of choice, whether it be food, booze, gym memberships, dates, sex, gossip, work, sugar, shopping, or TV. After all that, studies publish articles that question why nearly half of all college students suffer from depression, with numbers steadily growing. Why do universities only teach students that the world is made of impossible problems filled with cruelty? Why don't we ever teach students how to access the light, wonder, and joy?

If you take away anything from this book, I ask you to please worship yourself and one another. Offer praise to yourself and to those around you. Give compliments and learn how to accept them. Offer yourself and one another acknowledgment and recognition—big or small. This is more important than knowing how to critique. Any toddler can point at something and say, "That sucks." Anybody can bang out a negative review on their keyboard. The job of critics is supremely easy, and yet so many people cower around them and seek their advice and approval. Stop reading TV and film reviews. Why does anyone need a newspaper journalist to tell them what they should or shouldn't like? A critic's viewpoint will never be as valuable as your own. There's no one above you, dude.

Judging art is pointless. Systems that rank and rate based on competition and comparisons are playing with illusions. Primitive minds that believe in grades and authority maintain these illusions. These are not real.

Criticism is *easy*, while finding ways to praise, compliment, and worship an object or subject require careful observation, attentive listening, complex feeling, and thought. Adoration is an art. There's no one above me or you. Namaste. The divine in me worships the divine in you.

I don't understand why people choose to see a show or a movie based on other people's opinions published on some site, just as I can't understand people who seek their parents' approval for their life's decisions. That's the one upside to having detached myself from my parents early on and setting my own boundaries. I value my own opinion of myself more than theirs or anyone else's. When my parents visited me in LA for the first time, several friends asked me, "Are they proud of you?" I couldn't understand this question because it felt so irrelevant. Whether it be their pride, shame, or indifference, I never let my parents' opinion influence me or my life's decisions, so this question did not register with me because I'm already proud of myself.

I remember my dad asking me at age four: "What do you want to be when you grow up?"

I replied, "An artist." He told me, "In that case, I will do what I can to support that dream." Despite my family's poverty, my parents sent me to afterschool classes for art, dance, singing, writing, and swimming since I was in grade school. They took me to libraries and bookstores so I could read whatever I wanted. In this regard, I am proud of *them* and grateful for their support of my creativity, which helped me face my traumas rather than hide from them. I am proud of *us* for maintaining a relationship, and I'm grateful to us for figuring it out. We're still figuring it out. I am proud of myself for always renegotiating my boundaries in all my relationships while also learning how to better prioritize my health and safety and unlearning what does not serve me. It's a work in progress. It will remain so until the day I die.

One February evening a memory from thirty years ago surfaced from the marsh. It was my sixth birthday in my family's roach-infested one-bedroom apartment in Brooklyn. It was the first birthday I was celebrating in America. My mother had put together a birthday dinner for me on our coffee table, and the setup had such a charming crudity to it. There were bowls of rice, grilled fish, and banchan, as well as orange juice in gaudy wine glasses and a very elaborate cake from a local Italian bakery. So many elements clashed on this table, and yet to my mind's eye now, it shows my parents doing their absolute best with what they had to show me love and appreciation. Today that birthday dinner could not appear more complete and right in my mind's eye. It's taken me thirty years to recall that memory safely back into my consciousness.

There's a photograph of this birthday that my dad took on his Olympus point-and-shoot film camera through an automated timer. My six-year-old face in that picture reads to me as happy but tinged with an apologetic question that wonders whether she deserves any of this celebration. I keep turning to that girl, saying, "Yes, you do. Don't be afraid. Let it in." My daily task is to combat any limiting beliefs that tell me I am inherently defective, unlovable, and undeserving of anything good.

My parents took a risk and moved our family to New York. After living in other cities abroad, I've come to realize that I feel very at home in the States because of the freedoms this country affords me. It's a privilege to live here, and I do love my life right now.

The political is always personal. My personal experiences shaped my political views, and that is why I always stand on the side of the marginalized and the rebels. I sing praises of those who fight for what they deserve—safety, love, and freedom.

Sing praises of yourself. If saying affirmations seems stupid, just know it's about as stupid as calling yourself and others stupid. Whenever I hear me say nice things to myself in my head, I find it easier to say nice things to others. That's just how it goes.

Ahnyoung haseyo? The divine in me worships the divine in you. Namaste.

FALSE IDOLS

Gu and Mi-jeong's relationship represents the intersection of larger sche-mas in South Korea's social economy, which is universally apparent in all capitalist nations. Mi-jeong works at a credit card company. Gu is from the underworld of gangsters, gamblers, playboys, and booze. Gu profits from people who drink at his club and bars to escape their drudgery. Many clients pay their tabs with credit cards or leave unpaid tabs open. Gu's alcoholism mirrors his clients' cycle of working unfulfilling jobs while unable to escape debt and then going out to drink, get high, have sex with strangers, sing, and dance, only to forget their problems temporarily while deepening their debt and unhappiness. Humans make irrational choices toward fleeting moments of escape while enhancing the trap.

Gu has a vague past life and a completely unknown genesis. What's evi-dent is that Gu is the head honcho of a massive club, but he started from the bottom as a male entertainer at a host bar. Host bars in South Korea are conceptually similar to Japan's. I recommend the 2006 documentary *The Great Happiness Space: Tale of an Osaka Love Thief* for a peek into this world, as well as the K-drama *Lost* (2021). A host or hostess bar is where people go to be entertained by hired entertainers over booze, karaoke, and dance. It's not dissimilar from a frat, sorority, or any other social club where people pay to belong. It's not dissimilar from strip clubs in America in the sense that sex is not an official part of the business but is silently expected.

South Korea as a nation is currently treated like a host bar for non-Korean hetero cis-women from around the world who fetishize pretty boys in K-pop groups and K-dramas. Min Joo Lee is a scholar specializing in gen-der and Korean studies. She and I were in a writing group together when we wrote our dissertations as grad students. Her ethnographic research was fascinating, as it focused on hetero cis-female sex tourism in South Korea by North American and European women. These visitors are nick-named "hallyu tourists," and they fly to Seoul to visit production sites of their favorite K-dramas and eat local street food. But many of them also go in search of a boyfriend. Lee writes, "Drawn to the characters they see on their TVs, they start to wonder if real-life South Korean men resemble the K-drama male characters, both in their looks and behaviors."[174] These women project their fantasies onto Korean men, believing that they're just like the characters they see on TV; "'romantic,' 'gentle,' 'handsome,' 'knights in shining armor' are just some of the terms that the tourists used to describe their idealized Korean man."[175]

At a host bar, however, these projected fantasies are fulfilled for the right price. The young men who tend to these women say and do anything to make women's fantasies come true for the time that the hosts are hired. Hosting is an emotional labor, as it requires listening and companionship.

Sociologist Arlie Russell Hochschild defines *emotional labor* as "the management of feeling to create a publicly observable facial and bodily display; emotional labor is sold for a wage and therefore has exchange value."[176] Hochschild conducted an ethnographic study of emotional labor among flight attendants and bill collectors, observing how services like flight attending require workers to be exaggeratedly nice, while services like bill collecting require workers to be exaggeratedly vile. These two labors are two sides of the same coin in Gu's profession.

Gu started his job as a host, then quickly elevated into the rank of a "madam" or manager and eventually the president of his own club within a year. He was excellent at his job because gambling or womanizing never distracted him. His unbridled temper and ferocity make him a top-notch bill collector. Gu harnessed his shadows to dominate others and escape the insufferable job as a male entertainer. Toxicity is Gu's norm. Because it's normal for Gu to treat others like trash, he can't help but treat himself like trash with his incessant inner self-criticism and alcoholism.

Gu tells Mi-jeong, "When I'm clearheaded, the people from my past come rushing to me. All of them. Even the dead ones. When I wake up in the morning, those people who were resting come to me one by one,

---

174 Min Joo Lee, "Why Some Women Are Traveling to South Korea to Find Boyfriends," *The Conversation*, March 10, 2022, https://theconversation.com/why-some-women-are-traveling-to-south-korea-to-find-boyfriends-175905.

175 Ibid.

176 Arlie Russell Hochschild, *The Managed Heart: Commercialization of Human Feeling* (Berkeley: University of California Press, 1983), 9n.

endlessly. I destroy all those people who come to me in my head, swearing at them. When I sit like that for an hour, I get exhausted. It feels like sewage coursing through my body. 'Let's get up. Let's drink. If I drink, all these people disappear.' That's why I'm more considerate when I'm drunk than when I'm sober." Gu's monologue here vividly expresses my daily emotional flashbacks that turn into obsessive thoughts. My zombies. All the addictions I've struggled with in my life served to flee from these voices.

Whenever I go into autopilot mode, my mind wanders into the most dreadful corners. All the faces and words of people who assaulted, antagonized, and rejected me dwell there. They're like ghosts tucked away in the dust that stalk me whenever I do the dishes, fold laundry, walk, drive, brush my teeth, shower, and so on. They blindside me with my most humiliating and agonizing memories. I want these people out of my head. What business do they have wandering around inside my mind? I want them gone. So I rage. I take all my fire and throw it at them. Suddenly, I'm caught in their sticky net, and I can't get unstuck. I'm fighting them. I'm swearing and screaming at the unreal, but my heart rate is up, my whole body's tense, and I feel defeated, small, and helpless, tangled up in imaginary wars that erupt endlessly inside my mind. It makes me sick. That's why I drank as if I had a death wish. It's because I did. I enjoyed getting wasted. I wanted to black out because it was the only way I could turn off my head, which is an endless disaster channel. Where the hell is the remote for my brain?

Mi-jeong replies to Gu that she feels the same way—that she's built her life around preserving and maintaining her hatred for certain individuals, and that is why she has no will to live. I see this all the time, and it's encouraged in our society. A professor I knew in grad school once told me that when she writes a paper, she imagines what her worst critic might call out in her argument and uses that to fuel her writing. I remember thinking how exhausting and painful that sounds. What an awful way to live and carry out a career—constantly looking over one's shoulder, anxiously anticipating an attack. How can anyone truly be free if they build their career around what their enemy and critic *might* say or do to them?

I like this Yogananda quote that I have on my wall: "Be certain that you have made a good selection and refuse to submit to failure." It's so much easier on our mind/body and heart to move with self-trust rather than fear of what others might say or do. I lived my whole life with that shit because other people wanted to control me and dictate my life. I still struggle with the residue of that shit, but my goal is always to move forward with self-trust toward self-love. Whatever agendas other people wanted to fulfill by putting their hands on me is their fucking problem, not mine. I refuse to carry that with me by thinking paranoid thoughts all day. I take daily steps to remove that residue. It is a daily and moment-to-moment commitment. I do it to relax the aches in my whole being. It's a mindset. Choosing to flip this switch doesn't cost a thing.

THE DRAMA OF THE MOON AND THE SEA

I can't binge watch television the way I used to. It's just not possible anymore, just like it's impossible for me to drink alcohol or binge eat mindlessly.

Since the day I was born, I've always had the luxury of living by the ocean—in Busan, in New York, and now LA. I regularly drive up the Pacific Coast Highway and park myself by the beach to space out into the water for hours at a time. It's my favorite way to meditate until "I" disappear. It's not that different from watching TV, except it's far less stressful.

Korean American video artist Nam June Paik said that the moon is the oldest TV, but I think the ocean is a far more interesting channel—way livelier and always changing. The ocean's waves are created by the moon's gravitational pull. So romantic, no? It makes more sense to declare the moon the oldest remote control and the ocean our TV. The surface of the ocean's currents looks like the fuzzy black-and-white picture on TV, flickering with the promise of a concretized image that never emerges except in my mind's eye.

During one of my seaside meditations, I began having an emotional flashback. My hands and feet went cold, my breaths grew rapid, and my body constricted. The scenario was a conflict, and I was defending myself with such grit and rigor, like an attorney trying to get an innocent person off death row. Suddenly I broke through the stratosphere of my mind's theater and heard myself ask, *Wait. Who am I defending myself against? There's no one here. Why am I fighting while armed to the teeth when this is a fake scenario?* Once this hit me, I could not stop laughing hysterically. My flashbacks used to cause so much dread and anguish. While cracking up, I realized that my flashbacks now have no control over me. I'm the one in control, and my inner drama queen is so completely lovable and hilarious to me now. I honor and validate her, but that is all. She's nowhere near the wheel now. She knows her place. I'm the one driving this vehicle. I'm free to take myself wherever I please.

I heard myself say a curious phrase recently. I wasn't sure what I meant, but it rang true as I declared, "I no longer want to identify with myself." By this I mean I cease engaging with the dialogues and visuals in my head with ego, and instead I just observe—watch the drama erupt inside then die down just as quickly as it erupted—folding down like the waves, bowing to me.

I once heard Laurie Anderson advise to *feel* an emotion and not *become* the emotion. This all points to the television of my mind. It's just drama. It's not real, so why get lost in it?

My trauma survival has endowed me with gifts. Catastrophizing and the endless monologues inside my mind conjure scenarios, story ideas, and punchlines effortlessly every single day. Sitting down to write is the most natural thing for me to do. This is just one precious facet to my shadows.

What is drama? I think of drama as black lines on a white page that come together to form an image that keeps changing until it evolves into a scene. The scene draws our emotional attention and mind's curiosity as we try to make sense of the images, funneling them through our past histories by relating, understanding, and being moved.

Pathos gives drama its substance, and drama moves me. Isn't it interesting how we use that term—*move*? Moving images are "movies" not just because they move but also because they cause inner movement. When I say, "I'm moved," I'm saying I had an emotional shift. Something energetically changed inside of me as I watched something outside of me projected through a screen. Lines on a page come together to form multiple scenes, which get strung together to become a story. The size of each line varies.

My past traumas create the thicker lines, but I can always reimagine that. That's why I make art. If I want to change the lines on my sketch pad or the lines in my script, I can do it very easily through re-creation. When I create, I ask myself why I do it, and the answer's always the same: *To move and be moved.*

In Dan Sanat's graphic novel *A First Time for Everything*, the teenaged protagonist Dan struggles with anxiety about entering high school. Dan confides in his teacher, who tells him, "All I can say is that when you get to be my age, you realize life is full of pain and joy, and in the end all those moments shape you into who you are, for better or for worse."[177] I love this quote, but I would cut out "for better or for worse." The way I see it, everything I experienced shaped me. Not damaged or improved. No adjectives or descriptors. I am just lines on a sketch pad and lines in my mind's script. Lines are stacked up within me like the logs stacked up at my grandparents' house in Hapcheon that my halmŏni uses to make a fire every morning. My experiences are now just lines waiting to be built into something that moves us toward greater freedom.

FEELING SAFE IN LOVE

I recently dreamt I was at my parents' house in New York. It was nighttime. I had a letter and two DVDs that I needed to mail, so I put on a pair of boots and walked out of the house and headed for the post office. Suddenly my dad ran out, chasing me. I yelled in fright, but he caught up to me and said, "Give me the letter. I will take it to the post office for you." He was expressing a fatherly protectiveness, a willingness to help, and a need to feel purposeful.

I asked my dad what time it was. He said, "It's eight." I said, "Well, the post office is closed now, so it wouldn't make sense to go anyway." I turned around and went back inside the house, where I noticed that the DVDs that were supposed to go out were forgotten. I silently blamed my father for forgetting to take these DVDs, thinking, *There he goes again—not meeting my needs.* But later, when I woke up, I realized it was *me* who hadn't taken the

---

177 Dan Sanat, *A First Time for Everything* (New York: First Second, 2023), 255.

DVDs out with me in the first place. I was needlessly blaming my dad in my dream, even though he was just coming out to help. I was rejecting his love and good intentions.

In the same dream my mom was in the kitchen. I opened the refrigerator door and grabbed a plastic water bottle that had already been opened. As I was about to drink it, my mom urgently said, "That's been sitting in the car for a while." I silently chastised her for doing something like this *yet again*— hoarding what should've been thrown out in the first place but leaving it in the fridge for me to consume and potentially harm myself. I poured the water down the sink and said, "I want to watch TV." My mom immediately handed me the remote. She said, "I'm going to bed. I'm tired." I said to her, "But it's only eight." When I looked at the clock, it was 9:33 p.m. It dawned on me that my mom is now older, so she goes to bed earlier than she did when I used to live with her.

I walked over to the couch and found it covered with a billowy orange comforter and pillows. When I sank into it, the orange comforter and pillows were intensely warm. I turned on the TV and saw channel listings and titles. One of the titles that stuck out to me had the word "love" in it. I felt myself grow sleepy and shut my eyes. That's when I woke up.

In my analysis of the dream, I saw my parents making efforts to please me while I repeatedly discounted those efforts by tracking their mistakes. I had been in a self-protective mode for so long, but as the couch full of warm orange blanket and cushions show, I am now safe. There is no need for me to be defensive. It's safe enough to trust and relax.

The orange blanket and pillows were the same shade of orange I see Hindu and Tibetan monks wear, signifying the purification of fire. In Korean shamanism, red and fire are used to ward off evil. Both of these elements are in my Asian zodiac. The year of the fire rabbit is 1987, which denotes justice and the summer season—a period of abundance and vitality. The year I was born is when South Korea finally implemented the democratic constitution that it upholds to this day. The red fire of justice during that summer of the June Democracy Movement ignited the activists who marched for nineteen days to protest the dictatorship. This fire that dwells in me reminds me what

238

I'm made of. These shades of root and sacral chakras remind me that I am supported, grounded, and secure.

At this point in my recovery, I've come to realize that everything I need is always provided for. Everything I needed *has* been provided for. Blame and anger arise when there is a concretized expectation from others for my specific needs: *Why didn't they take better care of me? Why didn't they pay closer attention? They should've been better. They should've been perfect. They should've done this, that, this, that—then perhaps I would have avoided those disasters.*

I know my parents never intended to inflict lasting harm onto me. They were just trying their best with what they knew and had, just as I have.

My youngest maternal aunt, who is a practicing Buddhist, taught me to accept ourselves and others for how we are: "Everyone in this present moment is complete. We are doing our utmost best right now." It took me years to understand what she meant by this. It's up to me to stop pointing out everyone's shortcomings and honor their being in this moment as enough, just as it is up to me to accept myself fully as I am.

There's a phrase that filmmaker Werner Herzog frequently repeats when describing his impression of nature, such as grizzly bears and volcanoes: "Such monumental indifference." Monumental indifference toward what? Toward the human drama!

I find such grace in that monumental indifference. Thank you, grizzly bears, for never judging me. Thank you, volcanoes, for not giving two shits about my worst shames. I find such freedom knowing that our earth shares these qualities. I am comforted. I am filled with courage to confront my worst fears with zero trepidation—only full trust. I see the love I am gifted with because I am getting exactly what I need to just *be* part of the expansion of what is, has been, and always will be—the constancy of this world's evolution. I'm just here for the ride, man.

I do not identify with my past tragedies. I do not even identify with my "self." I am not just this body. I am only this present moment in my awareness. This calm, still center is my eternal home. I am my future, which builds continuously with my present and past, knowing precisely how to accommodate me best—a warm orange blanket and pillows on the couch with the remote so I can flip my mind's channel to whatever I want. It's all love. I feel joyous and free. Thank you for sharing this ride.

Anyway. Class is now dismissed.

ABOUT THE AUTHOR

Grace Jung is an internationally touring stand-up comedian, writer, scholar, filmmaker, and actor who is in season 4 of *The Joe Schmo Show* on TBS. Grace is also a former Fulbright Scholar with a PhD in Cinema and Media Studies from the University of California, Los Angeles. Her academic articles are published in numerous peer-reviewed journals. She is the author of *Deli Ideology* published by Thought Catalog Books and a recipient of the Academy of American Poets Prize at Pace University. Grace lives in Los Angeles where she hosts her podcast *K-Drama School*. Follow her on Instagram @gracejungcomedy and @kdramaschool.